W9-AOB-971

SHOCKS 7 • 8 • 9

THE POETRY READING
A Contemporary Compendium on Language & Performance, edited by Stephen Vincent & Ellen Zweig.

Momo's Press   1981   San Francisco

THE POETRY READING: *A Contemporary Compendium on Language & Performance*
© 1981 Momo's Press.

All rights reserved. With the exception of material otherwise copyrighted, no part of this book may be reproduced in any form without the permission of Momo's Press and the author(s).

The production of this volume was variously and partially funded by the Coordinating Council of Literary Magazines, the National Endowment for the Arts, a Federal Agency, the California Arts Council, and The Zellerbach Family Fund.

This volume appears simultaneously as the final issue of *Shocks* (magazine), and as a Momo's Press book.

Momo's Press
45 Sheridan Street
San Francisco, CA 94103

Library of Congress Cataloging in Publication Data:

THE POETRY READING

Bibliography: p.
1. Oral interpretation of poetry—Addresses, essays, lectures. I. Vincent, Stephen. II. Zweig, Ellen, 1947–
PN4151.P6   808.5'4   81–11077
ISBN 0–917672–11–9   (cloth)
ISBN 0–917672–10–0   (pbk.)

Book Design and Cover Art by Jon Goodchild.

Special and grateful acknowledgment to Gail Larrick for her careful editorial eye and assistance.

Typsetting by Eileen (Opie) Ostrow at the West Coast Print Center, Berkeley, California.

Printed in the United States of America

First Printing

for the makers,
the charm

CONTENTS

The POE TRY REA DIN G

THIS IS A BOOK OF READINGS. A book of language. A book of how language is able to occur. Several of the ways. Specifically poetry. We have worked to cover the field. Histories. Living oral sources. Performance pure. Just the poet.

And then the poet amplified. Into contexts. The Street. The Coffeehouse. The Big Auditorium. Into machinery. The cassette. The tape. The record.

And the poem. Just a spoken space. Then amplified as variously. With dance. Video. Music. Back to the page.

And the occasions. The self. The lovers. The City. The Mountains. Gods. The devils. Birth to Death. The people. Humor, pain, ecstasy, joy—the works.

The poet. The poem. The constant rendez-vous with language.

STEPHEN VINCENT
ELLEN ZWEIG
Spring 1981

13

Histories

FROM "SOUR GRAPES"

William Carlos Williams

The epidemic over, April 1918 was as lovely as ever. The war was on its way out; German ambitions would be beaten, and I had an invitation to go to Chicago to read my poems in the studio of a certain Ann Morgan. I was to go alone. Kreymborg had preceded me by a month or so, and it was a great occasion. . . .

I talked that night before some press club, read some poems and recited, improvising as I went, the story I later wrote for *The Knife of the Times,* "The Buffalos." I never performed better. You could hear them breathe; it nearly frightened me out of my purpose. Ben Hecht, Carl Sandburg, Mitch Dawson, and Marion Strobel were there. I later wrote the poem, "A Goodnight," for Marion Strobel. Harriet Monroe particularly admired it.

It was April, the air next day was delicious. It was a romantic interlude. So much so that on the return to Newark and home the mood continued with a girl bound for the East to meet and marry a student about to graduate from West Point. We sat up until late that night, together, after she found out that I was a writer, a poet. Women are strangely impressionable before such apparitions. She seemed *not* to want to go on with her journey.

When I arrived home I was dazed to realize that I in fact *was* married, and when I greeted my kids I couldn't imagine what had happened to me.

From "Sour Grapes," *The Autobiography* of William Carlos Williams, New York: New Directions Paperbook, 1967, pp. 161–162.

From "Projective Verse"

Charles Olson

First, some simplicities that a man learns, if he works in OPEN, or what can also be called COMPOSITION BY FIELD, as opposed to inherited line, stanza, over-all form, what is the "old" base of the non-projective.

(1) the *kinetics* of the thing. A poem is energy transferred from where the poet got it (he will have some several causations), by way of the poem itself to, all the way over to, the reader. Okay. Then the poem itself must, at all points, be a high energy-construct and, at all points, an energy-discharge. So: how is the poet to accomplish same energy, how is he, what is the process by which a poet gets in, at all points energy at least the equivalent of the energy which propelled him in the first place, yet an energy which is peculiar to verse alone and which will be, obviously, also different from the energy which the reader, because he is a third term, will take away?

This is the problem which any poet who departs from closed form is specially confronted by. And it involves a whole series of new recognitions. From the moment he ventures into FIELD COMPOSITION—put himself in the open—he can go by no track other than the one the poem under hand declares, for itself. Thus he has to behave, and be, instant by instant, aware of some several forces just now beginning to be examined. (It is much more, for example, this push, than simply such one as Pound put, so wisely, to get us started: "the musical phrase," go by it, boys, rather than by, the metronome.)

(2) is the *principle*, the law which presides conspicuously over such composition, and, when obeyed, is the reason why a projective poem can come into being. It is this: FORM IS NEVER MORE THAN AN EXTENSION OF CONTENT. (Or so it got phrased by one, R. Creeley, and it makes absolute sense to me, with this possible corollary, that right form, in any given poem, is the only and exclusively possible extension of content under hand.) There it is, brothers, sitting there, for USE.

Now (3) the *process* of the thing, how the principle can be made so to shape the energies that the form is accomplished. And I think that can be boiled down to one statement (first pounded into my head by Edward Dahlberg): ONE PERCEPTION MUST IMMEDIATELY AND DIRECTLY LEAD TO A FURTHER PERCEPTION. It means exactly what it says, is a matter of, at *all* points (even, I should say, of our management of daily reality as of the daily work) get on with it, keep moving, keep in speed, the nerves, their speed, the perceptions, theirs, the acts, the split second acts, the whole business, keep it moving as fast as you can, citizen. And if you also set up as a poet, USE USE USE the process at all points, in any given poem always, always one perception must must must MOVE, INSTANTER, ON ANOTHER!

So there we are, fast, there's the dogma. And its excuse, its usableness, in practice. Which gets us, it ought to get us, inside the machinery, now, 1950, of how projective verse is made.

From "Projective Verse" in the *Selected Writings of Charles Olson*, New York: New Directions, 1966, pp. 16–17.

18

Poetry Readings/ Reading Poetry:

San Francisco Bay Area, 1958–1980

Stephen Vincent

In 1958, IN RICHMOND, across the bay from San Francisco, I was in the twelfth grade. In Mrs. Weatherby's English class, a history of literature, the mandatory play was *Hamlet*. We had come to Wordsworth about the time of the *Howl* trial in San Francisco. Beatnik life exposés filled the *Chronicle*. Grant Avenue seemed like a bizarre heaven of music, strange poetry, weird characters—a break from the Eisenhower ordinary. That spring I went over to the Grant Avenue Fair with my friend Bob.

The afternoon was sunny, with a slight bite to the wind, and flooded with people. Up Grant were coffeehouses, booth after booth of craftspeople and artists, lots of sandals and canvas paintings. Inside a storefront two black musicians were playing, one the congos, the other a flute. Across the street, on the corner of Vallejo, a black poet stood on a crate, literally yelling down his poetry:

You who come down here in your Edsels
You with the deodorant in your arm pits . . .

One hand held the text, the other swung and finger-pointed through the air like an angry preacher's. Later I would see him putting his arms around a white woman, apparently a friend, swinging her around in a dancelike step on the sidewalk, before scooting down the street towards Vesuvio's.

Bob and I walked up the street and stared through the front window of the Coffee Gallery, amazed at the intense concentration of two men playing chess in the window and the big audience that perused each move. Then, as we turned back down the street, about an hour later we came to a big crowd at the corner of Vallejo and found another man up on the box, surrounded by a huge crowd of at least a hundred people. Again, the man read with one hand holding the text and the other arm reaching up like a prophet's, his fingers circling and pointing with the movement and intonation of the language. A huge web, a gigantic celestial web was approaching, getting ready to circle and embrace the human spirit. The poem was a big buildup for a beatific apocalyptic future. Between the serious lines, the poet would set a comic smile on his face, as if he were both poking fun and believing the vision at the same time. As the web in the poem got closer and closer to earth, he circled his hand over the shiny red bald head of a man who was almost pressed against his navel, and the crowd laughed.

That Sunday afternoon sticks clearly in my mind. In a sense it was my first poetry reading, the first time language struck out of the air like that, literally lighting up the ears. Whether or not it was great poetry— who was I to know?—the acoustic effect was enormous. A breach was taking place. Someone was taking language into the open, making it tangible and attractive. The two people were Bob Kaufman and Allen Ginsberg, and their histories, especially Allen's, are pretty well known. My friend Bob and I would carry copies of *Howl* in our back pockets for the rest of the semester.

The Early 1960s:
Sacred Texts and Populist Publications

After four years away at college, I went to San Francisco State in the early 1960s as a graduate student in creative writing. There I began to hear poetry in a regular way. The Poetry Center, begun in the late 1950s under the direction of Ruth Witt-Diamant and Robert Duncan, presented a series of readings each semester. While I was at State (1962–1965), the director was Jim Schevill, assisted by Mark Linenthal. Every other week in the Gallery Lounge, one or two poets read. The mix was rather broad. I remember hearing, from the Bay Area, Duncan, Kenneth Rexroth, Lew Welch, Gary Snyder, Jack Gilbert, and Helen Adam; from the Midwest and the East, John Logan, Robert Mezey, and LeRoi Jones; and from England, Charles Tomlinson. For me the Tuesday afternoon ritual was deeply important. I was paid $2.50 to set up the folding chairs in rows of perfect arcs facing the podium, and then take them down again. It was a special gestalt, as if a unique architecture were required to get an accurate rendering of the poet's true voice.

Indeed, at their best, readings in the Gallery could give the poem a purity of enactment. I vividly recall John Logan reading an autobiographical poem about going to a circus when he was a child. At one point, with incredible precision, he described one ladder being balanced on a ball, then another ladder at an angle on the first ladder, and then, after a precarious pause in which the whole work seemed barely balanced in mid-air, he allowed the comparison "as tenuous as a soul." I remember Charles Tomlinson describing with such careful accuracy the process of taking a knife to swivel the skin off the edge of an apple. At four o'clock one afternoon, Helen Adam sang her spooky ballads, among them the one about the hair of the first wife emerging out of the grave and threading through the house keyhole into the bed and around the bodies of her husband and his second wife.

With the audience carefully seated to face the podium, the Gallery became a special place in which the visiting poet could reveal the poem as a finished and, ideally, dazzling object. Such work gave the immediate world a refreshingly alive sense of shape as well as connection with some sense of poetic tradition. Orphiclike, the poet was back from a journey into some private comedy, heaven, or hell. The act of reading was similar to a religious act of sanctification.

As an audience, whether awestruck, bored, or occasionally a mixture of both, we were critical witnesses to the poet's achievement. As creative writing students, we found the experience much more personal. The reading series gave our own work an immediate sense of public possibility. We could hear the work of others and sense its value or lack of value to our own work and lives. The presence of published poets further built the possibility of becoming published, successful, known, and going on a college tour, still a phenomenon in those days. Equally important, the last reading of the semester involved the students. Each of us was allowed to read for from five to ten minutes from our own work to what was usually a big Gallery Lounge audience. As scary as those occasions could be, reading from behind the podium in front of those rows of people gave many of us our first public identity as poets, as well as an experience of that Orphic tradition. That experience, though personally crucial, was a mere fragment of what was beginning to occur in the Bay Area.

As long as I have been aware of the local poetry situation, two branches of writer–workers have existed. One branch includes those who are essentially writers of texts; for them what is written for the page is a form of poetic sacrament. The content might arrive from a variety of sources, but its final presentation as a book is crucial. David Hazelwood of Auerhahn Books and Graham Mackintosh (who would probably not like to be thought of as religious) of White Rabbit Press were the two printers essential to the creation of this tradition that began to flourish in the late 1950s.

Implicit to the tradition is the notion that the purest possible embodiment of the poem is engaged through exceptionally skilled typography and design. The choice of type, the spacing, the use of particular elements, the choice of paper and ink—all are considered crucial to the movement, the shape, the music, and/or the voice of the poem. If the printing process is abused, the poem is muddied. This obsession with printing, at least initially, was not meant to be confused with preciousness or false elegance. The printer was just as physically engaged with the work as was Charles Olson's image of the poet in "Projective Verse." Syllable for syllable, he was constantly dealing with the question of SPACE. In the working dialectic between the poet's manuscript and the total recources of the printer, a book of poems could reach its most powerful realization.

This particular emphasis on the making of the book, the poem as sacred text, was clearly not shared by every poet and publisher. City Lights Publications probably most notably represented the antithesis of this position. From the start of the Pocket Book Series, Lawrence Ferlinghetti clearly wanted to make the poet's work as inexpensively and universally available as possible. His was a populist intention—the book as a momentary depository for the poem on the way to the people. Books, in that sense, are staked on an oral or spoken-and-sung concept of writing, where the ideal poem becomes a provocative part of the public's imagination and memory. Certainly that kind of vision made it possible for a copy of *Howl* or Gregory Corso's *Gasoline* or Ferlinghetti's *Coney Island of the Mind* to end up in my back pocket in 1958.

On the other hand, books from White Rabbit by Jack Spicer or Robert Duncan, or books from Auerhahn by Michael McClure, Philip Lamantia, or Charles Olson were unlikely to be accessible through the same local bookstore route. Not until I went to State did I find the work of these poets in the library in Special Collections in the Humanities section, then overseen by Robin Blaser, a member of the circle around Jack Spicer and White Rabbit Press. The assumption, I believe, was that the audience for the poetry would find its way to the books (which usually meant being a friend, being on special subscription lists, or going

22

to a collector's store specializing in poetry), as opposed to the populist approach.

This division between sacred and populist was also mirrored in how and where poetry was performed. In the 1950s most of the writers published by Ferlinghetti thrived on public engagement—Kaufman and Ginsberg on top of the crates on Grant Avenue; Ferlinghetti, Rexroth, and Kenneth Patchen reading to jazz in the clubs and making recordings; and the joint readings that would fill Fugazi Hall in North Beach. It's difficult to imagine Spicer, Duncan, or Blaser reading or even desiring to read in similar circumstances. They read in formalized situations—at State or on KPFA, Berkeley's public radio station, but rarely in a totally open public format. As attractive as the writing could be, the poems were being written to confirm a spiritual space, one that was shared ideally by a "community of poets," which, I believe, was perceived as separate from the very community the more populist poets were trying to reach.

These two separate traditions had a big bearing on the making, publishing, and performing of poetry in the Bay Area in the 1960s and on into the 1970s. In this period a curious mesh occurred between both traditions. The poets, the printers, and the poetry wavered between powerful public commitments and retreats in spiritual or, some might say, aesthetic separation. The struggle was clearly heightened by the fact that the 1960s turned out to be much more explosive than any decade since the 1930s. Events were so powerful that poets, poetry, and the processes of publication and performance could not help but be radically altered.

The Mid-1960s:
Poems in Street, Coffeehouse, and Print

The 1960s brought poetry back into the street, although not immediately. When I arrived at State, the City was quiet. Most of the activity generated by the Beats had worn thin. Few coffeehouses held readings. With the exception of readings at the San Francisco Museum of Art, sponsored by the Poetry Center, one could hear little public excitement. Except for Jack Gilbert, who had won the Yale Series of Younger Poets award in 1962 and who was hardly considered friendly to the Beats, the dramatic figures of the 1950s were in retreat or simply out of town.

Events in the City began to accelerate. The local Congress of Racial Equality (CORE) organized what became a series of demonstrations that gave San Francisco a tense and embattled spring. Thousands of people demonstrated at the Sheraton Palace Sit-Ins, the Auto Row Sit-Ins, and the Lucky Market Shop-Ins—and hundreds were arrested. The demonstrations marked the beginning of several movements that radically altered the feel of the City. An electricity in the air gave a new sense of attention to the variety of people and action in the streets. Language became prominent again. The local *Chronicle* and *Examiner* newspapers and the TV stations were totally out of touch with the meaning of events. People suddenly had an intense desire to hear a new language that would allow a clear grip on the events that were radically changing our lives.

The first poets to step into the breach were Lew Welch, Gary Snyder, and Philip Whalen—at the "Freeway" reading on June 12, 1963, in the Tenderloin at Old Longshoremen's Hall—folding chairs and squeaky hardwood floor. Jack Spicer, I was told, was sitting behind me, swollen red with drink, not taking matters too seriously, with a band of friends. But serious enough to come. Lew had done the advance work. Ralph Gleason, the late jazz columnist for the *Chronicle,* had devoted a whole column to Lew's work as a poet, how he had cracked

Lew Welch, Gary Snyder, and Philip Whalen before the "Freeway" reading, 1963. Photograph by Steamboat

up and gone off to the Trinity Alps for two years, how he had just come back. With a hall full of at least 500 people, it was a great way to reenter. Gary read what are now well-known Sierra poems in a quiet voice. Philip read his poems real fast, moving through his manuscript backwards, flipping pages left to right. It was too quick until he settled into a long poem about the City and the Sheraton Palace Sit-Ins—a great piece of rant and outrage, published eventually as "Minor Moralia." He juxtaposed the political events of the City against two high school girls discussing homework and dates on the bus, totally oblivious to the protests and arrests shaking the City. He had the audience riveted, hungry as we were for a *real* depiction of both our political aspirations and a direct sense of what was happening on the street. Whalen had immediately established himself as a troubadour of local truth. And then Lew came on; he read exquisitely, as he was then capable of doing, of his return to the City, coming down Highway 99, of bizarre encounters with old friends. Reading his *Hermit Poems* he juxtaposed the cosmic and harmonious aspects of mountain-stream-pebble formations with the incongruous run-ins of City life. With a charming and hilarious wit, he collided the urban and mountain world.

As a reading, "Freeway" was enormously important to what was to occur in the next few years. It was a declaration of space and position. The space was both the City and the country, with a definite West Coast fix. And the poet's position became that of public person. The reading put the poet back in the position of responding to the City in an *actual* way, letting the poetry move as the City does, responsive to the edges, to the corners, to the voices that flood our City lives. Built out of a democracy of eye and ear, the poetry would help create a culture where language would have a genuinely liberating function. There was definitely a politic and ethic to the new stance: It was the poet's community responsibility to make accurate perceptions, not false metaphor. The music emergent would be part of the cure, the liberation. Jazz was part of the medium: Charlie Parker, Miles Davis, Eric Dophy, John Coltrane, Thelonius Monk were essential guides to how the language could break, lift, and move.

I remember Lew Welch saying this to me and some of my friends one night when we met by accident at the Juke Box, a now long-gone bar, near the corner of Haight and Ashbury. He had just finished giving a class on Gertrude Stein at the University of California Medical Center. What he said sounded fresh and available—so possible. He talked for three hours straight. I was high for three days. Suddenly all that time I had spent wandering City streets or through the Panhandle, marching in Auto Row picket lines, at Playland or the beach, the whole flow of information made sense, made a poetry possible. Taking the lead from Kenneth Rexroth's earlier work, Welch, Snyder, and Whalen began to provide an insistent example of poetry that constantly moved between the City, the coast, and the mountains, acknowledging the West as an authentic space in which to work.

For the next few years, the coffeehouse was primary home of the poetry reading, much as it had been early in the second half of the 1950s. In 1964 the Blue Unicorn was the base for much of the San Francisco activity. Located on Hayes Street, a couple of blocks above Masonic, on the other side of the Panhandle from the Haight-Ashbury, it was one of the few coffeehouses outside North Beach at the time. Gene and Hilary Fowler coordinated a weekly reading series there. Poets submitted poems, and then two or three were invited to read each week. Never fewer than twenty or thirty people made up the audience. When we students from State read, we were immediately aware of the challenge of reading in an off-campus situation.

Unlike the Orphic atmosphere and precise set-up of the Gallery Lounge, the Blue Unicorn was in many ways an extension of the street. (A motorcycle might be warming up outside during your first poem, or a drunk might come in off the sidewalk. The audience could be quite diverse; it was never quite clear where everybody came from. But that was the romance of the Coffehouse: It was *in* the move of the City.) A tension rose between those of us who were students and the other poets, who were most often fiercely anti-academic "drop-outs." The going assumption was that anybody connected to a university or college was insulated from the "real" or "actual" world. Not getting a degree and writing "on your own" implied a definite purity. In spite of these tensions, the Blue Unicorn readings could be lively and loose. People cheered or laughed with lines that *hit* them or bantered back when the poet made off-hand remarks between poems. The real test was to read compelling work, to feel it strike a chord in the context of the City. That was the trigger behind the act. I'll never forget reading my own "495 Words for John Coltrane," a long sentence done while listening to "A Love Supreme," just writing down all the backyard action through my window—the colors of the laundry moving in the wind, the blue Clorox bottle hanging from the line, the singular woman sunbathing in another yard, the cats in their black, white, and orange colors hopping the fence—all done to the shifts in the music. The power I felt in the reading, the clarity of the silence between the lines, and the sense of the music and images registering in the audience were part of the possible wonder of giving readings at the Blue Unicorn. Even if it meant sitting through the dullest imaginable stuff (readings in coffeehouses were still novel enough to be a source of excitement to keep things going through the worst), performing was a quick, to-the-point acknowledgment of your work and a relief to the anonymous and isolated character of City living.

The Blue Unicorn became the second home for many of us. Along with Gene Fowler and Hilary Ayer, Ed Bullins, Jim Thurber, Doug Palmer, David Hoag, Steve Gaskin, David Sandberg, Norm Moser, among many others, read and often dropped in during the day to rap. Influenced by the populist example of Lew Welch, many of us shared a common desire to make a stronger contact with the local. Doug Palmer and Jim Thurber, sandwich-board style, took to writing poems for people on the street for money or barter, for which they were arrested on the charge of "begging" on the sidewalk in front of City Lights. Doug, with the support of Gary Snyder, who taught during 1964 at the University of California, Berkeley, began an IWW local for poets, musicians, and artists. For five dollars we got membership books and started a series of public readings at the loft offices on Minna Street, near Third and Howard. The combined impulse of much of the activity was to get the town back into poetry, music, dance, and good living, without which, as Lew once wrote, "The City is only a hideous and dangerous tough big market." Or, as Philip Whalen put it in "Minor Moralia,"

The community, the sangha, *"society"—an order to love; we must love more persons places and things with deeper and more various feelings than we know at present; a command to imagine and express this depth and variety of joys, delights and understandings.*

It was a call for a socially anarchistic utopianism with poetry leading the way that would resonate throughout San Francisco, Berkeley, and the West for several years.

With the "Freeway" reading began a process that led to a huge number of readings and an outpouring of books and magazines by local writers and publishers. The intensity of much of what happened might be seen in direct proportion to the growing resistance against the expanding Viet Nam War and the violence against civil rights activists. Although much of the work was not directly political during this period in Bay Area history, poets who were identified with both the hermetic "text" and the populist oral traditions assumed a much larger public stance. The 1965 University of California's Berkeley Poetry Conference, not long after a massive university spring teach-in against the war, had the effect of acknowledging the genuine relevance of the current work. The conference staged readings by most of the important local writers, including Snyder, Welch, Whalen, Duncan, and Spicer, among many others, and, in addition, Charles Olson and Robert Creeley who, though from the East, were part of the important Black Mountain College influence on the local scene.

Wittingly or not, the conference set the stage for the presence and arrival of a number of important books. In addition to White Rabbit Press and Auerhahn Books (then in the process of becoming David Hazelwood Books), publications were coming from Robert Hawley's Oyez (Press), Donald Allen's Four Seasons Foundation "Writing" series, and James Koller's and Bill Brown's Coyote Books. In 1965 alone, White Rabbit published *Language* by Jack Spicer and *The Fork* by Richard Duerden. Oyez presented *On Out* by Lew Welch and *The Process* by David Meltzer. Four Seasons issued Gary Snyder's *Six Sections from Mountains and Rivers without End* and Ron Loewinsohn's *Against the Silences to Come*. And Coyote Books published *Dark Brown* by Michael McClure.

Magazines and poetry broadsides were flourishing. Mimeograph was the hottest and cheapest way to get things out quickly. David Hazelton's *Synapse,* David Sandberg's *Or,* and Gino Clay's *Wild Dog* were three of the better known mimeo mags. Offset publications included Clifford Burke's *Hollow Orange,* Len Fulton's *Dust,* and *Coyote Journal* from the press of the same name. Many of the presses put out broadsides of current poems. In mimeograph format, they were given away as "free poems among friends" at demonstrations or on campus corners. Oyez (Press), and the San Francisco Art Commission did separate and beautiful series of letterpress broadsides of Duncan, Meltzer, McClure, Brother Antoninus (William Everson), and many others.

What happened among many of the writers at this time was a genuine crossover from the hermetic fine press format to more public forms and then back again. The work of Philip Whalen, for example, could be found in a small, beautiful, letterpress edition printed by David Hazelwood at the same time it was mimeographed in *Synapse* or handed out (by him) in hand-lettered, offset-reproduced broadsides. In a sense it was the best of all worlds for a poet: He or she could have the work printed exquisitely by Graham Mackintosh or David Hazelwood with a design and typeface ideally in accord with the full intention of the poem (although, as Robert Duncan argued, there could be huge disagreements there); or, with the new proliferation of presses and magazines, the work could be made widely and cheaply available. Behind the burst of activity was the desire to make the work as accessible as possible. An openness to the time stood in raw juxtaposition to the horror of the war and racial outbreaks in the civil rights struggle. It was a genuine reaching out to audience.

As disparate as the poets were, what unites most of the writing of this period is the human and sensual sense of exchange between language and audience. (Jack Spicer's book *Language* of 1965 is, for example, the most open and accessible of all of his books.) The books, the magazines, the broadsides, and the ever-present poetry reading—which grew into the "Monster Reading Against the War" and finally the "Be In" festival—generated an echo effect between voice and text. (Often poems read in public would influence whether or not they were published by an editor listening in the audience.) For the successful poet of the time, and for the devoted listener, the poetry established an urgent but confidently shared kingdom. You can hear it in the hand-lettered broadside:

> DEAR MR PRESIDENT
> LOVE & POETRY
> WIN—FOREVER:
> WAR IS ALWAYS
> A GREAT BIG LOSE.
> I AM A POET AND
> A LOVER AND A WINNER—
> HOW ABOUT YOU?
> Respectfully Yours. Philip Whalen 10:III:65

The poetry began to gain a national audience. The reading scene for several of the poets moved to campuses and centers across the country. Grove Press and Evergreen Review (with the editorial influence of Don Allen), Harcourt, Brace & World, Inc., and New Directions published books by Brautigan, McClure, and, eventually, Snyder, Whalen, and Loewinsohn. Although the college student textbook market may have been the strongest influence on the decision to publish these writers, it was one of those rare times in which a non-academically developed reading audience helped create the way for the national publication of poetry books. Many of the poets, including Joanne Kyger, Spicer, Welch, and Meltzer, could go no further than the small fine presses. Given the production standards and improved distribution of White Rabbit and Oyez, that mode could be considered preferable— and a way of staying true to the intentions of your work. (Many New York presses had a history of dull-looking poetry books whose designers had terrible reputations for trying to reshape spatially open poems into conventional stanza forms!)

For the younger poet, the presence of a relatively large reading audience in the mid-1960s made mimeograph or offset publication of a book by any of the new small presses as attractive as any other, and definitely quicker. Lenore Kandel's *Love Book* was printed offset and staple bound by Stolen Paper Editions in 1966. The attention it acquired caused an obscenity trial for Lawrence Ferlinghetti and City Lights Bookshop. Other popular books, without the same legal complications, were done by Keith Abbott, Eugene Lesser, Doug Blazek, John Oliver Simon, and Gene Fowler by other small presses. In 1966, Doug Palmer edited and produced *Poems Read in the Spirit of Peace and Gladness*, a 230-page anthology of work by thirty-two poets who had read at the IWW loft on Minna Street. It included work by Mary Norbert Körte, Luis Garcia, John Oliver Simon, and James Koller, among poets who are still active today. Along with being a successful local book, it was the fruition and full indicator of work influenced by the older, more established poets.

Looking back, it's hard to escape the impression of an era in which street, academic, and hermetic poets somehow magically joined to make the Bay Area light and wind vibrate with poetry in the face of violence and war. The urgency and popularity of public readings combined with the publication surge of books, many of which still hold their weight and power today, help confirm that impression. I say *impression* because I was unable to maintain my participation in that experience. In 1965, with the military draft breathing down my back, I joined the Peace Corps. Just before the Berkeley Poetry Conference I was sent to Kalamazoo, Michigan, for "training" to go to Nigeria, where I taught

English and creative writing at the University of Nigeria, Nsukka. It was a hard choice to make in the middle of the happening of so much.

The Late 1960s:
The Language in Trouble

. . . Wednesday I was working again for Julia, and met Tim Reynolds. Later he gave me a ride to the Wednesday nite reading. Robert Duncan had been scheduled but decided for some reason to not be on the program, so it was Rexroth, and Antoninus. Ginsberg had been selected to fill the Duncan gap. He read first and it was nothing until he actually started reading a dream like poem he had written about trying to bumfuck LeRoi Jones and trying to get Jones to protect him in the coming racial war. Then esp-ically enuf, he read a letter he had received from Jones at about the same time he was having the dream that told him, "because of the fantasys you and other white Americans insist on having is precisely the reason why it must be destroyed." Ginsberg read this like it was a one liner, and everybody but myself guffawed. It seemed far too serious to me, and without time to think about it my mouth involuntarily opened and I bellowed, "RITE!"

This made the Glide very tomblike, absolutely quiet for a few seconds. Nobody knew who had hollared. I was barely conscious that it had been me. Then Ginsberg repeated much softer, "rite," then he said, "rong," began to waver between the two words like a metronome who simply didnt know. "Rite, rong, rite, rong, rite rong rite rong rite rong." I was annoyed with myself because I hate people who interrupt poetry readings, and now I had done it, not only had I done it, but I had done it to the most famous and least likely to be interrupted poet around.

Andy who was standing behind the seats, began to say, "its all rite," timed to coincide with the rite in the rite rong chant, which had begun to sound like a Tony Blank riff. "Its all rite, its all rite, its all rite with me," Andy crooned. After Ginsberg was off the stage and there was a brief break, I noticed Garry Grimmett and gave him a copy of the Bukowski book on my way up to apologize to Ginsberg. But I started talking to him about it, that it had been involuntary and so forth, even tho I did certainly believe the truth of what Jones had indicated, truth that these people had no business laffing at, and Ginsberg went into a, well then you get into absolutes, as tho absolutes were odious to him, and I just backed quickly off, he seemed so unimpressed with the foolishness of his position and out of touch generally. *

It's hard to define quickly the condition of San Francisco when I returned in late 1967. The public forms of poetry were in deep trouble. The Haight-Ashbury had become the temporary seat of the City, taking

---

* From an episode at Glide Church in San Francisco during the Rolling Renaissance Readings in the summer of 1968, recorded in *Valga Krusa* by Charles Potts.

that status away from North Beach. Haight Street—still so quiet when I left, and noted for its paint, hardware, and barber shops; two gay bars; Connie's, a Carribean restaurant; and Andy's, a Russian bakery and coffeeshop—had become an incredible din of activity. Anytime, day or evening, hundreds of young people were hanging out on the street or in the numerous new coffeehouses, head shops, record stores, and clothing boutiques. A new experimental movie house had backing from an LA investor. The local "B" movie theater had been renamed The Straight and remodeled with a performing stage and an enormous hardwood dancing floor. Laura Ulewicz's I and Thou coffee shop was running a regular series of readings coordinated by Bill Anderson, and David Gitin was just beginning another series at The Straight with a live radio hookup at KPFA. *The Oracle*, the often wonderful, multicolored, over-sized tabloid, was still coming out somewhat regularly and with work by Whalen, McClure, Welch, and poets I did not yet know; the poems were centered on mandalas, or set in the shape of mandalas, and splashed through with any number of colors. Clifford Burke had moved over from Berkeley to open his Cranium Press on Cole Street, just off Haight. With his own letterpress equipment, he was trying to popularize the fine press elegance and strengths of the work done by Hazelwood and Mackintosh. In addition to books and *Hollow Orange*, he would do innumerable broadsides (on pretty papers with colorful inks) that would be handed out free on the street and at anti-war demonstrations. (At about the same time, Graham published Richard Brautigan's seed book. Packed into a folder, the "book" was a collection of flower seed packets with a Brautigan poem printed on the back of each. Richard and Graham gave the books away to both friends and strangers.) Off the top, the City, especially surrounding Golden Gate Park and the Haight-Ashbury, still appeared to be a potentially powerful situation for poets and poetry.

In actuality, it was the beginning of a long period of silence for local poets. Many things had happened since I had left in 1965. Jack Spicer had died (in August of that year), leaving White Rabbit Press in spiritual shambles. Robin Blaser, Harold Dull, Stan Persky, and eventually George Stanley had left to live in British Columbia. Lew Welch was in alcoholic straits, focusing what energies he had on Mt. Tamalpais rather than on the City. Philip Whalen, terrified of the increase in street violence, and Gary Snyder were either in or off to Japan.

In an odd way, the poets and the language that had given permission and form to the changes in the mid-1960s were no longer needed. The lone poet as performer and evangelist of personal, social, and political change had been replaced by the rock star and the group. Country Joe & the Fish, the Jefferson Airplane, and the Grateful Dead—let alone Bob Dylan—had clearly taken their impetus from the poets. But more than the loss of an audience to music or to the technologies of sounds and rhythms, the new emphasis was on experiences that were essentially nonverbal. Language, especially poetry, was seen as the back and not particularly important edge of what could be felt and envisioned on drugs, in the ecstacy of dance and sound, or, on a more worldly level, in the urgencies of political street action or the communal pleasures and pains of operating a collective home or farm. I remember once asking Max Finstein, a poet whose book Clifford Burke was publishing, if he were writing any new poetry. He had recently moved to New Mexico from San Francisco to join the New Buffalo commune; he was back in town for a short visit. He was kind of snitty. "It's a 103-acre poem," he said and got up to leave Clifford's shop. *To say you were a poet was like assuming an unevolved or reactionary position.*

By the fall of 1968, harsh and violent political struggles had replaced the pacifist and utopian anarchism proposed by the earlier poetries. The first trial of Huey Newton, Eldridge Cleaver's speeches, the State strike and its suppression, the endless demonstrations against the war, seemed to put poetry further on the back burner. It was a time of action and choice. *Poetry was a refuge from the real.* A speech in the park by Bobby Seale, then co-chairman of the Black Panther Party, contained the news, a combination of anecdotes, analysis, and vision in what was usually an amazing display of vocal fireworks. Before politics he had been both a drummer and a comedian, and he was clearly a poet of revolution, though nobody called him a poet. Poetry in and by itself was now considered too personal, too indulgent, and too divorced from all the various collective callings. I remember when the poet Charles Potts flipped out, talking nonstop for days until Thorazine calmed him down. It's as if he thought everybody had stopped listening—that kind of despair.

In August of 1968, as a part of the Rolling Renaissance, a City-wide series of events commemorating the art, music, and poetry of the 1950s and early 1960s, a huge reading was held at Nourse Auditorium. Featured readers were Welch, Ginsberg, Snyder, Whalen, Brautigan,

33

and Ferlinghetti. David Hazelwood sat in a big overstuffed chair on the stage; the event was partly in honor of the huge contributions of his press, and he was retiring from printing. The authors he had started with had been picked up by national presses. The spirit had been popularized. The reading was both a commemoration and, in part, a death knell to a generation's participation in the City. Welch, in fact, read his essay about the value of going to the country which would later appear in the *digger newsletter*. I left at intermission thinking the event would go all night. It was deadly.

The huge influx of people seeking Haight-Ashbury liberations, the huge consumption of drugs, combined with police and unsympathetic community reaction, had turned most 1965 visions on a downward spiral. Rapes, indiscriminate police street crackdowns on anybody who appeared to be under the influence, muggings, black anger at the apolitical and indulgent character of the hippies, the simple fact that many people freaked out behind the perceptions they experienced on drugs—all contributed. One day, a talented writer who hung out at the I and Thou, a speed freak, jumped off the Golden Gate Bridge and survived—one of the few to do so. He came back and wrote a good play about ping-pong as a metaphor for the going-public psyche. Many were just not able to survive. It was as if more was being released into the culture than could be dealt with, at least on the level of language. With the exception of the determination of Clifford Burke, most of the active publishers of the mid-1960s had closed down. Graham Mackintosh was about to move to Santa Barbara to start printing Black Sparrow's line of poetry books, and Oyez was heading for several years of quiet. Most of the mimeograph and offset publishers had quit or moved out of town. As Lew put it:

. . . the Meth Freak hippy pushers have got so big the Mafia is moving in and pushers in the Hashbury are getting murdered. Three at least. *And* the acid is untakeable because it may be STP (an Army drug developed to pacify or wipe out the enemy, the trip goes on for 72 hours and 4 of my friends, some of them very strong, are now in loony bins), not to mention the bad shit LSD with Meth in it. Gary, people, good ones, are blowing their minds irreversibly. Like, gone. Away.*

A community had begun to disperse. Songs about going to the

---

* Lew Welch to Gary Snyder in a letter, August 9, 1967, from *I Remain:* The Letters of Lew Welch & the Correspondence of His Friends, Volume Two: 1960–1971, edited by Donald Allen (San Francisco: Grey Fox), 1980.

country, even if that meant Marin County just across the Golden Gate Bridge, became very popular.

A Personal Interlude

It's hard to convey the degree of distrust in language, especially the language of poetry, that occurred in the late 1960s. Between what were portrayed as the nonverbal visual and emotional powers of LSD and the lies that were perpetrated daily by the government in support of the war, words were simply seen as divorced from the reality of deeper events. As a poet, you could go two ways with language. One was underground journalism, such as in Bill Anderson's fine columns for the then-left-leaning *Bay Guardian*. The other way was to take poetry into a deeper and fuller association with the physical as a way of restoring its power. Silence was also a possibility: The image of Robert Duncan walking through Washington Square wearing a black armband in protest and holding a vow of silence could be poem enough.

Perhaps it's typically Western American to finally doubt language and to opt for the physical gesture as the only convincing form of communication. The book is often seen as beside the point, or looked upon with suspicion. And when the voice in the public poetry reading became questionable, it was natural to search the body as a way to insure, or to give testament to, *the fact* of the poem. In 1968, as the poetry reading scene disappeared, one of the ways to go toward a physical experience with language was to participate in Anna Halperin's Dancer's Workshop on Divisadero Street at the very foot of the Haight-Ashbury. Anna, I believe, was demonically pleased to have writers in her workshops and events. In her view, language was an art secondary to what could be discovered and experienced through movement, especially through contact improvisation.

That spring, she presented a ten-week series of *Myths*. Each Thursday night I went down to her studio feeling as if I were Hawthorne's Young Goodman Brown going to join with the saints and the devils of my own unconscious and physical underworld. Usually on condition of participation in the event, the evenings were open to the public, and sometimes up to a hundred people were present. The instructions and structures were quite simple. Language rarely came into the events.

One night, Anna broke us up into groups of ten, giving each of us a blindfold. After putting the blindfolds on, we were told to hold hands in a line; the last person in the line was to move from that end to the front, while all the rest of us kept our hands gripped. We could make sounds, but we could not speak. It seemed simple, almost inconsequential, as she proposed the structure. In reality, after two hours, when the lights were turned back on, I realized it had been like experiencing a medieval allegory in all its aspects: Only four people of the ten had made it through our line. Intense pain, ecstacy, boredom, loneliness, an absolute sense of connection, animal levels of ferocity, and angelic-seeming erotic levels of touch occurred through the hands I gripped on either side of me and through the various bodies that passed among us. They climbed up and down our legs and torsos as if we were tough mountains or warm valleys or as if, as in Ovid's *Metamorphoses,* they had been suddenly transformed into lions or goats. Alternately diverse and then communal sounds emerged from our various actions. The transmission of energy and the changes were enormous. Indeed, it was as if within the altering patterns and polarities of our line, the demons, the dreams, the whole residual history of the culture was simultaneously held and released.

   The Myths were a high-risk situation; eventually and unfortunately there would be physical violence at the Workshop (almost as if it were inevitable that the "outside" horrors of the culture had to break through the liberating structures of the rituals). But in terms of poetry, *The Myths,* as well as many of Halperin's other exercises, proposed a place where the language of the body could become the poem, where what was experienced as flesh could become sound, could become word. Instead of an external occurrence or sign, the poem could be felt and realized as a part of a healing ritual, where the language vented and mended the personal and community cracks. In turn the audience's experience of a poem would be felt as a full physical and vocal exchange. Going back to Olson's proposition in "Projective Verse," the line could move according to the intelligence of the total organism (psychic, physical, and mental) in the making of the poem *as well as* in the listening. It was a way to create community when there was little or none.

   The work at the Dancer's Workshop, which included beginning to take regular "movement" classes, had a huge effect on my own work, especially as a teacher. I was leading the Poetry Workshop, sponsored by the San Francisco State Poetry Center, at the Downtown Extension in a basement auditorium in the old building on Powell Street. The place became the center of many writing experiments involving movement, sound, and language. I was insistent on finding how a poem could be created and then both perceived and integrated fully into the response of the listener.

Sixteen students attended the workshop. We usually began with exercises that focused on one word. Fruit, because, I think, of its sensuality and seeming innocence, was popular. We took, for example, the word *apple*. Standing in a circle we went around one by one, repeating it over and over again. High pitch, low pitch, soft, quick, hard, or very slow. One person said it, and the rest of us echoed, in an exact-as-possible imitation. Then the vocal gesture became physical. Arms opened and closed to the rhythm and sound size of the syllables. After five or sometimes ten minutes, the process came to a close with a definite collective sense of a particularly known and shared *apple*.

Then I took fresh apples from a bag, giving one to each member of the circle. One by one, we placed the apples into a pattern on the hardwood floor. Everyone worked on the pattern, adjusting it until we were satisfied with its shape. Then came a new period of naming in which the ground rule was to be factually specific as to what was there in front of our eyes. Metaphors were not allowed. *Green. Red. Stem. Black. Brown. Bruise. Dimple.* We stayed as close as possible to the actual, letting the simple phrases and words adjust to what was there. Gradually a vocal shape emerged, a complete picture, and then silence. We broke and then ate the apples.

This process, after we had written from the outside and then the inside of a particular apple, led into a similar exploration of poems. For example, one night we took a poem by Denise Levertov of exactly seventeen lines, one for each of us, and each person was responsible for repeating his or her line from memory. We were in a circle. I turned off the lights. We went around seventeen times, repeating the poem from memory. At first the individual lines sounded stilted and tense, much the way language can sound at cold poetry readings. But gradually, through the process of repetition, the poem began to assume its own independent shape and sound, where the integrity of the actual work seemed to take on a life of its own. The sound was specific to us and what we brought to the poem. If it were raining outside, or spring, or if someone close to the group had died or given birth, these events would undoubtedly influence the shape and tone of what happened.

When the saying of the poem came to a completion, we turned on the lights and wrote, each person using his or her Levertov line as the first phrase from which a poem or paragraph would be improvised. After half an hour, when that was finished, we read the Levertov around again, this time adding the new lines. At the end of this reading, it was as though the Levertov poem, at least in this context, had extended into the life of its listeners as far as it could go. In the process, the poem managed to elicit the creation of a mythology and a strongly felt, though momentary, community.

In the late 1960s and early 1970s, this kind of vocal and movement exploration with audiences at public readings was practically impossible even to consider, at least in the Bay Area. The political turmoil of the time was the overwhelming preoccupation of both public and poets. Media drama, center stage, was a country falling apart. Experimenting with language, movement, and sound to create environments was seen as apolitical and indulgent, no matter what the actual content. There was a vulnerability about the process that was probably too scary for the time. (The Living Theater, which incorporated many of these techniques of ritual and audience contact, is an obvious and remarkable exception to this view.) When the poet was invited, no matter how physical his or her presence, the poet remained in the pulpit. A poetry of statement was primary. Not until the late 1970s with the emergence of sound poetry and performance art did some poets begin to cross these boundaries.

The Early 1970s:
The New Diversity

In the early 1970s, important shifts began to take place in what was heard. Historically these shifts may have marked the end of a certain renaissance of what was essentially white, middle-class activity. Out of whatever despair, in the spring of 1970 Lew Welch walked off into the Sierra, apparently in an act of suicide. Janis Joplin was dead. And it was hard to want to hear another record by the Jefferson Airplane. It was, however, the beginning of a genuinely multicultural alteration in what had been a primarily City-based, white-male-centered poetry.

In the East Bay, taking the lead from Judy Grahn and Alta, a strong body of feminist writers began to emerge. In San Francisco, propelled by the promotional and organizing energies of Roberto Vargas, there began a whole series of readings by Third World writers of Latin, Asian, and black origin. Writers up and down the Coast began to command attention. Bolinas had become a refugee center for a number of New York-identified writers, including Tom Clark, Bill Berkson, and Lewis MacAdams, as well as Joanne Kyger and David Meltzer from the City. Later they would be joined by Robert and Bobbie Creeley. Down the Coast at Santa Cruz, a number of writers, including Mary Körte, Morton Marcus, and George Hitchcock, got active in readings and publications, including George's already well-established *Kayak* magazine. In the City, in addition to Third World activity, a large number of writers (graduates of State, North Beach surrealists, people who had not been burnt out by the narcotic ravages of the late 1960s) began to make their work public.

A new order of writing was gradually established. No close identification was apparent among the poets. The initial diversity made things potentially fiery and exciting. Magazine and book publications were still few. The reading was a way of getting work to the public as a form of oral literature in which audiences began to speak about poems they had *heard*. (This was yet a few years before National Endowment for the Arts small press grants began flooding stores with everybody's books!) In the fall of 1970 I began teaching at the San Francisco Art Institute. In the library, with its great view of the Bay, Jacob Wiener and I started a reading series. We made a habit of inviting three or four poets every other week from all aspects of the community: Bolinas, the East Bay, graduate students at State, people from the Mission and North Beach. Both of us were amazed at the late Friday afternoon turnouts of fifty to one hundred people. We were definitely involved in a new surge.

The spirit of the readings was initially tentative. Occasionally you could sense a kind of competition to give a sensational reading, to capture a crowd. But poets were still unsure as to whether or not the reading was a viable form. No one wanted to get into an imitation Ginsberg or repeat the evangelical tone of Welch and the other Beats. Prophecy seemed archaic. At the same time, especially among feminists and Third World writers, an anger and urgency, a sense of pronouncement was growing. The question was how to relate to an audience in a compelling way. Most of the poems were centered in the voice, the processes and sounds of speech—whether declarative or conversational —and sometimes the work moved into song. Physical presence and a sense of dialogue with the listener seemed required. That possibility of exchange raised the audience's energy. In addition to attending to style, the integrity of the sound of the poet's voice, people were coming to

39

deliver and hear content. It was the beginning of the assumption of differences: the world of Bolinas, women, Latinos, Asians, blacks, City, country, and eventually the world of gays. Depending on where you were coming from, the new work could be liberating or threatening or, at least, amusing. It was definitely a new and diverse turf.

It was also the beginning of an enormous eruption of activity. In the fall of 1971, the Berkeley Poets Commune organized a large three-day poetry festival at the University Museum in Berkeley. The festival marked the first real attempt to unite at one occasion both established writers such as Robert Creeley and Joanne Kyger with the divergent groups of emerging, younger writers. Among several readings, Judy Grahn read with Alta and Susan Griffin as a feminist testament. And, equally important, a large Third World presentation included the work of Jessica Tarahata Hagedorn, Thulani Davis, Al Robles, and Janice Mirikitani. It was the first large exposure of new writers who had previously been heard only in small readings. The festival set up some of the main currents that constituted Bay Area writing for the next several years.

From 1972 on, readings began to spring up everywhere. In Berkeley a regular Wednesday night series was started at Cody's Books. It still continues. In San Francisco, Tuesday readings were begun at the Intersection, a nondenominational coffeehouse. They were coordinated by Tom Cuson with the eventual assistance of Steve Shutzman and Barbara Gravelle (who began a Monday night series for women's work). A few blocks away, on Grant Avenue, Carol Lee Sanchez took over the Wednesday night open mike to start a popular series at the Coffee Gallery. Another series began at Panjandrum Press on Saturday nights. In addition to the regular on-campus series, the Poetry Center began to stage large readings at the San Francisco Museum of Art. City Lights Bookstore, until Fire Department regulations intervened, held massive readings at Project Artaud, a warehouse artists' community, drawing up to 2,000 people for Allen Ginsberg and Yevgeny Yevtushenko, on one occasion, and Andrei Voznesensky on another. Between 1972 and 1976, rarely was a day of the week free of a reading or poetry event somewhere.

The activity made possible the publication of *Poetry Flash*. Initially the *Flash* was a two-side mimeographed flyer with a calendar of Bay Area readings and events. Edited by Jon Ford, it came out monthly and was distributed free in bookshops and coffeehouses. By 1973 an esti-

40

mated 500 to 1,500 people were attending readings each week. In addition, Poetry in the Schools, a project of the Poetry Center, funded by the National Endowment for the Arts (and, at the time, under my coordination), was placing poets in the schools all over the Bay Area and Northern California to do regular workshops and readings. It was by far the largest burst of activity since the middle 1960s.

An intensity and drive to be heard probably transcended the desire to be published. Fifty to a hundred people at a reading could initially be a much greater pleasure than the slow process of publishing and book sales. But *pleasure* was not the word to describe the tone. Much of what was being read was connected to a new political stance. The eruptions of 1968 had produced a constant source of personal transformation that found root and support in revolutionary politics. At its best, the language was attacking the very tissue of the country's social organization, whether racial, sexual, ecological, economic, or political. No situation was spared, nor were the ruling elites of poetry. Behind the attack was the spirited assertion of a liberated and changing identity, both individual and cultural.

You could hear the new tone when Susan Griffin read "On Being Asked by a Man What He Could Do for Women's Liberation," when Judy Grahn read "Edward The Dyke," when Paul Mariah read "One Mad Queen," when Roberto Vargas read *"Elegy Pa Gringolandia,"* or when Gary Snyder, one of the few engaged survivors of the 1960s, read his "Smokey the Bear Sutra." The language had a satiric, often savage bite. The intent was no less than to restructure radically what constituted *acceptable* American thought, behavior, and belief. The work was performed with and against the backdrop of intense moves and counter-moves in this country's political history. Not only was the Viet Nam war raging, but events revolved around George Jackson, Angela Davis, and the San Quentin Six; the Weathermen; the struggles to bring ethnic relevancy into schools and colleges; the initial gay and feminist protests and demonstrations; Watergate and the Nixon administration; the coup in Chile; the invasion of Cambodia, and on and on.

The mixed poetry reading became a place in which all the battles might be engaged. It would be wrong, however, to assume that all that was read went in the direction of the various liberations, or that white men, feminists, gays, and Third World writers were not without serious divisions. White writers (products of writing programs, or those with special affinity to surrealist, Black Mountain, and New York

41

Allende/Neruda Memorial Reading poster, 1973.
Reproduced from the silk screen by Rupert Garcia.

school writers) often faced Third World criticism that their work was too "interior" or self-serving. The view was that such writing lacked social context, relevance, and political commitment. It was writing as end in itself. Such writers were told that their work was racist, or, from a feminist point of view, the work was misogynistic, for refusing to acknowledge and respond to the new issues raised by women and Third World writers. Non-Third World writers would sometimes respond that writing done primarily from a racial and political base was limited because it could not engage the whole range of human issues and possible concerns of *language*. And both white and Third World male writers were damned by the women when they rejected feminist writing as unwomanly. It was a hot circle of writers and writing, to say the least. Nevertheless it was a period of contact, no matter how often blunt and bruised, in which the writing scene was not fragmented, as it currently seems, into several separatist camps of concern. At that time, on most any night of the week in North Beach, at Vesuvio's, Spec's, the Intersection, or Malvina's, it was possible for several kinds of writers to run into each other over drinks. The reading as a place of engagement with issues was played out all over the City and the Bay Area into the mid-1970s.

It was not just limited to the relatively small reading situations at the Intersection, Cody's, The Coffee Gallery, Panjandrum, and Minnie's Can-Do club but would periodically explode into larger scenarios, particularly at the Museum of Art, Glide Church, Fugazi Hall, the Longshoreman's Hall, and Project Artaud. The era of "the big reading" was definitely back, as it had been in the mid-1960s. Anywhere from ten to twenty poets were invited, and the evenings stretched from 7:30 to midnight. Different physical locations had various appeals. The Museum of Art put the work in a relatively apolitical context of *art* and social importance, no matter who was reading. Fugazi Hall in North Beach created resonances with the Beats. Longshoreman's Hall, near Fisherman's Wharf, held progressive "union" political connotations. And Glide, during those years, of all the settings, was undoubtedly the most provocative place in town—politically, socially, and racially.

Cecil Williams, one of the progressive Glide pastors, enlivened the church's community-based image. No matter what the event in the secular world—the strike at State, events surrounding the war, the struggles of gays, seniors, blacks, Chicanos, Asians, the demands of the SLA—Cecil was there as intermediary or negotiator, with whatever seemed called for. His services on Sunday, combining music and oratory with an insistence on community involvement and redemption, gave the church a dimension, a large and loaded sense of space in which almost any national or local disease could be put into focus for healing, banishment, or elegy.

The huge Glide readings, usually held on Friday or Saturday night, were often a large spectacle. The church holds about 1,500 people when it is full, both bottom floor and steep balcony. When the house lights are dimmed and the stage light focuses on the performer, the darkness about the place can be absolutely haunting. All the issues of the City and the Republic seem to float through the thick air; no matter who reads, their work is measured in the light of whether or not it grapples with the presence of oppression. In the early 1970s the darkness was loaded with guilt, anger, and grief connected with the war and issues of racism. Whether the reading was in commemoration of Allende and Neruda or a benefit for the bombed Bach Mai Hospital, it was as if the whole continent had tipped into one sanctuary to deal with Death. Whether Stan Rice was reading "Some Lamb" on the dying of his daughter or Ishmael Reed was recounting his satiric *Flight to Canada,* the dark side of the country was being tapped. Sometimes, especially during the Bach Mai benefit, the readings would spill into recriminations, with some Third World poets cutting into the ethnic oblivousness of some white poets, arousing guilt and anger. The place could get to feeling really crummy and hostile, until another poet would come on and raise the focus into more constructive directions.

The reading that remains strongest in my memory was at the Longshoreman's Hall. Sponsored by City Lights, it was a benefit for the United Farm Workers. The invited poets included Creeley, Duncan, Ginsberg, Whalen, and Ferlinghetti. Before the reading, Roberto Vargas persuaded Ferlinghetti that, given the nature of the benefit, it was strange that no Third World poets were reading. Consequently, Thulani Davis, Jessica Hagedorn, Janice Mirikitani, Serafin Syquia, and Roberto himself were added to the list. The turnout was huge; an audience of 2,000 filled the place. Perhaps because the reading was in support of progressive change and did not possess the elegaic spirit of the usual Glide reading, the whole evening had an up tone to it (with the exception of one crass, mad-mouthed drunk).

What turned the reading, however, was the acceptance of the 1950s by the 1970s. The poets from the 1950s had always made clear

44

the influence on their work of jazz, blues, and various La Raza and Asian sources. In the 1960s, however, there was already much criticism, mainly by Third World critics, of Beat indulgence in stereotypical and romantic depictions of Blacks, Asians, and Latinos. The potential tension between the "taker" and the "takee" transformed the occasion into a powerful and various experience of language with a multiple sense of origin, rather than a nostalgic "old boys" benefit. Serafin Syquia's poem about diplomatic ping-pong, the precise sound of the ball hitting the paddle before crossing back over the net, back and forth across the hyphens of America's diverse migratory nations, caught the edge of the evening, the audience riding the various lifts of the ball as it went from one poet to another. People left that place lifted, as if a truth and balance had been struck.

Up until 1976 there was a solid burst of work, both in readings and in publishing. Initially the publishing was secondary to the potential excitement of reading. Books and magazines, if they did at all, followed in the wake of the poet's voice. The emphasis was on performance. The intimate, collective process of getting together as an audience was encouraged by the urgency and the sense of hysteria of the times. It was social and more attractive to get together than to sit at home reading a person's book. That could come later, after the event. Then the poet's voice could resonate and possibly become more complex within the context of the printed page. In the early 1970s, it was quite possible the poet might not have a book. Even if she or he did, the poems in a reading might be totally new or different from those in the book: Things were moving that fast, or at least more quickly than most small press publishers.

Given the emphasis on and public success of readings, some poets naturally began to expand the format and shape of their work in order to involve actors, musicians, dancers, and their own instruments. Apart from the challenge of new forms, it was clearly a way to expand an audience that could grow tired of the poet-in-the-pulpit format. Those who were active in the changeover were Susan Griffin, whose play *Voices*, a poetic drama for six voices, was performed in several Bay Area locations, including a KQED-TV production. Ntozake Shange started working with Pamela Moss, the dancer, and from that work came the poems for her play, *For Colored Girls Who Have Considered Suicide When the Rainbow Is Enuf*. They performed the work in progress several times at places like the Intersection, Minnie's Can-Do, and the

Bacchanal, totally unreviewed, but before enthusiastic audiences before taking it back to a huge success in New York. Jessica Hagedorn established The West Coast Gangster Choir, a several-piece band with two singers, for the performance of her work. Julian Priester, the composer and jazz trombonist, wrote the musical arrangements; parts of the poems would be broken into refrains for the singers, while Jessica performed the poems from memory, sometimes going into song herself. When Jessica and Ntozake performed their work together, with the dancers and the music, they could stir a crowd to an obsessive frenzy, the language hit such a chord in the time. The Palace Monkeys, a group of poets that included Michael Koch, Renny Pritikin, and Anthony Vaughn, worked with their own instruments and other musicians to raise their poems into song or amplified narratives, with some following and success. The attention to poetry as performance was such that Lewis MacAdams, director of the Poetry Center, asked prospective poets for tapes of their work to hear how they might sound at a reading.

Though public readings were primary, they were ultimately a way of mediating back (or forward!) to the publication of books and magazines. With the exception of a few intensely oral poets, such as Max Schwartz, I have rarely met a poet who is not interested in releasing a book. At this point in history, the book was the way of confirming, or making concrete, what was experienced in the public reading. (It was also a way of taking the poems to audiences geographically distant from the Bay Area.) In any case a variety of new publishers began to flourish. Each one was generally reflective of the different pieces of the literary scene.

As the 1970s progressed, the Third World presence was increased by the activity of Victor Hernández Cruz and David Henderson and suffered the tragic loss of Serafin Syquia in 1973. Third World Communications published *Third World Women's Anthology* in 1973 and, in association with Glide Publications, produced *Time to Greez!*, a comprehensive anthology of local work in 1976. In addition, during the same period, Ediciones Pocho Che published *double back* volumes: *Primeros Cantos* by Roberto Vargas with *This Side and Other Things* by Elías Hruska y Cortés, and *Oracion A La Mano Poderosa* by Alejandro Murguia with *El Sol Y Los De Abajo* by Jose Montoya. Nationally, Random House published *Mainland* by Victor Cruz. And Momo's Press published *Dangerous Music* by Jessica Hagedorn. *Yard Bird Reader* and *Heirs* magazines variously also published the new work.

The number of women writers influenced by feminism increased dramatically. In addition to Alta, Grahn, and Griffin, new work by Beverly Dahlen, Pat Parker, Jana Harris, Stephanie Mines, and Julia Vose, to name just a few, began to be heard. Significantly, Shameless Hussy Press published Alta's *No Visible Means of Support;* Mama's Press issued *Let Them Be Said* by Susan Griffin; Women's Press Collective published *Edward The Dyke and Other Poems* by Judy Grahn and *Child of Myself* by Pat Parker. And Momo's Press produced *Out of the Third* by Beverly Dahlen.

The early 1970s also marked the rebirth of North Beach as a center for writers (a position lost for several years to the Haight), with the arrival of Beat-generation characters from all over the world. Harold Norse, after long exile in Europe, Jack Micheline from New York, and Jack Hirshman from Los Angeles, all in their late forties, formed an uneasy neighborhood triumvirate near which writers attracted to the 1950s Beat mythology began to congregate. In the spring of 1975, Bob Kaufman was brought out of a ten-year silence to give a reading at a packed Malvina's coffeehouse on Union Street. Though his voice was cracked with age, he read poems from his City Lights Pocket Book editions with the hypnotic, jagged, hip insistence with which he had undoubtedly read them in the 1950s. A scary experience. It was as though nothing had changed! The event hatched the revival of *Beatitude* magazine that again became a neighborhood organ. In addition to *Beatitude,* Second Coming press and magazine also published North Beach work with a special focus on Jack Micheline and its editor, A. D. Winans. City Lights published *Hotel Universe* by Harold Norse and *Lyripol* by Jack Hirshman. Public readings went hand in hand with these new publications, as well as the initiation of the annual San Francisco Poetry Festival.

Somewhat simultaneously with North Beach's revival, partly because of the returned presence of Philip Lamantia and the late Pete Winslow, surrealist work began to flourish. Equally important were the presence of Nanos Valaoritis, the Greek expatriate, by way of Breton's Paris, who had begun teaching at San Francisco State, and Andrei Codrescu, the Roumanian, by way of Paris, Detroit, and New York, and recent winner of the Big Table Award for his first book, *License to Carry a Gun.* Jim Gustafson, The Black Tarantula (aka Kathy Acker), Steve Brooks, Steve Shutzman, Tom Cuson, David Plumb, and Beau Beausoleil were all committed in one way or other to establishing an urban,

47

surrealist aesthetic that would be appropriate to the City. Panjandrum press and magazine, Isthmus press and magazine, Grape Press, Smoking Mirror Press, Journal 31, and Gallery Works were crucial publishers for the various writers. Divisions among the surrealists were, of course, rampant. In the work, however, there began to emerge an often harsh, though frequently anarchistically funny, multiple dreamlike image of the City's underbelly. (It was an image that in the later 1970s would connect easily with the local Punk music scene.)

Assertively open gay work could be found in *Gay Sunshine,* the new tabloid. It featured important interviews with Ginsberg, John Wieners, and Norse, and included large amounts of poetry with other kinds of reportage. Though not limited to San Francisco, it was the first local publication to provide a focus on gay writing with attention to poetry by Paul Mariah, Robert Gluck, and Aaron Shurin, among others. Manroot press and magazine, edited by Mariah, though diverse in editorial policy, also gave access to much gay writing.

As an editor and publisher of both *Shocks* and Momo's Press, I saw myself as a mender. Shocks were the reverberations I felt emanating from just about every writing quarter. The magazine and the press were a way of establishing a larger writing out of intense and conflicting fragments. The sum would be greater than the parts. It was time to break away from the focus on one writer over another, or the myth of the writer as isolated and independent hero. The intention became to establish contexts in which writers could occur in simultaneous situations. This intention was the impetus behind *The Day Book* issue of *Shocks* No. 5 in which six writers of various backgrounds (Andrei Codrescu, Beverly Dahlen, Susan Griffin, Jessica Hagedorn, Roberto Vargas, and myself) each took ten differently placed days over a sixty-day period in February and March of 1974. Each of us had a page per day in which we could write a poem, dream, idea, documentary, or story. The idea was to create a collective journal in which the various writings would vibrate off one another to create a larger dimension. This interfacing of borders and crossings of various writings and writers has remained the most serious intention of the press.

The work of all these various new presses and writers did not eliminate the work of writers established in the 1950s and 1960s. Several new and some of the older surviving presses committed themselves to sustaining the growth of these writers, as well as their responses to on-going events in the body politic. Sand Dollar, Tree magazine and press, Mudra, the Four Seasons Foundation, Grey Fox, and Cranium Press published various works by McClure, Snyder, Welch, Ed Dorn (who, in 1973, took up residence in the City for several years), Diane di Prima, and Robert Creeley. Most importantly, in terms of established poets, Turtle Island published Dorn's *Gran Appacheria* (1974), to be eventually followed by Wingbow's presentation of the complete *Gunslinger* (1977). Up the coast in Bolinas, Big Sky magazine and press would take care of much of the New York and local traffic with books by Jim Thorpe, Joanne Kyger, Bill Berkson, and Lewis MacAdams, among several others.

The early 1970s also marked the rebirth of letterpress printing. Influenced strongly by the example and teaching of Clifford Burke at Cranium Press, a number of new printers began to emerge under different logos: Holbrook Teter and Michael Myers' Zephyrus Image, Betsy Davids' and Jim Petrillo's Rebis Press, Wesley Tanner's Arif, Bonnie Carpenter's Effie's Books, and Five Trees original group of Jaime Robles, Cameron Folsom, Eileen Callahan, Cheryl Miller, and Kathy Walkup. Most of these presses were committed to preserving and expanding the traditions of lively and solid poetry printing initiated by David Hazelwood and Graham Mackintosh. True to that tradition, many of the printers, especially Burke, Teter, and Tanner, assisted in designing and printing books by McClure, Welch, Snyder, Creeley, and Dorn, as well as work of some of the younger writers, including Keith Abbott, Jessica Hagedorn, and Beverly Dahlen. Effie's Press, committed to feminist work, also partook of that tradition in making letterpress books by Susan Griffin, Adrienne Rich, and Mary Mackey, among others. In general, however, the letterpress process, for books, was too expensive and often too slow. Most publishers had to work with well-known writers to justify the financial investment. And, in terms of the politics of the time, many presses and young writers thought letterpress work was precious and primarily elitist. This debate was hot among many of the printers, who argued that their knowledge of printing and design gave strength and long-term reading power to a work. That photographic methods of typesetting and printing diminished the power was the corollary argument.

Some printers worked both sides of the fence. Avoiding the precious, but still making the work elegant and popularly available, Michael Myers and Holbrook Teter, for example, often used their shop to stick to the traditon of the 1960s free poem. They made broadsides in a combination of language and image that were usually an incisively ambiguous comment on national political events. The work was given away to strangers and friends, most often in The Pub, the neighborhood bar on the corner of Masonic and Geary. (As is done in Japan, their Zephyrus Image series on the Watergate Hearings should be preserved as a national treasure.) In a very real way the argument between letterpress and offset aesthetics always goes back to the tension between whether a poem is to be a sacred enshrined act or a popular and accessible document. That tension is always present in San Francisco in the circumstance of both readings and books.

The Late 1970s:
A Time for Assessment

Gradually the impetus, the energy of the early 1970s came to a stop. We are probably still too historically close to say what took the spirit out of the situation. Clearly much of the work had been animated by political turbulence, national and local. Perhaps it had been a circumstance of a unifying dream, and the dream had been broken. Certainly no energy could bring diverse poets together under the umbrella of "the big reading" for whatever progressive or funereal occasion. Fragmentation and separatism were in the air. A heated era, as they say, was gone. Or as one of my landlords said, "It's a luxury to live in San Francisco. If you and your family cannot afford it, you should move out."

It was time for a stop and a look around. As in the middle 1950s and middle 1960s, a certain number of poets had risen from the local to get national, or near national, attention. In terms of such success, it was clearly the woman's decade: Alta, Judy Grahn, Susan Griffin, Jessica Hagedorn, and Ntozake Shange all had gained national audiences and various kinds of critical acknowledgment. Among men, Victor Cruz and Andrei Codrescu both had national publishers and audiences. Though many of them would continue to read locally, to honor the audiences and sources of their power, their attentions and energies expanded East. (Ntozake, Jessica, Andrei, and Victor all moved to the East Coast.) No matter how interesting the work, the local media and institutions continued to provide only a minimum of support for local writers.

It was also a time for aesthetic questions. The poetry reading, no matter how popular as a format, often ended up putting real limits on the poem. Writing in response to events, or the presence of a large audience, made for a particular kind of poem, a kind of sound. "The disposable lyric," Keith Abbott called it. The work tended to become a commodity that the audience devoured and forgot. The movement of the voice, no matter who the poet, became a predictable lilt, or invective, or sincerity of tone. Part of the reason poets attempted to expand the form into music, plays, and so forth was to break out of these vocal binds. The poet's voice began to show its limits, especially as the social and political heat cooled. It became a time of parody, conscious or not. It was not that readings stopped entirely. They just became repetitions of previous readings. Steve Brooks, in his 1978 performance, *The First Annual Perennial Lonely San Francisco Poets Festival,* parodied fifteen different voices, introducing each as a different poet with a slightly fictitious name. Among them were the visiting Swedish poet and his translator, the surrealist expatriate writing in English, the feminist from Santa Barbara looking for love in North Beach, the pro-prisoner poet, the white Indian, and on and on. The *Festival* was a genuine celebration of the energies of the different poets, but, most importantly, it was a hilarious satire on the personal limits of the various writings.

By 1975 the National Endowment for the Arts began to grant money to writers, presses, and reading series throughout the country. The question remains whether or not the influx of money has had a healthy or divisive effect on the local writing community. The money, for example, established and maintains the West Coast Print Center, a low-cost printing facility for small press printers. The Center opened in 1976. On the one hand, it completely altered the economy and occurrence of poetry books in the area. Soon there were five poetry books where previously there had been one. The poetry book, whether by letterpress or mimeograph, lost the importance of its occasion. There were just too many books. Stores did not want them ("Nobody buys them"). Even the most open reader could not keep up with the saturation (especially if books from the rest of funded small presses in the country were included). The structure and expense of getting a book published had been broken, for better or worse, and a flood had taken its place. One of the first consequences was that the area's poetry letterpresses either suffered severe economic changes or were taken totally out of business. Clifford Burke left for Washington. Holbrook Teter and Michael Myers eventually stopped book job typesetting and printing. The other presses had to limit themselves to doing fine press work for well-endowed publishers or seek out grants to fund the making of their own titles. The art of printing, instead of poetry, often became the subject of the work. A lively, important, and powerful link between publishers, poets, and local printers had been broken. On the other hand, the Print Center could make the process cheaper and faster, and with the infusion of some of the local letterpress people, as well as outside criticism, the books typeset and printed there have improved greatly in the past five years.

The 1980s:
Where We Stand

Poetry in the Bay Area continues to feed from two directions. One direction addresses the local, the West. In it you find the mountains, the Central Valley, the coast, the shapes that occur in the City. It's made up of a language of particulars; the words emerge out of surfaces, people, and landscapes. The poet, no matter his or her resources, responds to immediate conditions. The poem is a psychic perception of his or her occurrence within a particular context. This tradition is alive in much of the work of Rexroth, Snyder, Whalen, Welch, Everson, Kenneth Irby, and was the paramount mode of writing in the 1960s and 1970s. The poem's intention, performed or read, is to create a communion between the material of the poem, the poet, and the audience. The poet is a healing transmitter, shaping and relieving the audience with a language true to our natural selves and place. You can get a pretty good sense of the totality of *this* landscape and the people through much of this work.

The second tradition creates a poetry whose methods are not necessarily derived from local shapes, nor is geography at its core. Its forms are internationally derived. It's a writing that sustains itself on the revision of older forms, taking, for example, Greek or Latin analogues, the nineteenth-century romantics, or the modern work of European surrealists, or Gertrude Stein, H.D., Zukofsky, and Pound, and shaping that work into a contemporary resonance of speech or voice. The writing creates at least a partial echo with previous writing and does not necessarily take place within an immediately perceived space or experience. I am thinking again of the '50s work of Duncan, Blaser, Spicer, and Stanley, writers of what I called "sacred texts." The world perceived is a pilgrimage of the spirit, a search for the appropriate spirit image. The quest of this work, especially with its particular attention to history and language, was not popular during most of the last two decades. Its evasion of immediate details was considered histrionic. The historic obsessions seemed aimed at increasing the size of the library. It proffered no secular cure.

It is the tension between these two traditions that impels much current writing. One direction moves toward defining what it is to be Western; it attempts to articulate what it is to be here in this ultimate refugee center. Is it East Asia, Northern Mexico, Indian territory, or a fringe extension of Western Europe and its various histories? ("This is the last place. There is nowhere else to go," as Lew Welch phrases it in "The Song Mt. Tamalpais Sings.") The unstable immediacy of our identity, I suspect, will always provoke a poetry immediately responsive to place. And the myth of the West, of loners and mavericks, of rebellious anarchists and pioneers, continues to make the work open to the radically political, ecological, social, and sexual. The poet remains a maker of movements.

The other direction insists on examining, making use of, and revolutionizing the various formal inheritances of the globe. Its impulse is to create a language that rises above the local context in such a way that the poetry resonates with an independent force and significance. Its intentions are genuinely international without any particular responsibility to the day-to-day local. The work has been recently most manifest in the "language centered" writings of David Bromige, Lyn Hejinian, Ron Silliman, Bob Perelman, and Michael Palmer, among others. The primary loyalty of the writing is to the making of literature. Though quite diverse as writers, their obsessive attention to formal and aesthetic questions makes the group the most active descendant of the groups that surrounded Duncan and Spicer in the 1950s.

In the next several years, I expect the work that will speak to us with the most validity will be possessed by the double edge of both traditions: the secular local and the international formal. There will be a continued obsession with what it is to be Western, what it is to be alone in a totally fragmented history without a prescribed identity. The poetry will work to forge a character and community out of that huge loss. Simultaneously, in awareness of that loss, the work will actively explore and make use of international materials. The myth and excitement that surround the Western loner will be seen as painful limits. (Lew Welch, in a sense, is a personification of that pain and failure.) Emerging out of both traditions, the poetry will be built from multiple resources. The mix of secular commands and aesthetic materials, though a constant source of acrimony and division, will create a writing with a much richer and more powerful formal identity. The public reading and the local publisher will make it possible for the argument to continue to unfold. It will be in this process that the writing of the 1980s will actively engage the crisis of the local, as well as resonate with our larger historical and global occasion.

THE FIRST ALL-WOMAN'S POETRY READING

Alta

3 YEARS AGO SIMON & I were very political. thru his politics he heard of
a new women's group. & he took me to the cafe to meet 2 of the women.
they told me the time/date for the next meeting & simon drove me there
& carried me up the stairs (i was pregnant by then & forbidden to walk).
so for the last few weeks of my pregnancy, i was part of a weekly small
group. except that it was large: there were 30 of us. we were all from
previous politics. all of us were into, besides our women's group, at least
one other political struggle. some of the women worked on the local
underground paper, including the wife of that paper's editor. i called her
one wednesday to remind her of the meeting & she said "o, alta, im sure
youre the only one in the group still speaking to me." i asked why &
when she explained the others were striking the paper & expected her to
back their strike & were calling her a scab, i said "well, im sure youll be
welcome tonight. do you want me to ask & then phone you again?" she
did. so when the women arrived i explained how jane was foolishly
worried that our outside political problems might bar her from being
with us as a woman. i finished & waited smilingly for their response.
well. it was my first experience with purging. cleansing of oneself by
removing the filthy member. dangerous physically & no fun socially.
when people's toes get infected, they dont cut them off. but maybe thats
not a sensible analogy? anyhow, jane got infected by loving her husband
more than 29 women she had known for 2 months, so she was unin-
vited. jeez did i feel stupid calling her back. "hey jane. you were right."

"yes, thats what i thot. well, thanks for trying."

but i stayed with the group. i always stay until i get purged. don't
ask me why: maybe im just desperate for company. & we worked

55

toward a city-wide conference for women. each women's group was to prepare papers on a topic. judy suggested "why dont you do a thing with poetry?" so it romped around in my head until one nite i decided to make up an anthology of all the poems i liked by women. i zoomed thru the bookshelves, pulled down all the women's books, & stared at them in horror. there were only 14. out of hundreds & hundreds of books. poetry, novels, astronomy, biology, geometry, history, psychology: of course there were books by women that i couldnt use for my poetry anthology, but how many of those left on the shelves were by women? jane austen, virginia woolf. & the rest? d.a. levy, jung, t.s. eliot, freud, shakespeare, malcolm x, emerson, richard krech, aristophanes, eldridge cleaver & 300 other men. either i had sold out my culture by denying its validity (& not buying the books) or i did not know of our culture & had been lied to all my life, or it did not exist. all the alternatives terrified me. in desperation i read all 14 poetry books & then pulled out the anthologies. i found only 6 poems relevant to the womens' struggle.

for the next couple of weeks i begged friends to bring books from their homes, the library, 2nd hand stores. anything. i found one more poem. to those i added one of mine, one by magda that she had shown me at her house a few months earlier; i requested drawings by the artists on the block & out came the first *remember our fire*. simon printed 500 of them & people loved them. it was the first women's poetry collection any of us had ever seen. to celebrate, i planned a reading with the poets from that booklet. the reading was scheduled for 2 months after kia's birth.

5 of the poets lived in the bay area. i called & 2 of them agreed gladly, i of course was eager, & i relate here the responses of the 2 others. julia said "what do you mean, a women's reading?" (told you we had never heard of such a thing.)

"i mean, just women. reading poetry. men can come listen if they want."

"just women. it'll be kind of flat, dont you think?"

but at least she came.

the 5th poet, the most famous for being revolutionary, said "o, yr from women's lib."

"yep."

"well, i dont go for all that. you all want to have abortions and work in factories."

"im having a baby in 2 weeks, & nobody wants to work in

factories. where do you get this shit?"

"well, when's the reading." so i told her & asked if she would come, cause i didnt want to put her on the leaflet if she didnt. she said she would come, but she didnt like women's lib. in case i hadnt heard it the first time around.

so kia was born & she & i lay around sleeping & trying to adjust to a new world of separation, & a week after her birth my women's group gave me a shower: (we did not dare celebrate before, in case one or both of us died) there was champagne, a stroller, blankets, diapers, powder & lotion, & bubbly slim glasses of champagne! it was lovely, & i smiled & cried, totally surprised. & totally touched that this women's liberation group was not "beyond" celebrating the birth of a child.

i scheduled the reading for our meeting night, so everyone in the group could come. there were 50 or more people to hear us, but only 2 from my women's group. i thot there must be some mistake: all our meetings had at least 10 people. so we waited for them, & for the famous poet. but they never came & she never came.

we had our reading. when julia got to the mike, she said "i had no faith in this reading since it was to be all women. i thot it wouldnt be good. so i only brought poems that i dont like very much, & now im ashamed." but the rest of us read poems we loved & the reading was a huge success. (youd think, since im a poet, i could say something less trite than "huge success"—but what? it was fun? people liked it? a lot? we all got revved up & wrote more poems? its all true—)

& at the next meeting of the women's group i cried out, "you celebrated the birth of my daughter, & i was happy & touched. the other birth, the birth of my work as a woman poet, the birth of our culture made public, you had no faith in! you, too, see me as a vehicle for procreation! you, too, are afraid to believe in our culture!" everyone sat, ashamed, quiet, until judy said "its true."

& simon was mountain climbing that night. he didnt think the women's reading an important birth, either.

For Women Poets, For Poetry: A Journal Entry

Frances Jaffer

November 20, 1978

Write about the women's readings that sprang up in the Bay Area in the late '60s, early '70s; what they were for women poets, for women's poetry, for Poetry. What they were for me.

WHEN DID FEMINISM erupt into poetry readings? I had stopped writing poems years before, taught that my concerns were not the concerns of poetry; better concentrate on cooking, fall in love, marry.

Marry the teacher, be "Mrs. Poetry Center Director." Spend ten years going to readings, mostly men's. Give parties for poets: "Frances, You're Queen of the Dips."

Then I read the poems in *Sisterhood Is Powerful* and Ann Stanford's anthology, *The Women Poets in English*—hardcover, expensive, authority for a timid wife. Could my rejected Louis poem have been a poem after all? Were my feelings an acceptable subject for a poem? Watching my son dying from a supposedly mortal illness: "Have I loved him enough?—Can five years be a Life?"

But I'd been told that the poem needed more visual imagery—needles, tubes, intravenous dripping, arms strapped to boards, mechanisms, images of his pain. They were not what obsessed me. He was unconscious. I was worrying about his five years of life, not about the mechanics of his present pain. And now feminism was telling me that I might have been writing a real poem, after all!

"Women's Poetry" was the theme of the Poetry Center's 1972 Spring *Intersession for Teachers*. Beverly Dahlen and Stephen Vincent

58

urged my husband Mark Linenthal and Stan Rice, the directors, to put on this ground-breaking, week-long presentation of the work of women poets—that energy! One after another, angry: Mary Körte, ex-nun; Janice Mirikitani and Jessica Hagedorn, angry; Susan Griffin, Jan Zaleski, Susan Garrett, angry: days of women's energy that took my breath, gave it back, started me—tentative, frightened—writing poems again.

Anxiety, controversy. Many women unwilling to hear the anger. Many men disturbed, bemused, uncomprehending. It was astonishing for men to be the minority: Stan, Mark, Steve reading among the women. A landmark moment, it seemed to me. I didn't know, then, that in the late '60s and the first years of the '70s there had already been a lively women's poetry scene in Berkeley—readings and presses, women encouraging each other. Alta and Judy Grahn had put together a women's poetry anthology, and there had been a reading from the anthology. Judy Grahn, Pat Parker, Susan Griffin holding workshops and readings. Jeanne Lance and Barbara Gravelle coordinating women's series. How many more I don't even know about!

And while Mark and I were out of the country in 1970 the Poetry Center had presented its first women's reading, with Judy Grahn, Pat Parker, Alta, and Lois Steinberg. Poets and audience sat together in a circle on the floor, and at Alta's insistence, water for all participants—feminism so new that Beverly Dahlen had to bring all the glasses of water, secretary-servant, and no one gave it a second thought—except Bev, of course.

No More Masks (edited by Florence Howe and Ellen Bass) and *Rising Tides* (edited by the Bay Area's Laura Chester and Sharon Barba), new anthologies of women's poetry, were devoured and discussed, legitimizing, I felt, our female literary "separatism," making poetry available to the many women who said to me, "I can't read poetry." I would reply, "Not surprising. Most of it hasn't been written with you in mind. Here, read some of these"—nutrition for the underprivileged?

Arguments. The idea of a female aesthetic? Nonsense? The language of critical praise: "terse, lean, dry, strong, spare, virile, ballsy." Imagine "soft, wet, curved, receptive, flopsy." Above all, imagine "LIMP"! Imagine many climaxes. Imagine anti-climax. Consider form as "extension of content." Imagine female content. Imagine the millennia of male domination of the world's intellectual life, formulations of

59

myths. Imagine women writing warrior epics. Imagine men writing sagas of sisters. Of mothers and daughters. In ancient Greece, in medieval Italy. Where literary forms originated.

Harold Bloom (*A Map of Misreading*, New York: Oxford University Press, 1975) writes, "The first true break with literary continuity will be brought about in generations to come, if the burgeoning religion of Liberated Women spreads from its clusters of enthusiasts to dominate the West. Homer will cease to be the inevitable precursor, and the rhetoric and forms of our literature then may break at last from tradition."

Arguments.

One catalyzing moment for me—a weekend poetry conference in Berkeley run by Susan Griffin (for the University of California Extension). Mostly Third World and women poets. Alta sitting on the stage, all of us clustered around her, babies crawling over our legs, Alta crying, some of us crying with her, some annoyed at her crying (I cried), her powerful unhappy story of trying to be wife, mother, publisher for the unpublished, flunking out of the U.C. writing program, determined not to give up.

Adrienne Rich reading "From an Old House in America"; when a baby cried, she stopped. Talked about the years she wasn't able to go to poetry readings because of her children. She asked if there was a man in the audience who would take care of the baby so that its mother could stay and listen, so that women would be able to hear the poem. Alta's husband took care of the baby.

Steve Vincent read "There Is a Woman in Me," a nonmacho poem about his warring relationship with the softer side of his nature, an oddly discomfiting, exciting experience for me. Susan read her *Tiredness* cycle of poems; was "tiredness," then, an acceptable subject for poetry? I was startled. Rich led two writing workshops (only about twelve women in my section—what a privilege), and she encouraged us to write the poems of our cruelty to our own children.

She was then writing *Of Woman Born*, immersed in this widespread, secret agony of women. I thought about my cruelty to four-year-old Duncan, hitting him with my flailing belt buckle—in the face!—pushing him down three stairs, desperate, out of my head with the troubles of my bad first marriage, inadequately mothered myself, no idea where to turn, psychoanalyst (male) trying to help me love "motherhood." Write—all that—in a poem? I couldn't.

And then Jessica Hagedorn and Ntozake Shange reading in a Third World section, following two men, disturbing, macho. The women's vibrant rhythmic angry singing shouting dancing poems—from their cultures in which women have so often been able (been forced?) to find ways to be electric, surging, powerful. The energy from that reading sparked the rest of my life. Shange read "Toussaint" and other poems I can't remember today by name—only that I left the conference and rented, for myself, the shack I'd been trying to convince Mark he needed in order to write his poems in solitude.

I told myself in advance that I didn't have to show any of my poems to men; I wrote with the idea of reading them, if at all, to women. One of the first was in response to Rich's frightening suggestion—a poem about my cruelty to my children: "Even in the Dark Linc's Head Shines." Rich wrote me that she read it (revised, a year later) aloud to her women's writing classes, and she said they gasped when they heard it. Young women wanted to send it to their mothers, astonished that a "cruel mother" could be someone they liked, someone struggling as they were to escape the net.

I would read these first efforts to women, often not poets, and invariably the response would be the same: a thoughtful pause, and then something like this: "Yes. . . . You know, when I—," and then responses out of their own experience. I knew then that I was on the right track. I had decided that at my age, fifty-three, a beginner, I wouldn't try to write "good" poems. I hoped that if I didn't try to write "good" poems, I might be able, even at that late date, to write some "true" ones, poems of my own experience and, by extension, other women's too.

I knew I needed help. It was hard to accept Mark's suggestions without arguing. I knew I had to have some help from a woman. Kathleen Fraser was by then director of the Poetry Center and was about to teach a class in special problems for women writers. I begged her to allow me to audit. She was worried—I was enthusiastic and had become articulate and talkative. Would I give the younger women who were just beginning to trust their own language out loud a chance to express themselves? I promised I would, and I sat in her class with SHUT UP printed in large red letters on a paper in front of me.

Approximately twenty-six women, from nineteen years old to my fifty-three, were in the class, and with Kathleen's tactful and effective guidance we discovered each other's poems. Our poetry flowered. In the following semester she taught the class again with new students, and I think these classes provided a nucleus for much excitement on the West side of the bay (and expanding).

There were student readings and a college-made television program drawn from them (all the student readings—men and women). On that television program seven women and only one man agreed to read! In local coffeehouses and libraries many of the readings were women's readings, a phenomenon previously rare, if not unknown. Women of the area, men too, flocked to hear them.

Activity in the East Bay was exciting and varied, but since I wasn't there and didn't know about much of it, I have trouble remembering or tracking down the facts, the sequence, who began what. Alta began the Shameless Hussy Press—as far as I know, the first women's press in the country. She virtually begged from door to door for money to get it started. And the Women's Press Collective, led by Judy Grahn, whose readings of *Edward The Dyke* and the *Common Woman Poems* electrified audiences. There were many benefit readings for women's literary and other programs. Susan Griffin's "I Like To Think of Harriet Tubman" and her funny, angry "Wear a Dress" particularly delighted me when I heard them later on. They stimulated political as well as literary activity. I heard Pat Parker for the first time in a large group reading—a benefit. She read "There Is a Woman in This Town" and brought down the house. I can't begin to list even the readings and poems that I can remember myself.

The Bacchanal, a women's bar, opened in North Berkeley, owned by Sande Fini and poet Joanna Griffin; the poetry readings held there regularly drew audiences from all around the Bay and beyond.

A fight developed in San Francisco State's Creative Writing Department over the curriculum for women writers, and the students formed a Women's Caucus. They wanted more women writers to be included in the list of "acceptable" subjects for Master's Degree oral examinations. This struggle spread into the city, with sympathizers everywhere, infuriating the conservative professors (not necessarily male). They wanted to make their own decisions without such input from students or community.

The Noe Valley Library ran a series of readings by members of the Women's Caucus. Women came from other communities to read with us. The Poetry Center under Kathleen Fraser's direction presented as many women readers as men, from all around the country—lesbian women writing publicly for the first time about their lives as lesbians,

Third World women, older women who had often been ignored until now; the excitement was high and stimulating to us all. As listeners. As poets.

Women were ignoring criticism from frequently uncomprehending and/or resistant males and their female counterparts (Yeats: "Did she put on his knowledge with his power?" The answer: "Yes. With emphasis on the pronoun"). At a writer's conference held at Foothill College in June, 1975, I participated in a panel discussion on the subject of women's writing. The interchange was excited, exacerbated, intense. Should anger be "transcended" to make—ART? Should there be a separate category of criticism for women's writing, not "lesser" or "greater," but different? The sections were crowded, tempers flared; it was all so new.

A "cluster." Here in the Bay Area. What now? Will it develop, grow, become a firm commitment, among women, among men? Or will the inevitable splitting and conflict that follows the excited unity of a first revolt prevent the continuing emergence of an authentic women's poetry to join, with equal authority, the poetry of men? Marxists, anti-Marxists, lesbians, heterosexuals, financial success, financial disaster, rejection, co-option—can aesthetic feminism survive these dichotomies?

I'm a pessimist, and I'm afraid. But perhaps it takes the optimism of youth to keep a revolt going after its first tenuous success. Or the tenacity of age? Both?

Write the next poem. And the next—.
And the next.

GETTING THERE A LITTLE LATE:

A Review of the *Kuksu* Benefit Poetry Reading

Barry Eisenberg

I GOT TO BE pretty good at predicting snow [during the winter of 1975], so I wasn't surprised to find six inches of new powder on the ground when I woke up. The lake by the cabin was dark and beautiful—fir trees so green and clouded with snow, and the tan oaks bent under, as always, in snowfall. How I loved to see snow falling [that winter], and I took off down the mountain with some regret at leaving home for three days.

As soon as I hit the pavement (an elevation drop of about five hundred feet), there was no longer any snow sticking to the ground, although it continued to fall all the way down into the Little Lake Valley (where Willits is located).

After trying unsuccessfully to track down a friend in town, I took off down Highway 101 and parked across from Andy's at the south end of town to wait for Peter Veblen and Mary Körte, who were going to the *Kuksu* reading* with me. About half an hour later, they came by and, after a couple of town trips, we took off.

We cut across the mountains through Lake County on Highway 20. The weather was clearing, and it was a beautiful, early spring morning. The redbuds were in flower (when the redbuds flower in Lake County, when the rhododendron blooms by the coast, folks make pilgrimages), snow powdered the highest hills, and the air was cool, fresh, and clean—the way it is after a storm.

After some car problems, we arrived in Nevada City, late for the reading, having missed Masa Snyder's classical Indian dance and Will Staple, and catching only the last words of Steve Sanfield's reading. But

---

*Held March 16, 1975, American Victorian Museum, Nevada City, California, for the benefit of *Kuksu*, a poetry magazine published by writers of the Nevada City area.

we arrived just in time to hear Gary Snyder. He read some old material from *Mountains and Rivers without End* and some new, aprés-*Turtle Island* material. Hearing the two contrasted, it was/is quite clear that Snyder's poetry continues to develop. His voice is surer, more lyric and whole than ever. Indeed, long after I had forgotten the words themselves, the soundness, substance, and coherence stayed with me. And yet as the reading progressed, it became clear that Snyder is just one of many fine poets living in the Nevada City area.

Some people commented that Snyder had read rather quickly and was very low-keyed, and I think that probably was due to the fact that he felt at home among the friends/poets whom he lives among and respects; he felt no need to dramatize or emphasize his own work; he gave a very comfortable reading.

A break was followed by some songs and poems by Doc Dachtler, a familiar poet who writes for his own enjoyment, without the pretensions or constrictions of "being a poet"; he's funny and full of earth. Steve Nemirov followed Dachtler with a muscular reading. I remember two poems especially: one about his work as a stone mason, and another about his walking and hitching twenty miles to see a woman, only to find her not at home, and having to walk and hitch back on deserted mountain roads at night without even so much as a kiss.

Dale Pendell, editor of *Kuksu,* closed the reading with a series of poems—including one long hunting poem—that brought the audience down to their roots. And it was the audience that made the reading exciting throughout. About three hundred folks showed up from all over the mountains, shouting, stomping, and dancing—to poetry! They were there to be turned on, and the poets gave them their money's worth with a live poetry rooted in the world; what might have been lacking in what the poetic intelligensia call technique was made up for with substance. Dale describes poetry as a "world-renewing event," and it was just that kind of experience.

At the close of the scheduled reading, poets from all over Northern California read individual poems. Two in particular remain in my memory: Phillip Suntree's reading/chanting of a jazz poem with drum accompaniment that had folks on their feet—Snyder was swinging his arms, snapping his fingers, and shouting; and Peter Veblen's beautiful piece, "Song of the Butterfly." After an exhibition of belly dancing, the whole affair broke into a free-form party.

I stayed with Dale for a couple of days, working on the finishing touches for *Kuksu* No. 4, talking poetry, and drinking brandy. During that time I came into personal contact with Steve Sandfield because of a mutual interest in the Grand Canyon. One night Dale lent me his car, and I drove over to Steve's. As I arrived, I was plied with Irish coffee in celebration of St. Patrick's Day and sat down as Steve was reading "Hansel and Gretel" from a remarkable translation of the Brothers Grimm. What ensued after "Hansel and Gretel" was a great poets-and-river-rats' rap session. Steve, who seems to be carrying on the poetic traditions of Jack Kerouac and Lew Welch, though his considerations are more rural, has coined a term for American haiku—"hoops"—from Black Elk's concept of the sacred hoop.

for Steve Sanfield haiku
a hoop of words
the power within

Synchronistically, there is the great classic poem by Kerouac (who was the all-time great American hoopster):

What's a rainbow, Lord?
A hoop for the lowly.

We wound up reading to each other poems about the Grand Canyon till late into the night. And I think in many ways this reading also renewed the world for those of us there. Which leads me somewhat fortuitously (by a commodius vicus) to the point of this review. The major strength of the *Kuksu* reading was that the poets were reading their poetry to friends at home. The experience was shared among audience and poets alike; there was no sense of performance. If poetry is to have any meaning to it, it must be shared. I have often found it strange to read before people I did not know work that was basically inspired by the love of friends and the life of my immediate environment. I almost always prefer nights like the one I spent at Steve Sanfield's—or just reading my poetry to the trees—to formal readings. The *Kuksu* reading was a marked exception.

There seems to be a gradually growing sense of place on Turtle Island [among many Indian tribes, the name given to the North American continent], and if our poetry is to grow it must grow at the grass roots. In cities there is a resurgence of the neighborhood spirit; people in rural areas have always needed, for practical reasons, tightly knit communities. I think the truly exciting things going on in poetry today are

66

not to be found at the conglomerate workshops of famous names but are taking place at readings all over the country—in rural communities and urban neighborhoods of which the *Kuksu* group in Nevada City is so emblematic.

KNOWN RENEGADES:
Recent Black / Brown / Yellow

Thulani Nkabinde Davis

TWO BOOKS—*The Dead Lecturer* and *Black Magic Poetry*—written by the same man, the first under the name of LeRoi Jones, the latter under Amiri Baraka, marked a very important change in the *sound* of poetry, as I recall the years between their publication. *The Dead Lecturer,* with all its shadows from Allen Ginsberg, Nietszche, and Sartre and its very personal direction, was a very important book. Vilified by critics, it was taken to heart by young blacks, who were shocked by the sad lyricism of "The end of man is his beauty." *Beauty,* one of the words to earmark the '60s, sounded so ominous and shattering:

> They speak of singing who
> have never heard song; of living
> whose deaths are legends
> for their kind.
>
>   A scream
> gathered in wet fingers,
> at the top of its stalk.
> (p. 3 1, *The Dead Lecturer*)

"A Poem for Willie Best," whose last line rang with an authentic sound that could not be denied, brought that precise language of the street firmly into the realm of poetry.

> Such a blue bright
> afternoon, and only a few hundred yards
> from the beach. He said, I'm tired
> of losing.
>   "I *got* ta cut 'cha."
> (p. 25, *The Dead Lecturer*)

This poetry, and *Dutchman's* insistence that "just murder would make us all sane," made it clear that poetry could have a direct and immediate impact on these lives we were living and could speak in the rhythmic and melodious tongues of the street and the blues. There was even more immediacy here than with Langston Hughes. To this day I still appreciate Baraka's unrelenting timing. *Black Magic Poetry* and his record *Black & Beautiful/Soul & Madness* put those closely aligned images into a rapid fire that became the imitated form among many poets.

New York

As a 17-year-old college freshman in New York City I thought the sounds in those poems matched the electricity in the city and of my own sudden growth. The digestion of those brutal noises of the south and its attack dogs, bombs, splattering windows, and latenight murders made these fiery staccatos and shouts, the congas and choruses seem the only way to make these messages heard. And hear/here again this word *beauty*. In the midst of all this:

Beautiful Black Women, fail, they act. Stop them, raining . . .
Ruby Dee weeps at the window, raining, being lost in her
life, being what we all will be . . .
(p. 148, *Black Magic Poetry*)

The sound of Smokey Robinson's "Ooh Baby, Baby," street harmony and the all-time hit for romance; a song with almost no lyrics suddenly had a profound new set of words. And Ruby Dee—wasn't she our cultural past too as that "raisin in the sun" that Langston Hughes and Lorraine Hansberry were warning us about?

Somewhere between *The Dead Lecturer* and *Black Magic Poetry*, or around 1968, some of us in the New York area had a chance to see and hear the Spirit House Movers, a group assembled after Baraka's move across the river to Newark, N.J. They performed at Ferris Booth Hall, Columbia University. The so-called poetry reading had, in a sense, disappeared. The Spirit House Movers were just that—"movers." Their colors and movement came from that old world none of us had seen except through its travelers to these shores. The "boot dances" from the mines of South Africa brought home the notion that the pronoun "I" not only had to give way to a black American "we" but to a world-wide "we." In those days every poet put his or her audience into as many understandings of "we" as could be imagined with one's own face and history. As the theoreticians of the "Black Arts Movement" were later to state, black artists/poets turned their work into the expression of our community, to be heard by our community. A poetry reading felt like family, like church, like a private communication between people who understood a special language, who knew romance to sound like Smokey and politics to be translatable to the common confrontations in any neighborhood.

All of this comes to my mind as I ask myself how "readings" have changed because art could not be separated from the political thought of the time, or the style of life that became associated with the nationalism so prevalent in our communities. Hearing Baraka read opposite James Baldwin at Town Hall at this time made all of the changes very clear to me. Baraka clearly and with a new melodiousness proposed a "new world." "The real work is the vision of the future," he said. Something new was called for in language as well: " . . . proposing something . . . might make you use language a little differently. . . . The language we speak as conquerors will be different than that we speak as slaves."

Language and sounds never heard in POEMS were everywhere. The (ORIGINAL) Last Poets, Gylan Kain, Felipe Luciano, and David Nelson were appearing in Harlem, down on the lower east side, and seemed to be all over New York in the summer of '69. These poets truly performed the work, moving from one poem to the next without introduction or indication of author. They worked without any pieces of paper and worked together, using three voices in most of the poems, improvisation and "riffs," gestures, movement, glances—the whole person of each poet. The Last Poets used street language, wonderful and provocative and sensual language, urban Puerto Rican language, sound language (rat tats and blee bop shoo bops), body language. They addressed "you," the understood community, and rapped to you, fought with you, seduced you, comforted you, armed you, got on your case, laughed with you, sang to you, made you sing, clap, and talk back. Poetry reading meant family, church, concert, theater, even film.

In the late summer/early fall, the Young Lords Party held a big benefit concert, which packed the Apollo Theatre on 125th St. It was one of those marathon events, complete with interminable equipment movings and mike checks, speeches, New York revolutionary style, and that highly charged idealism we all were feeling—and it felt good. More than the numerous bands and "celebrities," I remember the heat and the laughter and the poets. Felipe Luciano, acting in his official capacity as one of the Party's "prime movers," moved among the crowd and across the stage with a sense of having made the connection between the poems and the struggle.

Certainly Baraka insisted that art and artist must do the work of change, rather than remaining apart; certainly the Black Panthers had issued statements that the real work of the artist was revolutionary propaganda, but somehow Felipe, Kain, and Pedro Juan Pietri gave that idea real credence and a following. It may have been those elements of good looks, style, and performance, so unfashionable to discuss at the time, that helped them get the idea across . . . but their words and their sense of theater gave us all a lot of "food for work." (Good looks, a certain coolness, and a lot of theater shaped the appeal of black and brown social movements and their leaders all over the country. Any of us who did any of the envelope stuffing, typing, and general shitwork could tell you).

Kain, with appropriate respect for that legendary Harlem stage, gave his legendary performance of "Black Satin Amazon Fire Engine Cry Baby," and made us feel better than Smokey did, pleading for it at the footlights. Kain never *reads* poetry; he stands with his shirt slightly open and his heart bared and tells you, fingering your chin with his imagery, how it is. Moving only his insinuating shoulders, hips, and open hands, he approaches the audience with the manner of a would-be lover about to get over/or like an old friend who won't allow lies.

Pedro Pietri, poet laureate of the Young Lords Party, appeared in his trademark black attire, topped with the Party beret, and carrying a black attache case. He placed the case on the stage so that the white lettering on it could be seen: COFFINS FOR RENT. As he began talking a phone rang. He opened the case and pulled out a white telephone receiver and answered an office call. An explanation of the merits of renting over buying coffins in these hard times was followed by his classic "Puerto Rican Obituary." Pedro's urban video-flash sur-realism sets you into a rolling laughter/horror.

His rhythms, mixed Spanish/English/street stuff in "Obituary," snapped the audience through a labyrinth of anonymous, alienating, and yet extremely personal nightmares.

they worked
they were always on time

71

they were never late
they never spoke back
when they were insulted
they worked . . .
Miguel
Died hating Milagros because Milagros
Had a color television set
And he could not afford one yet
(*Pallante*)

Mortician to the oppressed spirit, Pedro first threatened us with Long Island cemetery, our own backstabbing, and reverence for white American culture, and then insisted we could still save ourselves.

I must return to the question of language. Some months later, Ntozake Shange and I encountered Pedro again, with a group of Puerto Rican poets at Riverside Church. This group included Jose Angel Figueroa, Ivan Silen, Felix Cortes, Alfredo Matilla, Jesus Pappo Melendez, and Etnairis Rivera. Pedro asked the small audience to sit on the stage and we performed from the floor ("this is not a show"). Ntozake and I had to conquer some nervousness caused by the fact that we had read in public only once or twice and were confined to the English language.

These poets read work about the conflict between Puerto Rican and American cultures, the landscape of "home," migration, the urban landscape, love, and (most noticeable to me) language. ("Learn how to say/*Como esta usted*/and you will make a fortune," Pedro read.) Here were poets taking issue with the oppression of the tongue I was using to take issue with oppression. And they took issue with the oppression of the misuse of the language they were being told they could not speak. It was, however, the same urge that black writers had to make the language spoken be realized and serve the community speaking it. This group took the poems then to Spanish-speaking churches all over Manhattan in the summer of '70.

Many, many poets were on the scene in New York in 1970 when I left for Calif. Yusef Inman, who had worked with the Spirit House Movers, had begun having poets appear with the music sets at The East, a cultural center in Brooklyn. (By 1972 he had a whole crew of poet/performers, including his sons and other children, who created some exciting pieces with musicians in the cultural nationalist vision.) Chant and the use of many overlapping voices were very important in their performances. An example of their work can be heard on *Alkebulan,* a record put together by Mtume. Askia Muhammad Toure was firing up his audiences with his collective anger. His voice shouted out the urgency of his vision of a black American Jihad. (I hear in the back of my mind a booming "DAGO RED, DAGO RED" indicting Harlem's death merchants.)

Archie Shepp, powerhouse tenor player and a "dean" of the lower east side in that era, was giving us a whole array of new images/sounds. I bring him into the picture now as his influence on poets, painters, and all kinds of artists has been great. The music of the so-called jazz avant garde (not sure what they were calling it) had taken on an increased importance as it addressed itself to the issues of the times. Other black music that tried vainly to keep enterprises like Motown and Stax records in the profits was rather schizophrenically divorced from the real world. This was the era of Aretha Franklin's blockbuster "Respect," "Boogie Down Broadway," "The Horse," "The Shing-a-ling," "The Tighten Up," Otis Redding's "Try a Little Tenderness," the Tempts' "Living in a Glass House," the Four Tops' "Loneliest Man in Town," and "Heard It Thru the Grapevine" by Gladys Knight and Marvin Gaye, both in their turns—but never was heard a word about the war, the increasingly competitive and thriving dope industry, the imminent ascendence of Nixon, the omnipresent murders . . . at least not until Marvin Gaye stepped out of that grand dancing procession in 1972 with *What's Goin On.*

Shepp did revolutionary theater, poetry, music . . . and did them all at once. His images invoked our conjuring, our power, our lyricism, our ballroom assassination, our tragic dope-ridden youth, the way we can sing a ballad in a bar. Archie Shepp left a stronger impression on me in 1968-70 than did a half a dozen other artists put together. One should still hear his incredible and haunting voice do "The Wedding," "Malcolm, Malcolm, Semper Malcolm," and the sounds of *The Magic of Juju; Live in San Francisco; Fire Music; For Losers, Blase,* and (from the '70s) *Attic Blues; The Cry of My People.*

And then there was that other "Haight Street" force in us. The year 1970 opened in New York with the glorious Fillmore East concert of Jimi Hendrix. While one could say that the masses of nonwhite people were not really involved in Hendrix's music, it would be impossible to say he did not leave a mark on us even then. Aside from the obvious impact made upon other black musicians at the time (which is well documented in David Henderson's fabulous *Jimi Hendrix, Voodoo Child of the Aquarian Age*), his sense of poetry and his original use of the blues structures in combination with a street surrealism shaped a whole generation of poets now in their early twenties. He also made possible the incredible metamorphosis of James Brown's sidemen into the Parliament/Funkadelic/Bootsy's Rubber Band conglomerate . . . groups that are producing lyrics that really snap with absurdist understanding (ah! *Funkentelechy vs. the Placebo Syndrome*).

And if one wonders about other roots of '70s poetry, with its "cosmic" aspects and its attention to the reordering of the world as part of the "natural" order of the universe, one has to check out Sun Ra. Sun Ra has long used poetry with music, dance, and film as a performance vehicle. Along with printing books of his work, he has used singers who recite, chant, and intone his messages. The poet Verta Mae Grosvenor spent five years as one of Sun Ra's multi-faceted group. ("Sun Ra/ and his band/ from outer space/ are here to/ entertain/ you/ now.")

In the spring of 1970 Sonia Sanchez returned to New York, bringing her chanting and singing sound from the Midwest back to Harlem. A much-quoted poem of the time sang out:

> I am a blk/ wooOOOOMAN
> my face
>   my brown
> bamboo/ colored
> blk/berry/face
> will spread itself over
> this hemisphere and
> be remembered.
>   be sunnnnnnNNGG
>
> (*Black Scholar*)

Listen to her record *A Sun Lady for All Seasons Reads Her Poetry*. She and Nikki Giovanni could be heard in Harlem at this time, just before Nikki discovered the New York Community Choir and recording. Sonia began to move towards Islam, and her poems rang in harmony with those new world sounds of Pharoah Saunders' *Tauhid* and the ubiquitous "The Creator Has a Master Plan," from *Karma*. Nikki moved from the jabbing and pungent "Nigger Can You Kill?" to the popular "Ego."

Carolyn Rodgers and Mari Evans used some of the elements of chant and song in their poems of black womanhood. Theater, once again, was used to lift their poems from the page. A memorable reading from a number of these poets was held at Alice Tully Hall in, I think, the summer of '71. Included were Rodgers, Kain, Luciano, Toure, Evans, and Jayne Cortez. Cortez' rich alto invokes the sounds made by bass players, and her poems invoke the spirits of the great horn players.

Larry Neal, reading work from the *Black Fire* vein, added a consciousness of be-bop and the use of horn riffs. His later work with an ensemble led by Bill Dixon moved towards a "guided" poetic improvisation. ("Bird Lives" is the piece I recall). A number of other important voices that I did not get to hear really until much later included Victor Hernández Cruz, Clarence Major, David Henderson, Quincy Troupe, Keoraptse "Willie" Kgositsile, and Amus Mor. (Other Midwest poets were known to me only through books, such as those from Broadside Press.)

To discuss the sound of all this poetry in contrast to its printed impact would be somewhat academic at this point. Theatrical performance of the work, the emphasis upon the sound of speech, and the involvement of music were used to give written work an unavoidable immediacy. Poets made conscious efforts to reach people who listened to music more often than they read books. We tried to close the distance created by printing and to give the audience a sense of community not possible in the individual experience of reading. Lastly, it seems that we were confronting and attempting to conquer the alienation promoted by urban education, housing, unemployment, experience with violence and war. A "poetry reading," or even poetry, had to reach out of printed pages and become physical.

These sounds, tones, cries, songs, even noises rang of recent and distant people and events. Their pace and volume matched the intensity with which the poet could feel these often traumatic moments. Many should easily come to mind: Malcolm's speeches and the gunfire of his death; Nat Turner's rebellion; Emmett Till's tragedy; Orangeburg, S.C.; Martin Luther King's life and death; the riots across the country; Fred Hampton's murder; the Algiers Motel; Franz Fanon; Cinque; and the life, times, and work of numerous black musicians.

The connection between the poetry, the politics, and the music was a visceral one. You could hear it vividly. Political statements using names known to us through the arts was common. Looking back over the material, it's apparent that John Coltrane, who died in 1967, is the single most lionized figure in the poetry of the '60s and early '70s. The significance of this fact should be obvious if one has any familiarity with his work. We had many heroes and many dead. The singers and horn players in us surfaced in a great rush of poetic energy. All that we had to live for, die for, and give to was so clear, and it had to be sounded, danced, sung, shouted out, and joined by everyone. Just a poetry reading wasn't possible.

California

On July 4, 1970, I experienced my first bit of San Francisco Bay Area culture shock by going outside to find it 40 degrees and foggy. I thought Joe Goncalves' poems must be right about this being the end of the continent and the end of the world. What a strange state of mind folks must be in to live without traditional seasons, I thought. It bothered me and my poems a lot. My second rude awakening occurred at the annual San Francisco Festival of the Arts. Literally hundreds of poets were scheduled to read in the square facing City Hall. When I got up and began to read one of my furious and fierce "New York" poems of unpleasant encounter, one of the park's white "residents" jumped up and attacked me. Very drunk and not easily dismissed, this man had to be hauled off by three men so that I could continue. He insisted that I could not talk about *his* people. So I discovered that poems really work.

Two years later at the Longshoreman's Hall at a farm workers' benefit reading, with 2,000 people assembled to hear some twelve poets, another drunk became enraged. The first poets to read included Ginsberg, Lawrence Ferlinghetti, Philip Whalen, and some of the seven third world poets who had bogarted at the insistence of Roberto Vargas. This time, a poem on the death of George Jackson created the scene. I had been working with a music group (complete with irrepressible congas), and I used the tightness of the music's rhythms to control the pace of my poems. I had also learned to make myself heard over a lot of other sounds, so I just kept on plugging as the man was pulled out of the room before he got to me. The music that the third world poets brought to that reading made it very special. I remember especially the bounce and biting irony of Serafin Syquia's ping-pong poem and those he did on salmon-working in the summer. Ginsberg, who was chanting and singing on the end of all things, was the only member of the older guard who seemed to appreciate the sounds. The other poets having properly ignored us and the poetry having aroused some tension, I was on my way off stage and HOME when Ginsberg stopped me, kissed the floor and my feet, and said, "Such music!"

These two anecdotes, say, in a way, a lot about my experience in San Francisco. I found my work changed a lot, and the work done with other third world poets had led me to associate my words more with music and musical rhythms. Such a wonderful, mixed, multi-lingual, multi-talented open-minded group I had never encountered anywhere. While at times it seemed the end of the world, the Bay Area is the beginning of much that will be important in the arts in America.

Everyone is probably familiar with what has begun there in previous years—the Bay Area's writers and their influence on other movements in other places. But in the '70s the Bay Area has spawned a coalescing of cultural groups that is hard to find in other regions. In her introduction to *For Colored Girls Who Have Considered Suicide When the Rainbow Is Enuf,* Ntozake Shange talks about the influence the third world artist groups had on her work as well as the work of feminist groups. Other documentation of the work of Bay Area third world artists can be found in *Drum Voices, Giant Talk,* the *Yardbird,* and *Y'Bird* issues.

I first met many of these artists at Glide Memorial Church in 1970. Here I heard Alejandro Murguia, Janice Mirikitani, Geraldine Kudaka, Roberto Vargas, Serafin Syquia, and Buriel Clay. They spoke then of "pocho" languages—mixtures of tongues such as one hears among Puerto Rican and Cuban New Yorkers. These poets came from such disparate places as Mexico, Nicaragua, the Philippines, Okinawa, and even Japanese-American roots in Utah. It was an amazing experience for me, and it led me then to participate in some of the most incredible readings I have ever witnessed. Among these, I recall some Easter morning services at Glide where we played music in the streets and recited before hundreds of people at dawn. There were readings to raise money and support to save the "I" (International) Hotel, a residence for elderly Filipino men; for the Welfare Mothers' Organization; political prisoners around the state . . . the list goes on.

In this period I met and worked with Jessica Hagedorn, Filipino poet, who has since become a close friend and collaborator. We were both interested in working with music and often performed together with musicians. With singers Linda Tillary and Ota, she later went on to form a band called the West Coast Gangster Choir that performed all over the West Coast. The sounds of the words and names intoned in her poems filled my head with all kinds of notions about my own past lives, so to speak . . . those far places from which I/we had come. Her use of the moment and the "scene" in the Bay Area made her work stand out and gave it an immediacy that I had not dealt with in poems.

Buriel Clay, whose humorous work combined street vernacular and a Texas drawl, also put me in touch with those stories that could be written from immediate family history, and all the migration that had taken place in our lives. The sounds of our many voices, with all their varied "colonial" training, made an unbelievable orchestra out of a gathering of poets: Diana Lyn's wonderful, slightly British tonality and all the images of Hong Kong mixed with Jan Mirikitani's clipping Japanese and Roberto's lyricism and repetition. He chanted "they blamed it on the reds," his voice moving in arcs, then jumping into rock 'n roll songs from the '50s and even "The Battle Hymn of the Republic," also with congas dancing him on.

Third World Communications, a group formed of these poets along with others like George Leong, Kitty Tsui, Elías Hruska y Cortés, Alfredo Garcia, and many visual artists, printers, photographers, musicians, filmmakers, video folks, and others, put out several books, including *This Side and Other Things* (Roberto Vargas and Elías Hruska y Cortés—a "pocho" book), *Third World Women,* and *Time to Greez!* (copublished with Glide Publications). (Each of these collections was the first of its kind.) We were probably one of the only group of poets ever to give regular dances and teach each other how to print books and put together television shows, as well as how to cook. (Tacos and lo mein, egg rolls, rice and beans, and tempura . . . herb tea vs. green tea . . . even all-natural Black Muslim Your Bakery blueberry cheesecake when we did readings on the road!) These poets brought all kinds of sounds and images to American poetry that enriched it beyond my ability to recount.

Then one must also mention Ishmael Reed's wonderful ballads and blues and his readings with bass player Ortiz Walton; Sarah Fabio's bouncing Tennessee rhythms and the arrival of Victor Hernández Cruz. Victor brought his "snaps"/New York rhythms to the Bay Area and in turn got stretched out by the landscape and eased into a slower more visual language.

In 1972, members of the collective filmed Jessica Hagedorn's *Chiquita Banana,* and local black poets worked on the San Francisco Black Expo. We were treated to the sounds then of a few other imported voices that included Gil Scott-Heron, Brian Jackson and the Midnight Band (D.C.), Gylan Kain (N.Y.), Calvin Hernton (Ohio), Ntozake Shange (L.A.), and others.

Also very important in the shaping of ideas for the performance of poetry was the music of the Art Ensemble of Chicago, who had done their first tour of Calif. not much earlier. Their influence was much like Shepp's. Their records, including the poetry of Joseph Jarman, were closely studied by a number of us. (Hear *Reese & the Smooth Ones, A Jackson in Your House, Message to Our Folks, Baptizum;* hear Jarman's *Song For* and check out his book, *Black Case,* Vol. I & II.) Other important work has been done by Jarman with Amus Mor in LIVE performance. Also to be mentioned, with particular reference to L.A. poets, are the performances of the Horace Tapscott Orchestra and Sun Ra. Concerts in L.A. that I had a chance to see featured not only poets but painters and craftspeople as well, who exhibited their work during the performance.

As so much work was recorded for radio broadcast at the time, I began to work with engineers, using taped music and orchestrating pieces for radio, most often with Glenn Howell and Roland Young for their show, *Oneness.* Poets in Calif. are afforded the opportunity to explore the use of theater a bit more than in other places, I think. The artistic atmosphere is more open, and poets have loyal audiences. Poetry readings are major social events in California and are considered respectable art forums. Thus they are held regularly and are well attended. (It is possible in Calif. to raise a considerable sum for a cause by having four poets in a hall!) For shaping one's sense of performance, nothing is better. Coming up with something new constantly becomes *de rigeur,* once there is an established and faithful audience. This alone allowed me to get the idea that I was a performer of my work as well as its composer.

And Back to New York

Returning to New York several years later, I found lots was going on uptown at the National Black Theater, under the direction of Barbara Ann Teer, and at other spots. Kimako was sponsoring lots of music/ poetry nights in Harlem cultural centers and book shops. Downtown, one could catch a little poetry at the New Federal Theatre, and in little places all over one might hear Oliver Lake playing solo saxophone and

79

reciting. The influx of musicians from St. Louis and Chicago around this time made a distinct difference, at first on the lower east side, spreading to Soho, and eventually to the whole New York scene. Members of the A.A.C.M. (Chicago) and B.A.G. (St. Louis) brought with their musical virtuosity a familiarity with theater that livened us all up. I like to joke about how they made the interminable rehearsal so fashionable, but they also encouraged the use of lots of funky blues stuff, march and parade sounds, steps, singing, poetry, and even costume.

The La Mama Workshop on 3rd St., several doors from the old site of Slugs', is now run by members of the Human Arts Association and has consistently involved poets in concert. Ntozake and I were probably the first to "integrate," so to speak, the Studio Rivbea, a music center on Bond Street. With dancer Paula Moss (who had worked with Ntozake in Calif.), we did a night there. Ntozake had brought a piece from Calif. called *For Colored Girls*. . . . Although Paula and Ntozke had performed to crowded bars in the Bay Area, this audience seemed to find it a rather odd evening. There was no explanation of the work, just performance, a planned sequence of poems invoking certain rites of passage, accompanied by a free movement over the entire space of the loft. The route taken by those twenty poems into the theatrical arena is now well known.

Later this idea was to expand during weekly "readings" at the Old Reliable on 3rd Street, an unheated backroom in a bar opposite La Mama. Other dancers came. Gylan Kain and other poets were appearing in a different arrangement each week, based on the common idea of creating ritual. Again, the evening would flow without much interruption in two or three "sets." Poets refrained from giving the usual "blah, blah" about what made them write the poem, when and all that, but rather, rose at an appropriate moment emotionally and addressed themselves to what was going on . . . testified. In the winter of 1976-77, another show, *Negress,* was done in a Soho loft by Aku Kadoga, Laurie Carlos, Shange, Ifa Iayoun, Amina Myers, and Michelle Shay.

Not far away on 6th Street the cafe idea was brought to life by Miguel Algarin, Miguel Pinero, and other Puerto Rican poets, and the Nuyorican Cafe was born. On one night in particular there I was lucky enough to participate in a real marathon . . . at least thirty New York poets read, including Pedro Pietri, Jose Angel Figueroa, Miguel Algarin, Willi Pietri, and even Victor Cruz. Poetry is alive and fun and jumping off the page in all kinds of transmutations of various neo-American

80

languages there. And there the question of social change is still alive.

In the winter of 1977-78, the Public Theater's Cabaret opened with a piece called "Where the Mississippi Meets the Amazon," written and performed by Ntozake Shange, Jessica Hagedorn, and me. We worked with a wonderful band that we called Teddy & His Sizzling Romancers: David Murray, Fred Hopkins, Anthony Davis, Pheeroan Aklaff, Michael Jackson, and, later, other horn players. In this piece we worked with the musicians to put together a work that flowed and moved through a range of emotions and kinds of sounds. We did the material from memory, took direction from Oz Scott, and tried to WORK the work.

The work moved thematically from poems on women to visions and dreams to music to love. With some changes as weeks went by, the same basic show, composed entirely of poems, was given every weekend for three months. We used costumes, performed the show in two sets, and choreographed our movements. We were amused to find one of our reviewers extolling even our dancing and singing ability—none of us can carry a tune. But it was very important in turning the work into an

Ntozake Shange, Thulani Nkabinde Davis, and Jessica Tarahata Hagedorn during "Where the Mississippi Meets the Amazon," at the Public Theater, New York, 1978–79. Photograph by Martha Swope.

evening of theater and giving the poems new ways of working.

For me, the process of memorizing (in complete terror!) and concentrating on "giving" them to the audience that could not have a reading access to them taught me more about the content of the poems than any previous experience. It has pushed me to try to do all readings from memory . . . with the intention of having the poems experienced by themselves, as works, without the intrusion of the writer's hindthoughts and aftervision. Whereas a few years ago I had thought this (and the improvisation that comes with it) could be done only by people like the Last Poets, I now see that it is a tool for finding my own voice/or *solo* as a friend once said. Those readings I have done alone, just doing the work for a 45-min. set, with only occasional moments of complete silence, have felt like meditations and singing, and seem far away from the classroom lecture kind of thing that I used to do. It is different even from a set with live music. Here the voice can be the whole band. All of these recent performances have been incredible fun for me and experiences that teach me about my work and about writing itself.

A lot of this experimentation with my work took place during my two-year stay in Washington, D.C., from the Bicentennial summer to summer 1978. There I had the pleasure of working with such poets as E. Ethelbert Miller, Michelle Parkerson, Larry Neal, Greg Tate, Mark Montgomery, Amma Kalil. They have lots of poetry marathons in D.C.—a real phenomenon that can involve fifty poets in twelve- to fourteen-hour sessions. I felt myself shifting from my life-long ambition to be a back-up singer for Aretha to wanting to be likened to Mavis Staples! No, seriously, now listen to that voice! Even talking, it's got you before you even know what the words are. Then D.C. also gave me another inspiration . . . Sweet Honey in the Rock! Now there are some female voices that will not be denied. It is *still* an ambition of mine to put together a night of women poets and Sweet Honey. Their a cappella tones and rhythms tell you what it's all about with poetry. Ethelbert asked me to work with the Ascension Poetry Series, which I still do with joy. It is really one of the best poetry series in the country. As part of that, Ntozake and I did a reading at the Folger Shakespeare Library that was one of the best I've ever done. The audiences in D.C. are extraordinarily warm, at ease, and familiar. There is nothing like them anywhere . . . and we had a great time. This was then recorded on Black Box, the cassette magazine—another D.C. institution. It captures, I think, what can happen when poets and audience have lots of fun.

Included in the "poetry" were pieces of plays, short stories, and even novels.

Jessica Hagedorn did one of the most difficult things in the world in the spring of 1978, putting together a one-woman show based on her work. This show, called *Mango Tango*, ran at the Public Theater. She worked with a band led by Michael Jackson, featuring the singer Ota, and carried the evening's material alone. It was lush and moving and fun.

Around the corner from the Nuyorican Cafe we now have the New Rican Cafe, which presented an excellent series of poetry and Latin music, put together by Sandra Maria Esteves. The new voices in New York are there and elsewhere in New York. Among the women: Sandra Esteves, Lois Griffith, Pat Jones, Yvonne, who not only bring new sounds, but also new forms and women-centered images. Two poets whose work uses a number of different personnae and voices as part of the form are Luis Reyes Rivera and Sekou Sundiata. All are wonderful poets who should be heard MORE.

New York is really just bubbling over with poetry/theater. It's hard to find a reading that confines itself any longer to an inert rendering of the writing on the page. Alexis DeVeaux, for example, is working with the theater/cabaret format at the Manhattan Theatre Club. Baraka, now back on the scene, invoked the role of the jazz singer in the David Murray Big Band concert last summer. He now has a play—*What Did the Lone Ranger Have to Do with the Means of Production?*—in production at the Nuyorican Cafe. Lois Griffith's "Bajun" accents have been extended into a one-woman theater piece for nine characters entitled *White Sirens,* now in "workshop" at the Public Theater. (Word has it that due to some protest made earlier this winter there will even be an Asian production there—unheard of in New York!)

But the Asian voices in New York are putting together their own workshops, readings, and programs. The Basement Workshop brings together many of the Asian writers and has involved writers such as Lawson Inada, Frank Chin, Fay Chiang, and Laureen Mar in their work. I'm hoping to see more programs put on there, knowing that New York could use the kind of third world energy created on the West Coast. The arrival of *Zoot Suit* from L.A.'s Chicano community also gives me hope that New York can see some of what it's missing.

Lastly, there have been quite a few interesting one-night productions, among them Oliver Lake's *Life Dance of Is,* music and poetry.

Oliver's poems were performed by Laurie Carlos and Jonetta O'Kelley. They moved about the stage so easily, letting the words slip out, that it seemed they were thinking these things as it went. As part of the Poets at the Public series Ntozake did a one-woman night called *Boogie Woogie Landscapes,* and June Jordan will be doing one with Bernice Reagan of Sweet Honey in the Rock. And as I bring this epic to a close, I am memorizing my "lines" for mine. *One Day the Dialogue Will Be Endless* takes me a step further, and I've persuaded Laurie Carlos to join in this presentation of the impossibilities of dialogue. When we try to talk to each other we start moving from poem to theater. The extensions of poetry reading keep leading me to unknown ground, where it's at for me.

As you may probably suspect, I have tried to cover most of what has been in the works in my travels among third world poets. Everywhere we are trying to go back to old poet forms/the community's song maker who rises to her feet in a gathering and makes the words give the story/how it has been/how it's going. In November, performing with Joseph Jarman and Famoudou Don Moye in their work *Egwu-Anwu* (Sun-Song), I felt it quite clearly. My poem (of the same name) came after the appearance of the Egwu-Anwu, a wonderful fetish-laden creature of two joined bodies that danced through in clouds of incense. Painted and in another nature of myself I gave my story of the mythical river village from which we all "blue like a one-star night" came with our songs. What happened to us was a possession belonging to the long past and to that moment, and I was just the voice. The song was all I was.

THE CIRCUIT/NEW YORK CITY PUBLIC READINGS:

A Short History

Harry Lewis

I ORGANIZED MY FIRST reading series in 1968 at Max's Kansas City. The Max's Kansas City Sunday Afternoon Readings, along with the first year of the Saturday Afternoon Dr. Generosity's Readings organized by Paul Blackburn, marked a turning point in the nature of public readings in New York City. The new format that developed with the success of these two series has become the dominant presentation form for public reading-performances in New York City: the Bar Reading Circuit.

Showcases for formal, credentialed poetry or prose readings have always been available in New York City. The best known of these, and the one of longest standing, has been the 92nd Street Y. These readings create, in effect, a museum. If a really fine writer reads, it means nothing more than that the writer has been around long enough to be given space. Little possibility exists for new talent to break into such a program. Organizers of so-called Discoveries Series take almost no risks and are very polite. In the late 1950s, the only words for a series like the Y's were "polite" and "safe." No room remained for anything unexpected or uncontrolled. It was a world for the appreciation of verse, not poetry. The situation was very similar to that so commonly described with regard to Establishment magazines. The young writers who were mapping their place had to find new means for presenting themselves publicly. They were demanding, as Robert Creeley has said, "the dignity of their own voice."

There was a growing sense that poetry was not an art experienced best in print. (That sense is very important to understand, since today poetry has fallen back, so strongly, under the cover of the printed word:

the poem on the page as the test.) That so many people give public readings doesn't change the fact that most poets can't read anything except the static word and that they find it very hard to write a poetry that is song. The monotoned poetry they do create is best read in a book. It is not made to be sung in public.

The poets and prose writers who wanted (needed) their own space turned more and more to making their space "at home." In New York City in the 1950s, they turned to their own magazines and small presses, and, following the lead of the San Francisco Renaissance writers, they took their work into the coffee shops and little book shops where they hung out. In effect, the publication of their work was homegrown and forced the public, which was in need of an art that was alive, to search it out in "the home" of the artist—in this case, down on the Lower East Side.

The most important readings in New York in the 1950s took place on East 10th Street between 3rd and 4th Avenues. The focus for the most active and regular series was the 10th Street Coffeehouse (run by Mickey Ruskin, who went on to make a lot of money and eventually open Max's Kansas City, and, most recently, The Lower Manhattan Ocean Club). Up and down that entire block and down as far as 2nd Avenue and over east from 2nd, smaller series were held in art galleries, book shops, and other coffee shops. But the 10th Street Readings were the standard by which to judge the whole scene. Those extremely successful readings were originally organized by LeRoi Jones (Amiri Baraka), Howard Ant, Paul Blackburn, and a number of others.

On Monday nights you had an open reading, which meant that anyone and everyone came and hung out, and if you put your name on a list you'd be called and given a few minutes (if you didn't push for more) to hold forth. The open reading was brutal and exhausting, but it generated a sense of energy like nothing you can find today (except in Third World communities).

On any given Monday night any number of better-known poets might be on hand (Jones, Blackburn, Allen Ginsberg, Diane di Prima, Joel Oppenheimer, or, later on, Diane Wakoski, Ed Sanders, Ted Berrigan, Carol Bergé, Armand Schwerner, Robert Kelly, Jerome Rothenberg), as well as many lesser known writers. There was a sense of competition. This was a jam session. The young came to make themselves known, and the older poets presented their work to show not only what they were doing but that they could still hold their ground. There was nothing polite about these evenings. Everyone was pushing and demanding to be heard, and if you wanted to be taken seriously you had to be good enough both as a performer and as a writer. Out of these Monday night open readings a young poet might finally be asked to a Wednesday night invitational reading.

The Wednesday night readings were more formal. They were announced, and the word was spread. They were well attended, even for unknowns. But they were far from polite. The audience was not made up only of quiet, head-nodding writing students, taking the whole thing very, very seriously. It was not at all uncommon for remarks to be made by people in the audience in approval or disapproval, and it was even more common for the reader to be ready to answer any comments. The give-and-take got heavy at times. These readings were more like living magazines. Poets and audience gathered to communicate about what they were doing. Each reading was a means of getting the latest news. (If a poet came into town, he or she was bound to drop in. Chances were, the out-of-towners would read at the open reading; if they stayed around long enough, they'd read on a Wednesday night.)

By 1965 this whole thing was breaking up, becoming formalized. The readings were more and more closed. Reading became a matter of who you knew and hung out with, which table you sat at. The open readings became places where younger poets read (often just to themselves) and where older poets would go on, to no particular point or purpose, about their own idea that they were poets. Open readings became places where you didn't really want to be heard. There was suddenly something negative about being at an open reading.

The whole nature of the animal was changing. It finally found a new institution. With the advent of the Kennedy vision of formal, organized, and packaged popular culture came the rise of the community "arts program." This took shape in the East Village with the creation of the St. Mark's Poetry Project (at St. Mark's Church at the Bowery). There was now money and a location for presenting large-scale programs. What the St. Mark's Poetry Project did was to institutionalize "the scene." It could now be administered.

The St. Mark's Poetry Project has become an institution and, as such, performs many valuable functions. There have been (and still are) a great many complaints about "The Project." But this all misses the point: Institutions cannot be expected to be spontaneous and innovative. Their very nature makes them representative of a particular group that has control. It makes very little difference who runs such institutions. The fact is that an institution serves those who subscribe to that system. Considering that, St. Mark's has been an amazingly active and successful center for a great deal of modern American poetry and related arts (theater, music, prose). It is still going strong and expanding the available space. *

Between 1965 and 1968 things dried up. "The Project" and "The Y" went on, but in between those two institutions, little else was happening. The only other active series that still tried to follow the old pattern of the '50s and early '60s was the IKON Book Shop readings (run by Susan Sherman) on East 2nd Street near 2nd Avenue. Established and new poets were given equal time, and all read to an audience that was usually jammed into a very small room. These were exciting readings, but the series in no way filled the gap between institutional readings and active contact with a live audience on informal terms.

Then Paul Blackburn, unquestionably the key figure on the New York City poetry reading scene from the early '50s to his death in 1971, opened it up again. Paul decided that the thing to do was to take the readings back into the public arena. The coffee shops were dead, but bars had become active hangouts for artists and writers. *He took it home again.* He followed the old formula: *Have the readings where we live.* That was now in the bars. He arranged to have a series on Saturday afternoons (it had to be held at a time that didn't interfere with anything else that was happening) on the premises up at a bar called Dr. Generosity's on 73rd Street and 2nd Avenue. He asked me to try to set up something downtown. I went to Mickey Ruskin at Max's Kansas City Bar and Stake House and hit him with the idea, pointing out that he owed his success, in many ways, to poets (Joel Oppenheimer had even named Ruskin's bar and restaurant). He agreed. For the next year Paul and I ran both series, and they were jammed every Saturday and Sunday afternoon. The average audience was sixty people—much higher for better-known poets and prose writers. The following year Paul moved to Cortland, New York, and I decided I didn't really want to keep running the whole thing alone. It passed on, through the hands of different people, and finally came to rest with Marguerite Harris, who

* A fire in 1977 which nearly destroyed the beautiful old church and dislocated "The Project," along with many other important community programs, was a great tragedy and points up the vitality and importance of "The Poetry Project" in the life of New York's literary community. Without it we are faced with a deadly silence or the gooey "literature" of the 92nd Street Y and its environs.

ran the series up at Generosity's until her death in the winter of 1978.

Within two years after what had been a small beginning, the setting up of readings in bars became a widespread practice. The idea is that the house gets the business and, in most cases, the poets get nothing but a little money from passing the hat. Blackburn and I had always set it up so that the house guaranteed $25 plus free drinks and free food. This way the readers were at least paid for their performances. It worked out very well.

Today so many reading series run in New York City that it has become necessary to have a poetry calendar (which lists only readings that have advanced schedules). Readings take place in lofts, in book stores, in private apartments, and in institutions, but still most actively in bars. Some of the readings are sponsored by Poets and Writers money, and growing attempts are being made to organize and control the reading scene in New York City.

Recently an arts administrator started investigating who ran the readings in bars and lofts and how they selected readers. The idea was that these readings should be standardized and controlled. Happily, this control is still a long way off, and concern about it might seem absurd, but the investigation is an obvious example of how the wide range of public readings have in effect become a new institution. Poets and other writers now *apply* for readings. Most of the readings are very predictable.

About two years ago I came back to New York City and started a new series. I wanted (pure ego) to show them all how it should be done. I wanted to prove I still had the touch, so I decided to run a series for a year. I asked the poet Brian Breger to run it with me. We were both tending bar at the Tin Palace (a jazz club on Bowery and East 2nd Street.) The bar was owned at that time by the poet Paul Pines, who wanted us to organize a series. We set it up in a new way. We made a Saturday afternoon available to a particular poet or group of poets and musicians. It was their day, and they could organize it however they wanted: a group reading, a music and poetry event, translations, conventional two- or three-person readings, and, on occasion, a super star reading. The house guaranteed $25 plus free drinks. The turnout, on the whole, was very good. The series ran through 1975-76 with great success.

That experience made some things clear to me: 1) Most poets, when given a chance to develop a program, will opt for very conventional readings; 2) the audience is no longer general (each reader or group brings on their own particular audience and the groups seldom overlap or communicate); 3) different groups resist any attempts to break down this separation; and 4) an individual series is as good and successful as the people who run it. In 1973, the most successful series in town was run by Chuck Wachtel at a bar called The Locale. In 1974 and 1975, Mark Weiss ran a very successful series at the West End Bar up near Columbia University. Other series go on but have become relatively small. The quality of the series depends on the editorial sense of those running things. The sharper and more varied the organizers, the better and more successful the series.

In the Third World Community you can still find a public situation where the reader and audience are open and in touch. Readings up in Harlem at the Frederick Douglass Center or the Harlem Studio Museum, or at the State Building on 125th Street, or downtown at the Henry Street Settlement or the Nuyorican Cafe, or very recently on occasional evenings at St. Mark's Project have an energy, variety, and intensity that lead to real excitement. These readings can go on for hours, and the audience stays and responds directly. This community comes to readings as a source of entertainment and learning (which is what they should be about).

Most of the readings these days are of limited appeal. There is no sense of an active community as is found in the Third World. The reason for reading doesn't seem to be to reach an audience with your work and let them know what's new and what's happening. Most writers read to pick up a little money and get their names around. The money is very little, and the ego satisfaction amounts mostly to the response of a small group of your close friends and, if you're known, your fans. (If you teach in the New York City area, you can usually count on your students; some readers make it a requirement.)

The mode might seem bleak, but it does allow for a wide range of performances. Things are more wide open now than they have been for years. The fact that less work seems to warrant the space is a problem not only of the readings but of the general literary scene in this country.

EUROPUEHSI

Victor Hernández Cruz

E very time I was going to California my mother thought I was going to another country; when I told her I was going to Europe she made me out going to another planet. Perhaps so. Days before the airplane flight I was on 11th Street talking to Pichon and Victor, one of the Roja brothers. We were discussing the new methods of selling dope on 11th Street; a place called RUSH features two fingers and a peeping hole, an outside door with a buzzer, and a teeny bopper with glazed eyes as a watch tower out on the stoop. We estimated whoever is in that locked basement was making 1 thousand dollars a day. I told the fellas yeah I'm going to Amsterdam for 9 days and they gonna pay me 600 gilders. What's that? Pichon flies. I don't know, we'll see, maybe it's slabs of silver.

In New York I got out of the bars and clubs and the yakity streets in preparation for my trip. I hit the library in search of Holland, in the Britannica and the Atlas—like where the hell was I going—to a hollow land, sunken, surrounded by a cup of water, the full moon a round chunk of Gouda? I was gathering informity like squirrels after their winter acorns. A land of senior citizens, it said, except for the swinging capital of "western youth." They are the damdest people; otherwise a good part of their livable land would be under water. Centuries back they were seafarers explorers thiefs, who even attempted to ransack San Juan in 1621 but were turned back by these Spanish *cañons* and crazy gypsy-looking *mestizos* with silver platters on their chests and what looked like silver bowls for hats. In the Fighting the whole town was burnt down. Three days later while people were beginning to uplift it one of the worst hurricanes of the century paid a visit, uninvited as always. El double-dutch treat. Ask Indonesia. There's more cream in Holland than anywhere else in the world. They have the potential for blowing humanity up. I whisked out the library like an Avenue B junkie, turned the corner on 11th Street, headed down the block, made my RUSH stop—sometimes there's a single file line in the hallway. This is technically an abandoned building purchased by the numbers people around the corner from the city for $1. They hire street hustlers to package and show their fingers; they have their schedule on the doorway as well as a price list: $3, $5, or $25. You ring the buzzer and they ring you in.

Suddenly you are in a small passageway with some stairs leading to the door with the peep hole. How much bro, a nickel, wham you got it, back out flow, constant motion.

ZOOM—DC 10 October 5th straight to Amsterdam 7:½ hours cheaper than flying to San Francisco. I was gonna rush to RUSH but thank devils I didn't, plain paranoia. I was sitting on the plane reading *España Invertebrada*, one of José Ortega y Gasset's books, cause inside I had a secret urge of making it all the way to Spain. Little did I know that the plane was loaded with well-intentioned literatis. Who? The likes of Kathy Acker and Ron Padgett, who was one of the panel members of the 1979 National Endowment for the Arts awards. I make this discovery when I went to the back to get some juice which was actually an excuse to mount conversation with one of the stewardesses. I barely got the juice on my lips when Ron Padgett who was back there talking to two others (Kirby Malone and Marshal Reese) recognized me, I guess from the time I read at St. Marks cause I don't really know him nor do I hang out in his circles. I don't really see many writers or mingle or platicate with many poetises types in New York, keeps to my self in the huge red bean. There I was thousands of miles over the Atlantic answering questions like " . . . what are you writing now . . . ? what are you writing next . . . ? how do you live . . . ? how do you work . . . ?" All I was worried about was getting off the DC 10.

One-World Poetry Festival 1979   Amsterdam

Dutch money looks like art post cards. Red, green, and blue money. Van Go face smack in it. Airport: it is two miles from the arrival gate to the baggage claim area. It seems the airplane should have kept going.

The Festival coordinators made arrangements for most participants to stay at the youth hostel Hans Brinker Stutel which was an improvement over the previous year (hum . . . what did they do? put them up in boats?) In this "stutel" they either put you in a room with two or with yourself and an empty bed or stacked you in a sleeping auditorium.

The festival was held at the Milk Weg, which is sort of like a youth cultural center featuring a restaurant, a cinema, a coffee shop, a bookstore, and a large performance area. The Poetry Festival ran performances for eight nights at the Milk Weg and at Ultrecht, a college town about 40 miles away from Amsterdam. Poetry overdose. Poets from the U.S., Hungary, Germany, Czechoslovakia, England, Netherlands, Sweden—O, and what else?—a Japanese apprentice guitarist who sang songs at one point about the beautiful people present. He cooks better than he sings; he made a last supper the apostles would have approved. The festival featured a few films such as *The Gerald Malanga Story*. Even Ricardo Sanchez had a bag with a film in it but didn't pull it out cause he said he had shown it the previous year. I missed both. From the U.S. came Ron Padgett, Simon Ortiz, Kathy Acker, Ed Dorn, Ricardo Sanchez, Bobbie Louise Hawkins, Gregory Corso, and este sirvidor. The readings were multi-lingual; poets sat in the audience with their heads straining like snapping turtles as their ears ventured into other languages; there was no translations except on a few occasions. This added spice and wonder. Lewis Macadams, who I forgot to mention with the above U.S. delegation, read not from text but off the top of his head. Mr. Macadams, who once criticized me for working on a poem overnight when he was working for the San Francisco Poetry Center, was scrambling up words second by second. In Holland too. Kathy Acker did a spoof on Erica Jong. Even the spoof was a goof. Two nights ago I had a dream where I saw Erica Jong do a spoof on Kathy Acker. Next year Benn Posset should invite Zsa Zsa Gabor; she is at least consistent. Simon Ortiz did an ancient Acama chant and haloed the whole place out. A poet is one who crosses linguistic borders with information. A Peruvian friend of mine told me that much of Cesar Vallejo's poetry is common folk sayings in Quechua. I'm sure that this is only an aspect of his poetry, a divine one. Bobbie Louise Hawkins read her poems and sang. The hashish really started going around. To the American contingent add Michael McClure whose poetry was *repleto* with botany and biological information; a woman fainted during his reading. Joanna McClure also read.

Gerald Malanga showed up from a half Frenchy direction. William Burroughs came as some kind of final blanket. During the P78 festival he refused to come unless they put him on the Concorde. They concorde him. Or was it the other way around or somewhere else? Anyway, 1st class and *mucho lana*. Ricardo (Panza) Sanchez interspliced his poems with the Mexican hit parade of the '50s. He had enough jewelery on him to start a shop. Throughout the festival Dr. Sanchez expressed an affirmative action attitude towards literature. We took pictures in the red zone and found a Spanish bar with mariachi music *y pistieamos*. Ron Padgett read fresh from his experiences as a NEA awards judge. At which is he better? Gregory Corso looked like a Santo Domingo jungle after hurricane David had gone through it. I don't know if Ira Cohen's friend made a facial cast out of gauze of Gregory. Ira Cohen is a poet who has been everywhere and looks like a skinny Allen Ginsberg. He had an arts-and-crafts young lady with him that was taking mug impressions of the poets. She cast them in white gauze, and they are going to start a museum with them. She and Ira Cohen kept going after me for my face. At one point he trapped me in the hotel elevator and asked me again. When I told him I didn't believe in leaving my image around like that he shot back with a racial slur about Puerto Ricans. If you ask Ira Cohen about the incident his own face will fall down.

One of the nights when I got back to the hotel from a wordy affair I found a huge brawl by the entrance involving the middle-aged manager and the Ivy League beer types from the Stella Artois across the street. I didn't know what was at issue but there I was in the middle of this heated rumble and everything was in Dutch.

SOUND POETRY is very popular in Europe now but it isn't anything new, according to Franco Bartolleni, who is not a sound poet himself. There were poets sounding away in the '30s and '40s. In Italy it has really taken on. Many of the Italian poets at the Festival were sound experts; there is actually an album which has seven discs of all sound poetry (that's both sides too). It was issued in Italy about two years ago. One of the sound poets riffing in English and motion came up with a big looking book and started to read:

text 1

text 2

text 3

text 4

text 5

text 6

Next he shuffled the pages like a deck of cards right up on the mike—what was he saying, that the text is useless?—so he uses it as a suggestive sound instrument. Are they saying that words are over with? What about experience? The best among all that was the woman who did the Hungarian alphabet without moving her lips.

Amsterdam and Mondayish and rainish so everything is laid back. I pull out a picture of my son and loneliness creeps in like fog over San Francisco. The song is the children's song and how pretty they are here. *El hijo de Benn Posset es divino.* He speaks not a word of English just Dutch, he looks like a white Eskimo, though we don't talk. He was always smiling and brings me things, like once he came over with a bag of peanuts. There is a Dutch look if you look. Even in the Rembrandts hanging at the Rijks Museum—he captured a crazy charm and blasted light through it. There is so much beautiful red hair it seems like they were dipped in paint.

Dusseldorf Germany on the Rhine

Arrived by train with a cold orbiting my skull. Dusseldorf is a big steel town. What is more boring than a German steel town? A slug race on a rainy day in Bernal Heights, San Francisco. When we got to town a plastics convention was going on. There were plastics representatives from every plastic corner of the earth. Small Japanese executives dressed in black suits with seven-foot-tall blonds. Nicolous Einhorn was host to Lewis Macadams, Bobbie Louise Hawkins, Gregory Corso, and yours truly for three days. Einhorn is of poetry cassette fame. Against great odds he has established an international poetry series, bringing to Germany many of the poets featured in his tape series and their allies. The building where the poetry readings are held is an ex-factory, featuring some broken windows. The place looks most unofficial, almost as if it were hidden from the authorities. The day I read at the building my attention was caught by two red juicy Cuban congas which were at the end of the main hallway. They were used by a conga drumming workshop that met on Wednesdays. That's right, people playing drum skins in Dusseldorf. So the town's established boredom has competition—Einhorn and his poetry series are contributors to that fire. Get down Dusseldorf be yourself and be other things too; in Puerto Rico we keep the Polish mazurka alive. On the night which Lewis Macadams and I read, Nicolous Einhorn, who is a professional technician when it comes to tape recorders, forgot to press the record button. Blank. The next night Bobbie Louise Hawkins and Gregory Corso read. Gregory came in the nick of time and greeted Bobbie by shouting: "Have you been flirting with these Nazis?" Just as if Gregory would have walked into the di Robertis Bakery Cafe on the Lower East Side (a place frequented by Galante)

94

and shouted to an Italian *señora* if she'd been flirting with these Mafiosis—we really have to respect his humor. The people at the reading were college students, professors, and international arty types.

Amsterdam Supplement

The whole festival took a boat through the canals towards the villages filled with cream and chocolate. We almost lost the boat. The skipper was smoking sin semilla and talking to a German beauty, forgetting to unhook one of the ropes as the water level went down between two gates which regulate the inner-city canals with the suburbs. We went and had lunch inside a post card. Somehow we got back.

The festival and the poetry was getting to be like the cheese. Brian Gysin read and Steve Lacy, a reed man, laced through his poem. Udo Bregar excused himself for reading in German. He is German. His new book is called *Identity Express*. Jean Jacques Lebel, a French journalist with a Brooklyn college professor's accent, got up on that stage and caught a fit; for his finale he threw himself on his back, opened his legs like a pair of scissors, and began having sexual convulsions: I'm making this up. When he got to his home base, Paris, Lebel wrote an article in *Liberation*, a leftist French tabloid, entitled "Poetry Party." He wrote the following paragraph about me:

> *voix tropicale qui chante*
> *comme personne avant lui*
> *l'opéra mambo des junkies*
> *catholiques colonisés des*
> *barrios portoricains.*

I guess he has touched on some aspects of my work, but like Houdini I can escape out of any sausage. Have you ever heard of *salchichon?* Due to my reading schedule I didn't get to hear Ed Dorn. One of the Dutch poets said he read fine but too long; thus Ed Dawn. Simon Vickennoog—poet, writer, and great master of ceremonies—gave me his copesetic, and he sits copesetic with me; he is a warm brilliant light. With all its pleasures, tensions, confusions, and clarity the One World Poetry Festival was a remarkable achievement of the contemporary creative spirit. *Vaya.*

New York/New Amsterdam

Got off that DC 10 like a cat after a mouse, went through customs like a breeze of air. The weather was warm and sunny. From the East Side Terminal took a cab to 11th Street. Unloaded and took a shower. When I hit the street I noticed that the whole neighborhood had a Wilfredo Benitez smirk on its face.

POEM

James Humphrey

For Jay Bolotin

The rain
turning to sleet
you & I
rolling along
a highway
in Massachusetts
in The Incomparable
'56 Oldsmobile
at night—early evening
in "summer's
light," but night
now, December 6th,
1972, drinking
good scotch.
The rhythms
of the car, the
engine, the
wheels, the
windshield wipers,
the heater—the
hunger there
in all of the car,

in all of you,
in all of myself,

if it can be put
into a word/words,

to survive.

The city we're approaching,
a building there, a room

in the building. The chairs
there, the blackness

of the room, the emptiness
there, like a poem

in a closed book. People
on their way there
to that room, people
gathering there
in that room, sitting
on the chairs, smoking,

talking, waiting for you
to sing your songs

& play your guitar,
& me to read my poems.

The night
around us. The

noises of the sleet
against the car. The

car itself. Us

Oral Sources

THE TALE:

An Account of Preparations for the Telling of the Makiritare Epic

David Guss

"Weaving the universe"—telling it in into existence or recreating it in every-thing they do—describes the view of the Makiritare of Venezuela as they examine the roots of their culture and the origins of the universe. In their epic tales, the universe is patterned similarly to the waja, *the serving basket, and to the division of space within the living quarters: All of life reflects the nature of creation. This night, the tale to be told was that of the* waja—*their story and origin.*

The people eat together. That's their way. First the men sit down to-gether—the *modeshi*, the young ones, on the outside; the elders, the core, at the center. The house is recreated in everything they do—the *annaca* encircled by the *asa* and around this circle the women. They arrive like waiters at a banquet, bringing food from the various houses—small clay pepper pots and large bowls filled with boiled fish or chunks of meat, paca, wild boar, the backbone of a bird. They leave huge buckets of a white mealy liquid with small drinking gourds floating on top. This is *sukutaka*, a yucca and water drink which is consumed in great quantities at every meal. The So'to never drink pure water. Strips of flat cassava bread—*u*—are slid on round woven *waja* baskets. This bread serves as silverware. Some men bring their own pieces of choice game hidden in cupped hands. Everyone sees it. Mothers slip sons fistfuls of aymara fish. Communal and individual needs both grace-fully served at the same time. Young boys wait to be handed their food, wait till their elders finish. It's a privilege to put your hand in the pot. Dogs chase discarded bones. Kicks chase dogs. Howling and laughter from the top down. The young one never speaks. The women are invisible. They enter the circle through shadows cast by candles and kerosene wicks, silently taking away bowls, leaving more food, setting down some water for use in washing. They'll eat later: during the day communally with the rest of the village women, at night in their own living spaces with their families.

The men hardly acknowledge them. There is no word for *thank you* in their language—just *eduwa*, "Okay." Just the acknowledgment of a role fulfilled. This is the way we do it. An arrangement. A truce in the war for the control of food. The outsider is unsettled by this segregation of the sexes—by their strict adherence to prescribed roles which restrict them to mutually isolated groups. There are no shared tasks. Work is either masculine or feminine—sky or water—and when necessity, such as the hauling out of a newly carved two-ton canoe, should force them to join hands, they will invent ways to segregate themselves in this as well.

Women plant crops and prepare food. Women carry—carry water and firewood, carry yucca and game, carry children. Women serve food and take it away, make *sukutaka* and *cashiri* (a sweet fermented yucca drink) or *iarake* (a bitter one). Men cut wood—clean *conucos* (gardens) and carve canoes, carve benches, *kanawa*, bows, arrows, spears, *yaribaru* and *suhui*, hunt game and fish fish. Women go out to get it. (Children gather wild fruit.) Men make houses, thatch thatch, wall walls, and weave: weave *sebucans* to press yucca, *manare* to sift it, and *waja* to serve it. Men travel. Women stay home. Men become shamans. Women don't. Women sing their own songs for their own work. Men initiate women. Women don't initiate men. They give birth to them.

Women's days are passed with women. Men's with men. Outside the house their lives rarely intersect. Except for the festivals (which define their roles), they do not gather together. They eat separately. They bathe separately. They work separately. Their lives are both interdependent and exclusive at the same time; determined not by choice but by tradition. There is dignity in this. It is the dignity of doing what is right and necessary, prescribed and unquestioned. One

Photograph by David Guss

is fulfilled because one fulfills. It is more than mere duty. It is living the way Wanadi showed us. It is recreating his life.

But the outside person is a little uncomfortable, a bit uneasy. If he is a man, the women's world will somehow elude him. It will be a silent place he wants to touch, but can't. To do so he has to enter the private space—the *asa*—where the men and women drop their guards (and roles) and blend into the fluid warmth of family.

This world is two concentric circles—like the basket; like heaven; like the men eating, surrounded by the women. The center is bottomless, infinite. The center is essence, the tree with its roots in heaven—Kahuña, the Sky Place. This is the body circling the soul, and the house looks like that—the *asa* circling the *annaca*. In the outer circle (the *asa*), the exoteric one, vision is easier. Here the extended families live, like the flesh around the core. Here is found life the stranger can bite into. Not that men and women completely shed their roles in the privacy of this family space, but all is carried out in a much more fluid and relaxed way. They talk openly with each other, shouting and joking, teasing and laughing, like a cast backstage letting off steam after a performance. They even share the same food bowls, although a woman would still never eat out of the same bowl as a strange man.

Here two fires are going and the warmth of bodies and laughter fills a narrow room. Three doors open out toward the river. Three doors open in toward the center. This is the house of the chief, Julio. The sun has already set, and his entire family, which shares this space with him and his two wives, is gathered together preparing dinner. There have been no communal meals now for several days. Almost the entire male population of the village is away in La Paragua building a shelter so they will have a place to hang their hammocks when they go downriver to trade. Julio's house, composed mainly of women and children, is the least affected by this exodus. The chief's house takes in all the village's orphans and strangers. The chief is the village host, and an extroverted personality is one of the main qualifications of his office.

The catch was good today, and this makes everyone happy. They are excited about the feast, more animated than usual. Sylvano, the Yanamamo boy who has lived in Julio's household for more than four years now, has brought in a giant aymara fish. This is more prized than a good sturgeon, and Mama, Julio's eldest wife, quickly prepares to boil it with hot peppers. She is sitting on a low wooden stool, skirt tucked tightly between her legs, shifting a log. A paca which someone has caught is being prepared at the next fire. A bowl of toads which Josero has brought in has already been set out. The people in Adujaña don't usually eat toads, and a lot of joking and laughter is going on about their appearance. But Josero is from another village, and toad is one of his favorites.

Josero is Mama's nephew. He has come from Santa Maria de Erevato with his new wife for a visit. He lost his mother while he was an infant. Soon after, his father and uncle were killed by Kanaima magic while on the Lower Paragua. Julio's household took him in for awhile but then decided to send him out of the jungle to be raised by Criollos on a ranch. As soon as he was old enough, he returned to Adujaña. He got a reputation as a playboy, and so none of the women would let their daughters marry him. The men didn't want him as a son-in-law either. They thought he didn't work hard enough. Finally, in frustration, he left the village and moved to Santa Maria, where he married the daughter of the local shaman. This was more than two years ago. Now he claims his in-laws are casting spells on his wife, preventing her from having children. He can't counter it or prove it. He doesn't know what to do. It seems black magic has haunted him his entire life.

Josero has good black boots, cut low around the calves in the style of a cowgirl's. He wears green, mirrored sunglasses and a straw cowboy hat. He can ride a horse and rope cattle and even knows the rules of chess. Dark and wiry, he likes to wrestle with the *modeshi* and body press heavy boulders. He's a basket maker, although distinctly mediocre, and is trying to adapt a new style of figurative carving into the Makiritare's traditional woodwork. This is the Criollo influence on him—the blending of the traditional form with the individual imagination. He has a high-pitched voice which shrieks and squeals at times. But he can speak Spanish and is willing to translate for me.

Josero missed a lot while growing up on the northern floodplains of the Orinoco. Now he wants to make up for it and is eager to learn many of the same things I am. Maybe he can learn how to protect himself against Kanaima and his in-laws. So much he doesn't know. We make a pact to find it out together.

A young, stocky girl with a shaved head and a torn dress is hauling in a bucket of *sukutaka*. There are children everywhere—lying in hammocks strung like rigging across the room, leaning against the thighs of bench sitters, dipping big pieces of cassava into little pepper pots, smiling shyly as elders aim jokes at them. Inchokwa is eight, maybe even ten. His name means "Old Man," and he is called this because everyone claims he stopped growing years ago. His mother is dead, his father is remarried and living in another household. Julio has adopted him. Inchokwa is just beginning the long initiation into manhood. Only over the last week has he begun the first stage, going out into the forest with the older hunters, trailing behind them and learning how it's done. Yesterday he carried home the liver of a wild boar which Sylvano had speared. People are teasing him about it now, calling him a big hunter. He pulls his knees up to his forehead and buries his face in his naked thighs with a smile.

It has started to rain outside now, and the downpour, combined with the smell of cooking meat, begins to bring in the hunting dogs. Bones are strewn around the floor. The dogs timidly come up to get them. The dogs are mercilessly kicked. The dogs run off with a yelp. Everybody laughs. Now the paca is ready, and Mama sets it out. She fixes a special bowl for me which Julio passes over. I sit down between Josero and his wife. The fire casts a soft, flickering orange glow against an emerging, receding backdrop of half-finished baskets and *bejuco* cords, arrows slid into rafters overhead, hammocks both up and down, red and black yucca graters—sharp sides toward the walls—powdered milk cans stuffed into corners, dog racks and thatch, gourd racks and thatch, people moving, people cooking, people sitting, people eating, people talking, people joking, people laughing.

And of them all, Julio is by far the loudest. That is his role. The chief is the one who speaks—speaks loudest and speaks best, speaks when others are silent. Speaks to his own people and to those who visit. He is not chosen for his birthright, his popularity, his strength, his wealth, his magical powers, or even his knowledge of the tribe's traditions. He is chosen for his ability to speak, his ability to motivate and direct his people, his ability to organize them and get them to work, his ability to console and cajole, to settle and avoid conflict, to appease, manipulate, and inveigle. He is the trickster. He has no law or manner of enforcement behind him. His only tool is the power of speech.

Julio is in his mid-forties. He has been chief now for just over two years. He deposed his sister Joseppa's father-in-law, Juan Castro, soon after the village came into contact with the whites. Some say it was the Venezuelan government itself which engineered his takeover. They wanted someone with whom they could deal more easily, someone with a little knowledge of Spanish who was familiar with the Criollo culture. Like many of the Paragua Makiritare, Julio had come from a headwater village on the Merevari. His grandfather and father had both been powerful shamans. Julio himself had been initiated as one but gave it up after his father died. He said: "You had to eat people to be a shaman. My father ate lots of people. I didn't want to do that." He worked in the diamond mines in the Guyanas for a while as a young man and picked up some Spanish. He also picked up a healthy appetite for white man's things. He dreamed of tin roofs and concrete floors, of electricity and bicycles, of spaghetti and rice, sugar and oatmeal, khaki pants and cowboy hats. He showed me a little one-eyed peep slide he had tucked away of two people fucking someplace far off. He also had a stack of scratched and underdeveloped slides of a wedding that had taken place up on the coast years earlier. He must have gotten these in a trade for something. Perhaps in La Paragua. He told me he wanted to wallpaper the roundhouse with newspapers. He thought that newsprint was beautiful and sensed the great power in it. He used to feel my beard and ask me if I'd bring him one some day. He was someone the Venezuelans thought they could deal with.

He is seated on his bench between the fire and the door, on the big smooth one which Mama, his first wife, often shares with him during meals. His red loin cloth is almost entirely concealed by his enormous belly. He reminds me of an African chief. He reminds me of Idi Amin. He reminds me of what he so often is—a con man in a loin cloth. He is holding his two-year-old grandson between his legs, calling instructions to his wives and the younger women, joking with Josero, making fun of Sylvano, rocking back with a high-pitched wild laugh, spitting out some phlegm, telling me to eat some toad, now laughing again, now talking with his sister Joseppa. She is standing in the shadows,

Joseppa is somewhat older than Julio. She is a very homely, sad-looking woman with pigeon-toed feet. In the village is an old black-and-white photograph which some unknown traveller had taken and then left there years ago. The lack of color in the photo seemed unnatural, so one of the villagers took some red and colored it in where the face-paint should have been. Joseppa is in the photograph, standing with four other women, all holding small infants. They are completely naked except for the traditional *muajo* bead skirts. They also have on long strands of beads criss-crossing their chests like bandoliers, beads around their ankles, beads below their knees, and beads around their wrists. They are wearing large, silver, triangular earrings. Today the women are all clothed in cotton dresses, not so much out of a loss of their traditional culture, but because beads have become unattainable in Venezuela, the import tax on them being over 100 percent.

Joseppa is one of the village elders. Whereas her brother Julio spends his days scheming up ways to turn his village into a sylvan Mecca of advanced technology, Joseppa is busy instilling the younger members of her tribe with the traditional values with which she grew up. Only a few days earlier a group of pregnant and breast-feeding women had asked for part of a catch of wild boar which some visiting Taulipang Indians had brought. For these women to eat any game hunted by dogs is strictly forbidden, and Joseppa was furious. She asked how it was possible that these women did not know this. She accused them of being lazy and easily distracted and asked them: "What will happen when we die? You young people don't know anything." Now she made all the women sit down and told them she would sing them the song explaining this taboo. She said: "Listen closely. Pay attention. It's hard to listen to these songs. You have to concentrate and learn them. If not, no one will know them after we die, and then what will happen?" Then she sang them the *Suna Semmadi*, (Teaching the Dog), a chant used to cure dogs who "have grown lazy and don't feed us anymore. This teaches them." Some say the dog has probably licked menstrual blood, and that's why it's lost its scent. They cure it with this song, holding its snout down a smokehole full of peppers until the dog is almost suffocated. The song also explains why women who are pregnant or breast-feeding should never eat any meat hunted by a dog. Joseppa knew this and taught it to the other women. The men present told me the language was very secret. They listened carefully, too, but they couldn't understand a word of it.

The men in the village have just built Joseppa her own house where she lives with her thirteen-year-old son Pedro and an adopted daughter. This is Marianna, Inchokwa's elder sister, whom Julio has sent to live with Joseppa so she will have someone to help her with her work. Before this, Joseppa had lived in her brother's household. She had been married many years ago to a man much younger than herself. The man, who was the son of the former chief, Juan Castro, had been forced by his parents to marry her. It was a political marriage, engineered to increase Juan Castro's base of support by allying his family with that of Julio. But soon after they had their first child, Joseppa's new husband took a second wife young enough to be her daughter. When he took this girl's younger sister for his third wife, Joseppa could no longer bear it and decided to move out. The alliance was broken, and Juan Castro lived to see Julio depose him.

Now small charcoal-covered clay pots cover the entire floor. As they empty, the women reach down and fill them with more broth and peppers, paca and fish. Someone screams "*u*," and more cassava is slid onto the *waja*. Everyone is eating now—eating sitting, eating cooking, eating talking, eating playing, eating laughing. The narrowness of the room intensifies the activity. The soft glow of light accentuates the intimacy. Fifteen to twenty people are in the room now, and the rain outside is falling harder.

The conversation between Julio and Joseppa has gone on for some time now and starts to absorb everyone in the room. Some sit silently, paying close attention, while others, like Victor, make sporadic interjections, and still others go on talking among themselves. And yet, an intensity and directedness begins to grow and, without anyone's planning or foreseeing it, The Tale is suddenly and spontaneously underway. It grows from a conversation to a collaboration to a performance. Joseppa knows the story. But Julio knows how to tell it. Joseppa feeds him the details like a prompter, leaning forward to accentuate a point. Julio takes it and elaborates, giving it color and sound, howls and chants. He compares people in the room to characters in the story. Everyone laughs. He is warming up. Arms wave. He takes a fragment and converts it into a half hour of monologue. Then he turns to Joseppa for what happened next. Bending forward from the waist, she unfolds her arms and opens her hands as if to present him with a gift: the next detail. Julio takes it and begins once again. People go on eating and cooking, laying out food and stoking the fires. Some play or talk among themselves, but most get drawn into Julio's animated telling of the tale. Others, who know the tale, offer commentary or a forgotten detail. It goes on like this for a long time, between Joseppa and Julio, between Julio and everyone else. It goes on long after the last pot has been emptied and the evening rain has stopped.

COLLECTING IN OGOJA

Stephen Vincent

In the summer of 1966, after a year of teaching at the University of Nigeria, Nsukka, I was invited by Peter Ogbang, a friend in the English department, to go to Ogoja Province. Peter had just received a research grant to tape some of the oral literature of his native province on the Cameroon border. For several weeks, evening after evening, we went to various villages and family compounds to record fables and the cyclic songs of birth, naming, coming of age, marriage, and war, and funeral dirges. We collected the epic materials of history and origins of the various branches of the tribe. Although the situations were artificial—we were recording songs independent of their usual occasions and situations (actual wars, deaths, or births)—the tape recorder often provided its own depth of response when Peter explained that we would be taking the tapes to other lands. The farther a song can travel, the more value it has. And although I could not understand the various Ogoja languages, I was moved again and again by the tone and seriousness, the commitment to the enactment of what were vital rituals, and the total choral interplay between the singer/performer and the village audiences that participated in each session.

It's hard to relate to a media-saturated Westerner (or any modern urban dweller) the deep power the spoken or sung word still holds in contexts almost totally separate from technological contact. In one remote village near the top of Mt. Obudu, even Peter needed an interpreter to understand the language. None of the naked young boys running around the square mud compounds had been circumcised. When we asked if this group had circumcision songs, the people laughed: Who would do such a thing to their bodies? Peter explained it was ritual habit for the tribal branches at the bottom of the mountain.

Since it is raining, we gather inside the watchguard's house and set up the machine. Fifteen people fill the small room. The door is open. Outside, the light rain is beginning to form puddles between the buildings. Inside, the chief sits on a small wooden bench under an ancient-looking shotgun hung from the low rafters. He explains our arrival, and then the recording begins. Pauline, a young mother, sits with her baby on a stool in front of the mike, at a slight angle toward me. Her warm gold face has the same angular classic features of a Vermeer. She wears a light green headdress, washed out by the rains, and her sideburns are literal arrowhead-shaped fringe scar tissue. She wears a pale gold low-cut blouse with a thin necklace of pure gold links.

Her first song is a lullaby. She rocks the baby, loudly knocking her fist against his upper spine. Her voice has a gentle, natural sound, and three other women chorus with her as they are suckled by their own babies. I cannot believe how, early in the song, the baby is fast asleep. The strong knocking on the spine, I think will surely keep him awake. (This work took place long before I became a father and learned that the rhythmic hitting of the spine actually relaxes a baby.)

Then, almost immediately, the singer sets off into two other songs in succession: a marriage song and a birth song. It's hard to communicate the strength of her voice. It comes up from her stomach, natural and committed, without any affectation of style. The song seems to come up because it has to come, has come before, and will come again, as though it waits to emerge on the ritual occasion. As the marriage song moves into full gear, the other women join her with what we might call Indian cat yells and stirs. In each song, they comment, back her up, and drive her on until the place is riddled by the energy of first the marriage and then the birth. The sounds are so intense it is like, or it *is*, the actual enactment of each occasion, with no sense of separation between language and subject.

Pauline is followed by a much older man. He sings a calling to war and then an elegy. The war song seems long and without conviction. (Down the mountain, one evening in a village on another occasion, we had recorded two men singing a similar calling; the song was so vigorous that other men went looking for their machetes, clicking them together to the rhythm. The situation began to get out of hand, and we had to stop the singers.) The elegy, on the other hand, emerges from a pure grief, "O-aye, aye, aye," and is for a recently dead father. The voice is clearly focused and carefully concentrated. The remembrance for the man is suffused with changing tones of appeal, lament, and anger. Gradually an incredible stress appears in the language. The dirge, Peter later explains, is much greater than a piece of personal grief. The voice appeals in several directions—to the people in the room, to the local gods, and to a whole history of ancestors. A complete cosmology and its code of existence is being asserted. The voice rises to an insistence of how valuable the man has been to the community and how great his loss. It becomes a universal elegy, not just for the death of a particular father but for the death of any person who has lived fully. The voice rises to an almost shrill pitch. The singer's anger is aimed toward the trickery, the deceitfulness of death. The singer's eyes stretch out to their fullest; his right forefinger stabs the air, punctuating the grievous tones in what becomes a futile gesture against the figure of death. Finally it is too much. He is overwhelmed. The trembling voice quiets. He appeals through the song to be allowed to stop.

The gesture is not rhetorical. The emotion of loss is enormous; the silence in the room is almost palpable—a definite, felt sense of death's finality. It's the momentary end of the cycle. Gradually people's voices begin to ease the man and each of us back into the context of a rainy day. Peter and I pack our equipment, give our thanks and good-byes, and walk two miles back to the mountain lodge and bar. For the next several hours we drink whiskey after whiskey. Birth, marriage, war, death—we have heard too much in too short a time, more than our systems can tolerate. The enormity is too heavy. Drink is the only way out.

Without the language, there would be no life; the complete cycle of songs, from birth to the grave, the epics of origin and history, all had to be sung, or chaos and dread would reign. The major responsibility fell to the singer. The physical force of the song, the weight, the tone, the power of each word, made possible individual and communal life, while simultaneously holding death in a vital perspective. The lower villages had been strongly changed by the way of the City that came in on the roads. Sometimes it was hard to record traditional songs and narratives without thinking they had become histrionic in the face of transistor radios, recorded music, advertising jingles, and the charismatic arrival of Western clothes. (Peter's younger sister, a high school student who had accompanied us up the mountain, spent the whole weekend engrossed in a James Bond novel!)

Peter, before going into university teaching, had been on the rise as a community leader, a symbol of challenge to the established politicians. When he gave speeches, three young men from his village traveled with him. They were his escorts and singers. Before he spoke in a village, they did public calls and praises to raise an audience. In his own village, the young men were popular as makers of song and story.

One night, just before leaving to return to the university at Nsukka, we decided to have a recording session at Peter's father's. He and his wives and fifty-one children lived in a large compound. He and Peter, his senior son, and each wife and their respective children lived in separate, cylindrical-shaped houses with conical straw roofs.

On this particular evening we wait until eleven in the evening. The women and children have gone off to sleep, and we gather with about a dozen men in Peter's house. (Later Peter explains that no rigid boundaries exist between men and women; women's counterparts exist for the men's situations, and in some events men and women singers join together.) We light a tilley lamp and set up the tape recorder. A couple of men bring in several calabashes full of palm wine and glass bottles of native gin. Sitting up on kerosene cans, for the next three hours the singers take turns as lead performers, while the rest of the men act as a chorus. The situation is more like a jam session than a competition (perhaps most similar to American blacks vying back and forth in the telling of *toasts*). But it is also a test to see who is the most alert and agile story teller, who can get the most attention and energy rolling. After an hour it is clear that the finest singer is Linus Ede Igbagiri—eighteen years old, short, a sharp wit in the quickness of his eyes, which dart almost mischievously inward and then outward to his audience. Peter later says no one tangles with Ede. His tongue is so sharp that his victims suffer for days.

The form of the telling is really a challenge. No written texts. None of the singers has ever been to a formal English-speaking school. The more dialects and languages, the more authority the song commands. This possibility is both political and aesthetic. The more languages in a song, the farther it can travel; it can be known in more villages and possess a larger power. In addition, the different dialects and languages, including Pidgin English, increase the stylistic possibilities of the poem, giving it all kinds of shapes and tones.

From the start of the night, each singer uses a similar technique of presentation. They create four or five stanzas of varying length. Between each stanza is a clear-cut pause in which the singer appears to generate energy and thought for the composition of the next series of stanzas. Although each stanza is created spontaneously, they are delivered with a definite sense of prosody, so that one stanza leads into the next. When a particular sequence of stanzas is completed, the singer signals with a sharp phrase or hand movement, and the rest of the men start a fixed rhythmic clap that combines with a specific chorus voice. The singer either joins the clapping and the chorus, or, especially as the song builds, he sings over the chorus until he signals the men suddenly to stop, at which point he begins another series of stanzas.

Ede is totally adept at the form. With light from the tilley lamp flickering back and forth across the faces in the room, his voice moves from a depth of seriousness to high mischievousness, building his phrases and stanzas up with great tension, enacting characters and plots, then turning it back over to the chorus, which he lets his voice surf up and down upon once he has the poem's movement up to full strength. The last poem of the evening, which Peter and I have translated here, took about one half hour; it moved into what felt and held like a militant, evangelical epic by the time he brought it to full resolution.

Superficially it is a praise poem for Peter, known in the poem as Ode Atiang. But clearly Peter is only the means through which a whole world view is generated. The work is at once personal, religious, communal, and political. It encompasses lovers, enemies, witches, local and military politicians, considerations for aesthetics, the audience, and death. Practically no facet of the community is left out of the embrace of the narrative. With Peter's help, I have included some explanatory notes and performance description.

> I just do not know how to start.
> I do not know how to narrate with my lips.
> God who gives suffering also gives reward;
> otherwise I had never dreamt
> that people like us could ever sit
> to talk history this way.
>
> You know that when you surpass somebody
> he can never really like you.
> Otherwise I would say Ode surpasses the whole clan;
> but who doesn't call his son his pet?
>
> In the olden days those who bought cars
> insisted that Linus Igbagiri must wash them
> before he could enter.
> But today I don't have to wash any car
> before I climb into it.

Is this not evidence I have arrived?

It's just that my lips cannot say everything.
Death does not tell a story
else I would insist on saying everything
even at the risk of Death.
But if thought is exhausted
man is dead.
Otherwise I would say many things.

The Okara[1] man calls me the "magnator of the ladies."
Even though I am poor I have become important
because everyone must write me
before he can see the king.
"If you love me, I love you not by force;
Salutation is not love,
love is blind."
Gentility without ability
calls me a drunkard.[2]

The road always leads to a house.
That is why we must agree
Atiang Ogah[3] surpasses his age group.
If you surpass anybody
he will never like you;
otherwise we could say
he has surpassed the clan.
Today if Atiang Ogah dies
nobody will blame him anymore;
Ode, his son, has made his name known
everywhere, in all lands.
I cannot exhaust my thoughts;
otherwise I would request audiences.

Who knows the pregnancy
that will give birth to a King?
They used to mock at our poverty
and our failure to own a car.
But now Ode Atiang owns a car.
Should Igbagiri go about singing it?
However, what I can proudly say, I will.

Those witches who take human life
have no wise heart;
if they are as wise as I
they will not take human life.
The witch must beware of her deeds.
The reason is quite simple.
Today our name is known in several lands.
Formerly Ogoja was called bush.

---

[1] White, literate.
[2] Roman indicates Pidgin English.
[3] Peter's father.

But today because of Ode Atiang
it is now known everywhere, Ogoja.

It's just that I do not want
to say much more.
Otherwise how could one
exhibit his drunkenness on the calabash?
The next day where would he put his wine?
Palm wine tappers do not deny one another
the use of their calabashes.[4]

Atiang Ogah has the strongest hands;
the whole village assembled and acknowledged this.
Why do others wrangle and contest him?
Witchcraft is not the wisest thing.
If they were sensible as Linus Igbagiri is,
they would not kill anybody.
The witch must beware of himself;
the reason is quite simple:
today our name is heard in several lands.

The glory of the family lies deeper
than enemies would think.
The village gives their consent
before the family achievements.
But the family does not give for nothing.
They give in the right place.
They don't give for nothing—
      yah-oh yah oh yah oh.[5]

They give in the right place.
They don't give for nothing.

Oh, Eliza Adigbo,[6]
when a woman is beautiful
Linus Igbagiri likes her,
and once I like a beautiful girl
I will die for her love!

If her husband has an arrow
let him shoot me.
If he has a gun
let him shoot me.
And if he has a stick
let him beat me.
If I die that ends it.
Death does not stew meat for Death.[7]

Look at these people running about!
Formerly Ministers pronounced Death on us.

---

[4]Concept of gratitude: ingrates to Ode are under attack here.
[5]Beginning of hand clap and oral refrain.Chorus and refrain are repeated about ten times before being brought to an abrupt stop.
[6]An appeal to a married woman the singer loves in a neighboring village.
[7]The heroic code of defiance.

Even poor Utugwang people paid tax of three pounds.
Aguii-Ironsi[8] got up and yelled oh-oh oh-oh oh-oh
and raised the alarm.
He thought and thought and declared,
"If you rear a slave
can he ever become your master?"

Those Ministers who used to ride in long cars
have now deserted the roads for the bush path.
Ode Atiang refused to go into politics.
Ukutia village assembled to insist on politics.
Ode Atiang said with his voice
he will not play politics;
it was not up to a week after
soldiers started shooting them.
Some of the politicians do not know
what to do for a living.
Some have become houseboys.
Some have become night soil men.
Some have become messengers
collecting two pence for garri.[9]
Michael Okpara[10] has escaped into the bush.
Aguii-Ironis has said
the slave can never become the master.
In the early days slaves were sent to labor at school.
But a slave can never become a master.
If you plant an akra[11] stand
it can never grow too tall;
you can bend the tree to harvest.
But these Ministers grew too tall.
The slave can never become the master.[12]

You must beware now the slaves know their fates.
They are after you, Ode.
But Aguii-Ironsi has cleared the way
for true sons[13] to become Ministers.
A slave can never become the master.
A slave can never become a son.
Aguii-Ironsi reduced taxes down to ten shillings.
A slave can never become the master.
A slave can never become the son.

---

[8] Aguii-Ironsi was the first mlitary president of Nigeria after the liberal coup in January 1966; he was actually dead, assassinated, by the time of this piece in August, unbeknownst to Ede.

[9] A foodstuff.

[10] Former Prime Minister of the East.

[11] A fruit-bearing tree.

[12] Enter the chorus with hand clap and choral refrain: "yah-oh, yah oh." Ede rides the chorus, repeating material from earlier stanzas, the pressure and quickness of lines increasing, then loosens the tension by drawing ironic references to his romantic prowess and exploits. Then he moves back into a forward-bursting movement of militancy and defiance.

[13] Dedicated, educated, having ideals and sense of belonging.

It is two o'clock in the morning. Glowing with the sweat of several cala-
bashes of palm wine, bottles of gin, to say nothing of making music, we move
out the door into the night. Outside, a half crescent moon shines down through
the tall palms to create a glitter on the straw conical roofs. After the farewells, a
clarity, quiet fills the air. Everything appears to be at rest.

*Peter and I returned to teach at Nsukka. We listened and reveled in the tapes
and finished this one translation. Unfortunately, Nigeria was sliding faster and
faster into civil war. By October 1966 two major pogroms had taken place
against the Ibos in the north. Nsukka was in the east on the northern edge of
Iboland. Refugees by the thousands began to pour down from the north. We
were in what would become Biafra in May of 1967. Political tensions made it
practically impossible for Peter to work. We had two sets of tapes. I was asked
to leave the country in June. My suitcase with the tapes was supposed to leave
by air mail. I crossed the river Niger and went overland to catch a plane to
Europe from Lagos. My set of tapes never arrived. Nsukka was the first town
captured by the federal troops. The university staff retreated south to the
Enugu campus. Peter had differences with the Biafrans. He fled to Ogoja and
then to Canada to study for his Ph.D. His set of tapes was lost in the escape.
This translation and the memory are what remain.*

WITH SARAH GREYS:
A Journal, a Talk, and a Dream

Howard Norman

Journal: May 30

Twelve early mornings in a row now I have met Sarah in the market to
hand down melons to her from high crates. She watches my feet work
their balance. I remembered today a childhood tag game in this market;
I had run a corner and taken flush to my face an entire hung seal. I felt its
whiskers and hard, dead mouth. Much of her time in the market this day
was concerned with a particular melon; she smelled it four times,
worried her fingers over it. Finally it was refused. I noticed that for some
reason all this put consternation on her face, not simply the look of
indecision. She has a game here: she gets attracted to the face of
someone browsing the market corridors—Norwegian, French Cana-
dian, faces of mixed Indian or Eskimo origins—and tries to locate its
twin among the pinched "faces" at the ends of melons or coconuts from
one Asian ship. Satisfied with her pairing, she gives me a kind of
hiss–whistle, holds the fruit up for my view, points the person out. Then
I must scrutinize her choices, and agree or not. "Look closer. . . . Maybe
you should squint," I hear, should I disagree. Anyway, she has settled on
various melons and, each with our carrying satchels full, we walked
from the market on a dirt and pebble road soon branching into three
roads, each ending on the steep cliff overlooking the Bay. Taking the
road furthest north, she said, "I did not taste melons until I was old."
Our road ended at the seals. We could not see them through the fog,
though we heard their barking through muffled distances. I must tell
here that Sarah keeps superstitions, seeming both to invent them for the
moment and drawing them up from her childhood woodland villages to

the East. This morning she determined the belief if we lingered too long near salt water our feet would barnacle and we would forever walk club-footed. She spoke directly to my face, and while knowing I heard this belief (quite unexpectedly, for we had stood at this cliff eleven times before without it taking effect) for the first time, she still held an expression which said, *Your intuition is vague at such perils. You should pay closer attention.* She decided it safe to stay until the fog cleared. I saw her shiver. In the cold her breath, barely a different color from the fog, clouded out like the shape of a pond floating on a lake. Instead of lifting, the fog seemed cut by the knife-cries of gulls who careened off with the pieces. Winds swept the rest away. In the new, clear day we saw below a wooden dock we had forgotten, which stretched out some yards from the gray rocks shore. We immediately began noticing out loud to each other how winter ice had again warped the dock's slats and buckled its stilt legs, and how repairs would be made. Sarah said the carpenters would tune their hammers to the sound of the remaining thaw ice breaking and sectioning off to floes, the cause of the distant surface thunder we have heard some weeks now. But our talk was designed evasion from what we both saw clearly on the dock: a corpse, a Cree man curled to himself, his clothes stiff. He looked to be floating on wooden waves because of how the slats were warped in undulations. We could hear thin voices rising from back where the dock met the land, though we could not see these people who had probably lifted a man from ice water. We stood a long time. The dock would not be cured of him by our staring. Then Sarah exclaimed, "Look! . . . at that! That seal . . . jumped from the water. To sun . . . on the dock. I have never seen one do that before. . . . " Her face held a bondage of seriousness I longed for, broken even by nervous laughter, but she went silent. Some minutes passed. Finally I said, "Sarah . . . that's no seal." "I do not want to hear nonsense any more," she said. Taking my arm tightly she led me back to the road.

"Sarah, listen . . . ," but she began speaking an intense almost tearful concern about this particular melon she had left in the market, saying her fingers and nose knew it was an excellent choice but some fear in her head talked her out of it. And how she greatly disliked believing things that way. Two years later I learned it was her half-brother on the dock.

She had spoken of a shiver illness, and pointed out those lines on her face he believed it left. She said, "That's when the Shaking arrived. Into my fingers." This shaking remained her entire life, especially showing itself mornings and whenever her fingers concentrated on something. When she stirred broth once, I saw her ladle hand tremor. As when she sewed. It was later told that in fever she called out for her son William Minikeses. He had been sitting next to her the whole time yet she beckoned him as if he were across the room, with small flaps of her hand as if fanning herself. He put his face directly in front of hers, and still he was asked to bring her son from the other side of the room. He stood, brought to the bed a chair over which his coat draped, set a limp sleeve in his mother's hand. He backed away. Clutching the sleeve, she thanked it, and fell asleep with a somewhat fierce look moored in sweat on her face.

Kusketasisew, *Greys,* is a verb. It is known of her that as a small child she was capable of playing tones of light on her face, standing in a place under shade trees so that her face would *grey,* and in summer's day's late sun liked to make a shadow wall of her chest, performing a repertoire of animal-shaped shadows on it from her hands—fox, duck, and sometimes tail-shapes and their movements alone. For those who hadn't a good eye for tails shadowed on snow as they disappeared into burrows or under fallen trees, guessing them was difficult. But she had a memory for tail-shapes, and when she mimicked them on her chest it often brought older hunters around to guess.

From a Talk with Sarah

In my life there was one—of all of them—one extraordinary winter, the longest one.

Well, when the night lynx decides to lengthen winter, all we have is this dance, to answer with.

At that time my husband, who was my third one, would organize a dance. He would put on the lynx claws *(shows they went on his hands)* and around his neck too . . . and it was a soft padded-foot dance . . . done lightly, as the lynx walks.

It was an asking dance . . . not wanting winter to go on forever.

"How did we insult you, lynx??" *(indicating that is partly what was asked, in the dance).*

"How did we ever do that . . . ?"

I am puzzled how we insulted the lynx, even after all these years . . . I can name the children who were lost in that winter.

There was Sarah Kenesabishs's child girl. I can . . . I could name the others, as they come to me throughout the day. . . .

At that time, in that winter, I was with my third husband. He was more an owl when we slept together . . . he hooted in a manner of an owl, both during love-making, and before. And after.

But it wasn't that way with the first one, who smelled the worst of all, but was the best provider. He was quiet during it all, but my second husband vented his own animal sounds . . . not human altogether, or a bird altogether . . . more . . . it was several animals breathing at once. I had to think hard from laughing. Sometimes that would be the case with me. I remember them all . . . good men, but the first was the best provider, though he smelled . . . the most distinctly. It was during that winter, I remember, that while sleeping with my third husband I often thought of sleeping with all three at once . . . just for the warmth of it . . . does that give you a further idea of how cold it was? Yes . . .

That was the winter of the flying meaze. They flew all over, and many hares died because of it. I can speak about this because I trapped many hares . . . did the *wayawesew* trappings, in which hares were caught. So it was I remember that year . . . a bad year for trapping, hares wandered away, there was little to eat for them, and it was hard. We all began our hunger-thinking, and there was much *tipiskooctopawin* . . . much of that, so that you can see how we were thinking during this time. So, then, here I'll remember about the freezing (liquids) . . . there was how snot froze in our noses . . . and blood from the rabbits froze on their hair, and on my fingers . . . just the short distance back home! Still, even to this day, I remember the small *waposmikenimos* all along my finger-nails . . . I tasted them. The taste has lasted, still, until now . . . as I speak of it.

Sarah's Dream

One night I was chased by bone ladles. . . . I thought they were all sleeping in their places. Some prefer to sleep in bowls. . . .

It happened they chased me. Some of them were clicking. I went running from them, ahead. . . . I heard them behind me, some were clicking. Some still had soup dried on them, so I knew animals in the woods smelled them go by, after me. . . .

I was chased into a clearing where it was lighter, because of the moon out.

It was there I turned on them, and called out, "Bone ladles! Bone ladles!" I shouted at them, out of fear. . . .

And it was then I found this out: They were not chasing me, I found out. Because they went by me, to the lake there. They . . . all the bone ladles went to the lake.

When they got to the lake, each one dipped into it. Then they were filled with water, and they lined up on the shore. . . .

That's the end. I began, I think, to wake up when I was calling out, "Bone ladles!" But I remember them lined up, filled from that lake . . . at the end.

THE POETICS OF PERFORMANCE

Jerome Rothenberg

Spoken July 1975 *at the annual meeting of the American Theater Association in Washington, D.C.*

There's a Seneca Indian song, a song that's part of a medicine society & ceremony called "shaking the pumpkin" or "the society of the mystic animals" or "the society of shamans," which I've translated elsewhere in a more elaborate form than I'll give here. But it's a key, in what it says, to the bewilderment I feel at where my own poetry & the poetry of my generation has taken me—to this place, for example, where I'm to be celebrating a poetry of performance in our time tied up in some ways we've yet to define to a poetry of performance in those cultures we may think of as "primitive" or "primary" or "primal." The words of the Seneca song, which I translated with the Seneca songman, Richard Johnny John, go like this (the title is our own addition):

> I WAS SURPRISED TO FIND
> MYSELF OUT HERE
> & ACTING LIKE A CROW
>
> I didnt think I'd
> shake the pumpkin
> not just here & now
> not exactly tonite
>
> I didnt think I'd
> rip some meat off
> not just here & now
> not exactly tonite

Now, I hadn't shaken the pumpkin before, hadn't sung before or sung before to a rattle: I hadn't done any of those things & it would have seemed foolish to me then to have done them. It did seem foolish but at a point I was doing them & it no longer seemed foolish, seemed necessary if anything I'd said

The first section of this talk was published in *Alcheringa*, New Series Volume II, no. 2, edited by Michel Benamou and Jerome Rothenberg. "A Post-Script" was published in *Performance in Post Modern Culture*, edited by Michel Benamou, Milwaukee, Wisconsin: Coda Books, 1976.

about it before had a meaning. My own origins, from which I'd been running for most of my grown life, should have told me as well, if I'd been able then to give them my attention; for the living tradition of the Jews is also "oral," from the mouth, & even in an age of writing, the word must be renewed by the processes of "speaking" & of "sounding." So Rabbi Yohanan ben Zakkai said (in the century that began the dangerous process of writing down a large body of the still existing "oral tradition," the records of discourse called THE MISHNA): "He who reads without melody & repeats without song, concerning him the scripture says: therefore I also gave them statutes which were not to their advantage." It's by this sounding & voicing (this near eruption into song) that the attention is brought to focus on the sources of the poem, the song, the discourse, in the prior act of composition (making or receiving), which was itself an act of focusing attention. In creating that attention, that intensity, the Senecas, who are otherwise as removed as we are from the primitive condition, begin the ceremony by invoking those "mystic animals" who were the first keepers of the song, who came once in a vision to a hunter lost & wounded in the woods, to cure him & to leave him with a set of keys by which to summon them again.

The ceremony begins in darkness, then the rattle sounds, & makes a kind of light, a heat, that moves around the circle of those joined in the performance.

(At this point there follows a chanting, with rattle, of the opening songs to Shaking the Pumpkin, *translated by myself & Richard Johnny John.)*

Now, what has happened here, at least for me, isn't a series of separated events or actions but a totality that I no longer want to break into its component parts: to isolate the words, say, as the poem. For my experience is the experience of everything that happens to me in the act: the movement of my arm, the sound (& feel) of pebble against the rattle's horn, the way that breaks across my voice, the tension in my throat, the full release of breath, the emptying that leaves me weak & ready to receive the next song, the song occurring, rising out of memory, becoming voice, becoming sound, becoming physical again, & then returning into silence. And it's also this room, this time & place, these others here with me. The event is different from the event of composition (in this case, to further complicate the matter, involves a second composition-by-translation), but the poem is everything-that-happens: & if it is, then to insist that it's only part of it (the words), is to mistake the event, to miss that total presence.

Before I'm anything else, I'm a poet & (living in the time I do) a stand-up performer of my own poetry. It's better for me to *do* poetry than to talk *about* it. I do it first & then I sound it: This is doing it a second time, a third a fourth a fifth time, to renew it by the sounding. My performance is this sounding of a poem: It is renewal of the poem, the poem's enlivening. Without this sounding there wouldn't be a poem as I've come to do it(though, since I work by writing, there would be notes about the poem as I intended it). This is the return to voice, to song, as the poet Gary Snyder speaks of it; it is one side, the impulse toward the oral, toward a poetry of performance, as is that other side, discourse, that the poet David Antin speaks of. Poetry becomes the sounding—

Jerome Rothenberg in performance. Photograph by Suzanne Graf-Morrone

not the script apart, the preparation or notation, but the sounding. Where there's no writing, the sounding truly renews the poem, creates it in each instance, for here there's no poem without performance. Writing, that strange aid to memory, eventually becomes its surrogate, displaces memory itself— that first, great Muse. The poetry *sounding* becomes the poetry *reading*. This is the condition under which most of us work. If others would go more deeply into orality, would bring composition & performance together in a single improvised event, that would also be welcome. But I would like to describe it as it now is for me & why I've sought my model of the poem-as-performance (the poem in action) in the domain of what I came to call the "ethnopoetic."

As a stand-up performer the poet retains a solitary stance. He is in no way the playwright of the old verse dramas, but the central (typically the *only*) figure in the performance in which he *must* play a part. The part he plays is the poet-as-himself, performing in a theater as yet without an actor—or much of anything else besides what the poet brings: words & a voice. The difference between the poet and the actor is crucial: The basis of the poetry performance is in fact hostile to the presence, the manner, of the professional actor. That the poet as performer is otherwise motivated, otherwise related to the poem, is here a shared assumption: an insistence on a lack of separation between the maker & his work, & of a virtual innocence of any means of performance beyond the ones immediately to hand. The poet's delivery may vary, he may read easily or he may falter, he may digress, he may drift at times into a drunken incoherence, he may fulfill or disappoint our expectations of how a poem is spoken. Somehow it's enough that he risked himself to do as much as he could do: to stand there as a witness to his words, he who alone can sound them. That kind of witnessing is not without its precedents, as in the sounding of the written "law" within the Jewish Temple, where the reader (sounder) was the witness to the meaning of a text devoid of vowels. It is one arrangement (there are others) that maintains the oral basis of a poetry, its openness, once we've entered on an age of writing. In the poetry of our own time, with its use of an approximate & highly individualized notation, the measure of a poem (& much of its meaning) is likewise only clear when it's being sounded: in this case sounded by its maker. The poet when he sounds his poem is witness to the way it goes, the way it came to happen in the first place. He is in fact the witness to a (prior) vision, to an image-of-the-world expressed through word & sound. The failure to communicate is a failure to communicate his credibility: his own relation to those words, that vision. The actor may attempt to take his place (& in certain kinds of theater today the actors have become the makers & sounders of their own words), but as a witness to the *poet's* words, the actor's credibility has yet to be established.

There is a widespread idea that the poets of our time, the artists in general, have abandoned the possibility of relating to poets of other times as models: that we live without a vision of ourselves as historical beings but are locked into an eternal present, not so much an opportunity as a trap. I've never seen our condition in those terms—have rather seen us as freeing ourselves, on the basis of conditions in the world itself, to a wider, more generous view of the past, of the historical totality of human experience, than has ever been possible. This process has been going on at least from the time of the Romantics, & it has produced a number of new images, new models or visions, of the past, from which we now can draw. (Like any historical search, it functions to heighten our awareness of the present & the future.)

Increasingly the model, the prototype of the poet has become the "shaman": the solitary, inspired religious functionary of the late paleolithic. Partly this has been because of our own involvement with the kind of solitary, stand-up performance that I was just describing. But there's also a second side to it: the visionary & ecstatic, & a third perhaps: the communal. I won't concentrate on the last two (although they're in some ways the heart of the matter) but will try to focus on the shaman's (proto-poet's) way of going/ speaking/singing: his performance. In a deeper, if often more confused sense, what's involved here is the search for a primal ground: a desire to bypass a civilization that has become problematic & to return, briefly, often by proxy, to the origins of our humanity. Going back in time we continue to find diversity

& yet, maybe because we're looking at it from the wrong end, the picture emerges of an intertribal, universal culture (& behind it a poetics) that has a number of discernible, definable features. The most direct inheritors of this culture—up to their virtual disappearance in our time—are those hunting & gathering peoples, remnants of whom now exist as an endangered & ultimately doomed "fourth world." Far from being mere "wild men," mere fantasizing children, they had a world-view marked (Paul Radin tells us) by a strong sense of realism ("reality at white heat") or, according to Stanley Diamond, "(by) modes of thinking (that) are substantially concrete, existential & nominalistic, within a personalistic context" & supremely able to "sustain contradictions."

Here the dominant religious functionary is the shaman: He is the one who sees/the one who sings/the one who heals. He is not yet the bard, the tribal historian. He is not necessarily the speaker. He is typically withdrawn: experiences long periods of silence, other periods of exaltation. He may inherit his words, his songs, from others, or he may come on them directly in a vision or trance. He may be a prolific song-maker or he may be constantly renewing a small, fixed body of song. He may have helpers, but typically he works alone. He may improvise within the actual performance of his rites, but more often he will sound, will activate, the words or song delivered at another time & place.

So, among us the poet has come to play a performance role that resembles that of the shaman. (This is more than coincidence because there is an underlying ideology: communal, ecological, even historical: an identification, as Gary Snyder has it, with late paleolithic ideology & organization, seen as surviving in the "great subcultures" within the later city-states, civilizations, and so on.) The poet like the shaman typically withdraws to solitude to find his poem or vision, then returns to sound it, give it life. He performs alone (or very occasionally with assistance, as in the work of Jackson Mac Low, say), because his presence is considered crucial & no other specialist has arisen to *act* in his place. He is also like the shaman in being at once an outsider, yet a person needed for validation of a certain kind of experience important to the group. And even in societies otherwise hostile or indifferent to poetry as "literature," he may be allowed a range of deviant, even anti-social behavior that many of his fellow-citizens do not enjoy. Again like the shaman, he will not only be allowed to act mad in public, but he will often be expected to do so. The act of the shaman—& his poetry—is like a public act of madness. It is like what the Senecas, in their great dream ceremony, now obsolete, called "turning the mind upside down." It shows itself as a release of alternative possibilities. "What do they want?" the poet wonders of those who watch him in the role of innocent, sometimes reluctant performer. But what? To know that madness is possible & that the contradictions can be sustained. From the first shaman— that solitary person—it flows out to whole companies of shamans, to whole societies of human beings: It heals the sickness of the body but more than that: the sickness of the soul. It is a "mode of thinking" & of acting that is "substantially concrete, existential & nominalistic, within a personalistic context" & "supremely able to sustain contradictions." It is the primal exercise of human freedom against/& for the tribe.

Now, as many questions are left as are answered. Does the poem really heal? Or what kind of poem or song, or discourse, does heal—or sustain contradictions—or turn the mind upside down? What is the basis for seeing in cultures & poetries so far removed from us the kinds of conjunctions I've so far assumed? And if the move from the "oral" to the "literal" was tied up, as I believe it was, with the need of an emergent class of rulers for a more rigorous arrangement of society, why should we now expect a move in the opposite direction? It is as yet hard to say, for our whole poetics (not just our *ethno*poetics) is, like our life in general, up for grabs. What do we say about the function of our poetry, the thing we do? That it explores. That it initiates thought or action. That it proposes its own displacement. That it allows vulnerability & conflict. That it remains, like the best science, constantly open to change: to a continual change in our idea of what a poem is or may be. What language is. What experience is. What reality is. That for many of us it has become a fundamental process for the play & interchange of possibilities.

And it has come out of a conflict—more or less deeply felt—with inherited forms of poetry, literature, language, discourse: not in every instance but where these are recognized as repressive structures, forms of categorical thinking that act against that other free play of possibilities just alluded to. Against these inherited forms, the conventional literature that no longer fed us, we have both searched for & invented other forms. Some of us have doggedly gone from there to a re-viewing of the entire poetic past (of any poetry for that matter outside the immediate neighborhood) from the point of view of the present. Here there are two processes involved—not mutually exclusive. On the one hand the contemporary forms (the new means that we invent) make older forms visible: & on the other hand the forms that we uncover elsewhere help us in the reshaping, the resharpening, of our own tools. The past, come alive, is in motion with us. It is no longer somewhere else but, like the future, *here*—which is the only way it can be, towards a poetry of changes.

A Post-Script—as improvisation—to the Preceding, June 1977

The fact of performance now runs through all our arts, & the arts themselves begin to merge & lose their old distinctions, till it's apparent that we're no longer where we were to start with. The Renaissance is over or it begins again with us. Yet the origins we seek—the frame that bounds our past, that's set against an open-ended future—are no longer Greek, nor even Indo-European, but take in all times & places. To say this isn't to deny history, for we're in fact involved with history, with the sense of ourselves "in time" & in relation to other forms of human experience besides our own. The model—or better, the vision—has shifted: away from a "great tradition" centered in a single stream of art & literature in the west, to a *greater* tradition that includes, sometimes as its central fact, preliterate & oral cultures throughout the world, with a sense of their connection to subterranean but literate traditions in civilizations both east & west. "Poetry is made in the mouth," said Tristan Tzara, & Edmond Jabès: "The book is as old as fire & water"—& both, we know, are right.

The change of view, for those who have experienced it, is by now virtually

125

paradigmatic. We live with it in practice & find it more & more difficult to communicate with those who still work with the older paradigm. Thus, what appears to us as essentially creative—how can we doubt it?—carries for others the threat that was inherent when Tzara, as arch Dadaist, called, circa 1917, for "a great negative work of destruction" against a late, overly textualized derivation from the Renaissance paradigm of culture & history. No longer viable, that great western thesis was already synthesizing, setting the stage for its own disappearance. The other side of Tzara's work—& increasingly that of other artists within the several avant gardes—was, we now see clearly, a great positive work of construction/synthesis. With Tzara it took the form of a projected anthology, *Poemes negres*, a gathering of African & Oceanic poems culled from existing ethnographies & chanted at Dada performances in Zurich's Cafe Voltaire. To the older brokers of taste—the bearers of western values in an age of chaos—this may have looked like yet another Dada gag, but seeing it now in its actual publication six decades after the fact, it reads like a first, almost too serious attempt at a new classic anthology. In circulation orally, it formed with Tzara's own poetry—the process of a life & its emergence as performance in the soundworks & simultaneities of the Dada soirees, and so on—one of the prophetic statements of where our work was to go.

Sixty years after Dada, a wide range of artists have been making deliberate & increasing use of ritual models for performance, have swept up arts like painting, sculpture, poetry (if those terms still apply) long separated from their origins in performance. (Traditional performance arts—music, theater, dance—have undergone similarly extreme transformations: often, like the others, towards a virtual liberation from the dominance of text.) The principal function here may be viewed as that of mapping & exploration, but however defined or simplified (text, for example, doesn't vanish but is revitalized; so, likewise, the Greco-European past itself), the performance/ritual impulse seems clear throughout: in "happenings" & related event pieces (particularly those that involve participatory performance), in meditative works (often in an explicitly mantric model), in earthworks (derived from monumental American Indian structures), in dreamworks that play off trance & ecstasy, in bodyworks (including acts of self-mutilation & endurance that seem to test the model), in a range of healing events as literal explorations of the shamanistic premise, in animal language pieces related to the new ethology, and so on.*

While a likely characteristic of the new paradigm is an overt disdain for paradigms *per se,* it seems altogether possible to state a number of going assumptions as these relate to performance. I won't try to sort them out but will simply present them for consideration in the order in which they come to mind.

---

* When I made a similar point in *Technicians of the Sacred* ten years ago, I attributed the relation between "primitive" ritual & contemporary art & performance to an implicit coincidence of attitudes, where today the relation seems up-front, explicit & increasingly comparable to the Greek & Roman model in Renaissance Europe, the Chinese model in medieval Japan, the Toltec model among the Aztecs, and so on; that is, an overt influence but alive enough to work a series of distortions conditioned by the later culture & symptomatic of the obvious differences between the two.

(1) There is a strong sense of continuities, already alluded to, within the total range of human cultures & arts, & a sense as well that the drive toward performance goes back to our prehuman biological inheritance—that performance & culture, even language, precede the actual emergence of the species: hence an ethological continuity as well. With this comes a rejection of the idea of artistic "progress" & a tendency to link avant garde & "traditional" performance (tribal/oral, archaic, and so on) as forms of what Richard Schechner calls *transformational* theater & art—in opposition to the "mimetic/re-actualizing" art of the older paradigm.

(2) There is an unquestionable & far-reaching breakdown of boundaries & genres: between "art & life" (Cage, Kaprow), between various conventionally defined arts (intermedia & performance art, concrete poetry), & between arts & non-arts (*musique concrete,* found art, and so on). The consequences here are immense, & I'll only give a few, perhaps too obvious, examples . . . :

• that social conflicts are a form of theater (V. Turner) & that organized theater may be an arena for the projection &/or stimulation of social conflict;

• that art has again recognized itself as visionary, & that there may be no useful distinction between vision-as-vision & vision-as-art (thus, too, the idea in common between Freud & the Surrealists, that the dream is a dream-*work,* that is, a work-of-art);

• that there is a continuum, rather than a barrier, between music & noise; between poetry & prose (the language of inspiration & the language of common & special discourse); between dance & normal locomotion (walking, running, jumping), and so on.

• that there is no hierarchy of media in the visual arts, no hierarchy of instrumentation in music, & that qualitative distinctions between high & low genres & modes (opera & vaudeville, high rhetoric & slang) are no longer operational;

• that neither advanced technology (electronically produced sound & image, and the like) nor hypothetically primitive devices (pulse & breath, the sound of rock on rock, of hand on water) are closed off to the artist willing to employ them.

(3) There is a move away from the idea of "masterpiece" to one of the transientness & self-obsolescence of the art-work. The work past its moment becomes a document (mere history), & the artist becomes, increasingly, the surviving non-specialist in an age of technocracy.

(4) From this there follows a new sense of function in art, in which the value of a work isn't inherent in its formal or aesthetic characteristics—its shape or its complexity or simplicity as an object—but in what it does, or what the artist or his surrogate does with it, in a given context. This is different in turn from the other, equally functional concept of art as propaganda, at least insofar as the latter forces the artist to repeat "truths" already known, and so on, in the service of the total state. As an example of a non-formal, functional approach to the art object as instrument-of-power, take the following, from my conversations with the Seneca Indian sculptor/carver, Avery Jimerson:

I told him that I thought Floyd John's mask was very beautiful, but he said it wasn't because it didn't have real power [the power, for example, to handle burning coals while wearing it]. His own father had had a mask that did, until there was a fire in his house & it was burnt to ashes. But his father could still see the features of the mask & so, before it crumbled, he hurried out & carved a second mask. And that second mask looked like the first in every detail. Only it had no power. (J.R., *A Seneca Journal*)

(5) There follows further, in the contemporary instance, a stress on action/ or process. Accordingly the performance or ritual model includes the act of composition itself: the artist's life as an unfolding through his performance of it. (The consideration of this private or closed side of performance is a little like Richard Schechner's discovery that rehearsal/preparation is a theatrical/ritual event as important as the showing it precedes.) Signs of the artist's or poet's presence are demanded in the published work, & in our own time this has come increasingly to take the form of his or her performance of that work, unfolding it or testifying to it in a public place. The personal presence is an instance as well of localization, of a growing concern wth particular & local definitions; for what, asks David Antin, can be more local than the person?

(6) Along with the artist, the audience enters the performance arena as participant—or, ideally, the audience disappears as the distinction between doer & viewer, like the other distinctions mentioned herein, begins to blur. For this the tribal/oral is a particularly clear model, often referred to by the creators of 1960s happenings & theatrical pieces that invited, even coerced, audience participation toward an ultimate democratizing of the arts. In a more general way, many artists have come to see themselves as essentially the initiators of the work ("makers of the plot but not of everything that enters into the plot"—Jackson Mac Low), expanding the art process by inviting the audience to join with them in an act of "co-creation" or to respond with a new work in which the one-time viewer/listener himself becomes the maker. The response-as-creation thus supercedes the response-as-criticism, just as the maker/particularizer comes to be viewed (or to view himself) as the superior of the interpreter/generalizer. It is this which Charles Olson had in mind when he saw us emerging from a "generalizing time," and so on, to regain a sense of the poem "as the act of the instant . . . not the act of thought about the instant." More dramatically, as a contrast between the involved participant & the objective observer, it turns up in Gary Snyder's story of Alfred Kroeber & his Mojave informant, circa 1902, in which Kroeber sits through six days of intense oral narration, the story of the world from its beginnings, & then writes:

When our sixth day ended he still again said another day would see us through. But by then I was overdue at Berkeley. And as the prospective day might once more have stretched into several, I reluctantly broke off, promising him and myself that I would return to Needles when I could, not later than next winter, to conclude recording the tale. By next winter Inyo-Kutavere had died and the tale thus remains unfinished. . . . He was stone blind. He was below the average of Mojave tallness, slight in figure, spare, almost frail with age, his gray hair long and unkempt, his features sharp, delicate, sensitive. . . . He sat indoors on the loose sand floor of the house for the whole of the six days that I was with him in the frequent posture of Mojave men, his feet beneath him or behind him to the side, not with legs crossed. He sat still but smoked all the Sweet

128

Caporal cigarettes I provided. His house mates sat around and listened or went and came as they had things to do.

To which Snyder adds the single sentence: "That old man sitting in the sand house telling his story is who we must become—not A. L. Kroeber, as fine as he was."

The model switch is here apparent. But in addition the poet-as-informant stands in the same relation to those who speak of poetry or art from outside the sphere of its making as do any of the world's aboriginals. The antagonism to literature & to criticism is, for the poet & artist, no different from that to anthropology, say, on the part of the Native American militant. It is a question in short of the right to self-definition.

(7) There is an increasing use of real time, extended time, etc., &/or a blurring of the distinction between those & theatrical time, in line with the transformative view of the "work" as a process that's really happening. (Analogues to this, as alternative modes of narration, performance, and the like, are again sought in tribal/oral rituals.) In addition an area of performance using similarly extended time techniques toward actual transformations (of the self, of consciousness, etc.) parallels that of traditional meditation (*mantra, yantra*, in the Tantric context), thus an exploration of the boundaries of mind that Snyder offers as the central work of contemporary man, or Duchamp from a perspective not all that different: "to put art again at the service of mind."

For all of this recognition of cultural origins & particularities, the crunch, the paradox, is that the place, if not the stance, of the artist & poet is increasingly beyond culture—a characteristic, inevitably, of biospheric societies. Imperialistic in their earlier form & based on a paradigm of "the dominant culture" (principally the noble/imperial myths of "western civilization" & of "progress," and so on, in a western or European model), these have in their *avant garde* phase been turning to the "symposium of the whole" projected by Robert Duncan. More strongly felt in the industrial & capitalist west, this may be the last move of its kind still to be initiated by the Euro-Americans: a recognition of the new/old order in which the whole is equal to but no greater than the works of all its parts.

Performance

From "The Duende: Theory and Divertissement"

Federico Garcia Lorca

. . . Once the andalusian singer Pastora Pavon, "The Girl with the Combs," a somber Hispanic genius whose capacity for fantasy equals Goya's or Raphael el Gallo's, was singing in a little tavern in Cadiz. She sparred with her voice—now shadowy, now like molten tin, now covered over with moss; she tangled her voice in her long hair or drenched it in sherry or lost it in the darkest and furthermost bramble bushes. But nothing happened—useless, all of it! The hearers remained silent. . . . There was only a little man, one of those dancing mannikins who leap suddenly out of brandy bottles, who observed sarcastically in a very low voice: "*Viva* Paris!" As if to say: We are not interested in aptitude or techniques or virtuosity here. We are interested in something else.

Then the "Girl with the Combs" got up like a woman possessed, her face blasted like a medieval weeper, tossed off a great glass of Cazalla at a single draught, like a potion of fire, and settled down to singing—without a voice, without breath, without nuance, throat aflame—but with *duende!* She had contrived to annihilate all that was nonessential in song and make way for an angry and incandescent *Duende,* friend of the sand-laden winds, so that everyone listening tore at his clothing almost in the same rhythm with which the West Indian Negroes in their rites rend away their clothes, huddled in heaps before the image of Saint Barbara.

The "Girl with the Combs" had to mangle her voice because she knew there were discriminating folk about who asked not for form, but for the marrow of form—pure music spare enough to keep itself in the air. She had to deny her faculties and her security; that is to say, to turn out Muse and keep vulnerable, so that her *Duende* might come and vouchsafe the hand-to-hand struggle. And then how she sang! Her voice feinted no longer; it jetted up like blood, ennobled by sorrow and sincerity, it opened up like ten fingers of a hand around the nailed feet of a Christ Juan de Juni—tempestuous!

The arrival of the *Duende* always presupposes a radical change in all the forms as they existed on the old plane. It gives a sense of refreshment unknown until then, together with that quality of the just-opening rose, of the miraculous, which comes and instils an almost religious transport.

—from "The Duende: Theory and Divertissement," a lecture composed and delivered by Federico Garcia Lorca during his stay in Havana en route from the United States in 1934. Published in *Poet in New York* by Federico Garcia Lorca, a new translation by Ben Belitt, Grove Press, 1955.

THE POETRY PERFORMANCE

Tom Schmidt

MY FIRST EXPERIENCE with performing came in music. In music no alternative to performing as well as you can has ever come to my mind. After about 15 years with music I began to get involved with the reading—I'll call it performance—of poetry, my own. Around that time I remember someone telling me the story that Yvor Winters thought a poem should be read aloud as badly as possible. If it could survive such verbal butchering it proved, yes, that the poem was a good one. Or, before a recent performance at the University of California at Irvine, I was warned to expect a cool response from members of the audience who were part of the university's writing program. Michael Horovitz, the English poet who is practically a one-man opera when he performs, had been received with icy disdain just a few months before. "Here they want a kind of flat reading that won't distract from what's on the page," my friend Roger Angle said.

What's on the page? Unless it's a poem meant not to be read aloud—a concrete poem which is a visual experience, say—what's on the page is exactly analogous to what's on a printed sheet of music: a notation or a map that is not more than a guide to the music. As a poem is a guide to the poetry. Xavier Villaurrutia says, "My pen traces [the poem's] coastline onto the page." The musician goes through notation to get to the music. John Cage says over and over, "The composition is not finished until it is performed." The poem is not finished until it is performed. The poetry performer guides the audience along the edge of a breathing promontory.

When I was nine my folks took me to a Danny Kaye movie about musicians traveling around the country on trains. Several pop musicians played actual parts in the film, jamming in the Pullman berths and all: the Dorsey brothers, Benny Goodman, and, in another car, Louis Armstrong. After the movie my mother asked me which of those instruments I liked best, and would I like to play one. The next day we walked down to Knudsen's Music Studio on San Pablo Avenue, and I told the man behind the glass display case that I wanted to play the trombone. I was captivated by some photographs on the wall of what I later found was Knudsen's vaudeville act in the '20s. A flat-faced young man standing stiffly in his tuxedo in front of large racks of instruments. It was said that he played one song using all 29 of them in less than three minutes. It was surprising to find that there were 29 instruments.

"He's too small to play the trombone, ma'am," the clerk said. "But he could start out on trumpet and work his way up." There was a terrible uneasy moment. I wanted to play the goddamn trombone, and, though I'm sure I didn't have the words to think it, I was hoping my mother saw through that bullshit and was going to stand up for me. She didn't say anything—which maybe wasn't so bad after all, now that I think of it—and I said, "Clarinet."

Luckily they had a nice used one for sale and easy payments could be slipped right in with the price of lessons. My first teacher was called Mr. Bomberg. He was a shriveled old violin player with leathery, hepatic skin who chain smoked cork-tipped Raleighs and snicked my fingers with the bow when I made a mistake. Or, when I leaned toward the music, straining to climb into some difficult passage—just about everything—he'd place the tip of the bow across my forehead and push me back in the chair as neatly as if he'd used the flat of a sword. "If you are going to play that thing you must breathe," he said. It didn't make sense to me, but I went on with it because sometimes it seemed like something I could do.

First I was asked to join the band at Knudsen's. Mostly accordians and Hawaiian guitars. I was terrified in the middle of so many bad noises. Then the grammar school orchestra—my lucky clarinet broke during my solo at graduation. In high school the teacher, Ernie Douglas, was a fine oboe player who was full of bitterness because he had to play saxophone on weekends in order to make the payments on his house in Orinda. And because about all he had to work with was us products of Knudsen's Music Studio. But in the eleventh grade the band played some tired warhorse—a Rossini overture, I bet—which had a long clarinet solo passage which I was chosen to play and which I somehow

135

decided to like. I practiced it a little, and we all thought it sounded pretty good. The first performance was at an assembly. At the appropriate moment I actually had to walk out in front and read from a special stand. I decided to put all of my underdeveloped heart and soul into it.

I was surprised how easy it was walking out there, the piece already moving well along. I remember Mr. Douglas winking as I passed the podium. I remember beginning to play. Then a strange thing happened. It seemed to me that the music was very beautiful, but it was as if someone else were playing it. There was a moment of terror calling out in a room far back in my mind, a voice in there pointing out that the notes on the page before me had blurred into a vague white blob. But the music went on and was fine and outside me. I was exercising *no conscious effort whatsoever* to play my clarinet. I was actually aware of my consciousness standing outside and watching the form of my body play the clarinet. And then. And then I was aware that the whole world had disappeared. There was one great moment when I was essentially blind. I not only couldn't see the music, I couldn't see anything but a fog of brilliant white light. And the music went on, lovely, outside me.

The solo ended and I was able to blink my senses back. Returning to my seat I felt a terrible vertigo, and, trembling, I was certain I would crumple on top of the flute section. Of course it was years before I told anyone about it. I had gone insane and would be institutionalized if word got around. It was something Mr. Bomberg never prepared me for.

That kind of experience is more available to musicians, particularly in collectively improvised forms like jazz where notation doesn't stand between the musician and the music, than to poets, who usually feel they're doing most of their work in solitude, even as the Blakes and the Spicers remind us we're never singing alone. The thunderbolt of communion that can wire up all the senses of five people jamming the blues probably seems like a kind of rhetorical indulgence to many poets. (Of course most schemes of pop music toss out electrified clusterfucks like small change. Or, in a slightly different space, Cecil Taylor says white musicians are "trying to cop a feel.") But it is the opposite of indulgence. What happens is each musician disappears—his senses of harmony, pitch, rhythm, form, tradition, technique, and finally his sense of his isolated self, disappear and become music, just music. And poets must disappear into their poems as well.

That is what a poetry performance is for. To make it happen, poets need to remind themselves that the poem resides, no, rides, in the body. As prose, the literary, rides the argument, poetry rides the breath. The breath is a column of air surrounded by the lungs and throat and mouth. The column of air is lifted off the earth, levered from the plant of the feet by the legs, hamstring, the guts. All of this is watched by eyes in the mind, and if I were talking about writing poetry I'd be talking about those eyes. But in performance the poem must become literally embodied.

Lately I'm working with a dancer, Karen Toepfer. We've worked out every arrangement of poetry, music, and dance available between us. I am learning that Karen's dancing with my poems doesn't function as illustration, but as an aura, a flame above the poems. I believe it draws the body of the audience toward the poem and through the poem. Karen also reads some of my poems, which gives me the chance to play flute behind them. I use no written music, but I've fallen into following her breath patterns as I breathe into the flute, another column of air. When it works the poem is given wings, a flying energy that soars right across the faces in the audience.

And there are even fragments of the event where I take part in the dancing. Karen said that if she had to play music I'd have to dance a dance. I have little fear of performing a poem or a song: I think it might be valuable in this context to consider the sheer terror I suffer at the prospect of dancing. Dance is the place where there is no machinery between your body and your art; when dance is notated it is notated *after* the performance. Dancers like to talk about dance as the first art. When I do this moving around, sometimes carrying a poem along with me, I often feel as if the chasm between my mind and my body is as wide as the Grand Canyon. Having worked so long with poetry and, most of the time, music so high in the brain, I sometimes sense that parts of me, some bridges, are nearly atrophied. But then, somehow, there'll be an earthquake of a moment when those terrible worn walls are drawn together and the connection is made. That is what a poetry performance is for.

That is the moment the poetry performance wants to hold for an hour, an eternity.

MAKEBELIEVE MUSIC

Jessica Hagedorn

> *love is like*
> *an itchin' in my heart*
> *tearin' it apart*
> *i can't scratch it . . .*
> —The Supremes

CHICAGO NOT A very pretty city this winter. We drive through the South Side for a tour of the neighborhood. Roscoe and Malachi are going to show me Muhammad Ali's house, and then on the next block, the series of mansions built by the late Elijah Muhammad for himself and his family. I have been in Chicago only a few hours. Everything grim and gray and cold. The wind cuts through my Paris fleamarket coat and I think my face is gonna fall off. "She ain't used to it," Malachi chuckles. "I keep forgetting—she ain't from here."

At a neighborhood bar where integrated couples hang out and peanut shells litter the floor, Malachi starts talkin' about the "music of the mind." How everytime you turn on the radio you only hear escapist music, and never the kind of music the Art Ensemble plays. "And I don't blame the people for their ignorance," Malachi continues. "It's just that—," he paused.

"They don't have a choice," I suggest. "They listen to what's been programmed for them, and that's all they know . . ." And, I betcha, a child could just as easily learn to dance to Malachi's "Tutankhamen" or Lester Bowie's "Barnyard Scuffel Shuffle" or "Banana Whistle," as they do now to Michael Jackson's "Enjoy Yourself," which you hear every twenty minutes on AM or FM radio.

Copyright © 1977 by Jessica Hagedorn.

"Ain't nothin' wrong with it," Malachi says. "I like to dance and have a good time myself. . . . But all that IZ MAKEBELIEVE MUSIC—the man singin' about how he'll love you forever when everybody knows they're rushin' to City Hall everyday to file for divorce. . . ." We laugh. It all brings us back to what makes us keep doin' what we're doin', despite everything we know. . . . Maybe it's those people who flock to hear our performance the following night at the Body Politic, a little theater on the North Side of Chicago, where I get my first glimpse of the Playboy skyscraper and fantasize bunny rabbits hopping in and out of Mercedes-Benz limousines.

We rehearse the next afternoon, after I make reservations to fly back to San Francisco during an intense scene with Roscoe. "I don't care about performing tonight," I mutter. "Fuck all those muthafuckas . . ." Remember all those warnings in theater school—"Don't ever get involved with people you work with." I throw a fit. "I'm leaving this city!"

Roscoe convinces me to go on with the performance and leave in the morning. I calm down. Malachi has phoned twice to ask why we're late for rehearsal. I am nervous. A performance with Malachi Favors on bass and Roscoe Mitchell on saxophone—what am I doing here? It's not like working with your own band. I think of the Gangster Choir fondly. I do like my R & B, but it's on another level tonight. And this *is* Chicago.

The rehearsal goes smoothly. Malachi listens to what I want him to do. I give directions shyly, in a halting voice that holds back tears. "This is a poem of celebration," I tell Malachi. "It's about dancing—it's about joy." Malachi nods, begins plucking his bass. I start to recite *Canto Negro*.

With the Gangster Choir, I always wait for the chorus to chirp "Shake/shake/children of the jungle. . . ." That's my cue. I wrote it in. I arranged it, with Julian Priester's melody in my head. But this afternoon there are none of the four vocalists I usually have with me, no electric guitars and Echoplexes and drummers and Fender bass players, their naked chests gleaming with sweat. It's just me and Malachi, and what I can do with my voice and my conviction. I forget about my private torment. I allow the poem and the music to lift me out of myself, and it works! Just what the doctor ordered . . .

I formed the West Coast Gangster Choir two years ago. I remember holding rehearsals in the cramped garage of my former house by the beach. Nine people gathered (we still had the piano player then) to follow Julian Priester's instructions. His arms flailing the air from time to time, he pounded a "Latin Percussion" cowbell with infinite patience to keep us constantly aware of the ONE in time.

This was my concept of where I wanted the "poetry reading" to go—an extravaganza of voices and moving bodies playing instruments that would hypnotize an audience numbed by the pomp and circumstance of academia, forgetting that the origins of poetry are oral and physical—even Robert Bly cops to *that*.

The "poetry reading"—I've always felt uncomfortable with that term. It is detached and academic to me, visions of young women wearing tweed suits and tortoise-shell glasses, clearing their throats and "reading" about their anima rising and libidos pulsating in trembling, Sarah Lawrence-type voices. Holy shit—not me!

"Oh, Jessica," folks would say, "are you reading tonight? Where are you doing your reading?" It conjures up images of astrologers—and, while I do believe in the connection between magicians, psychics, and poets, I am not a reader. Most of the time I keep the paper in front of me only as a shield between myself and the audience. Plus those podiums are always good to lean on.

The concept of the Gangster Choir—shades of the old "Doo-wop" school, Smokey Robinson, the Flamingoes, some Hector Lavoe chanting, always the tropics lurking in the background, the way we sing, the way we put it out there, the message in the music. The poetics of our lives, this is what I am interested in. It's already been monumentalized in what critics snidely refer to as "pop" music—but very little has been said about poets doing it for themselves. There were those beatniks talking about urban madonnas, but that was an elite and very white cult of people.

We got our own folks now—Pedro Pietri and Papoleto, Victor Cruz and Ntozake Shange, Thulani and Al Robles, and the countless others too numerous and beautiful to mention. We are only scratching the surface and sometimes, like Ntozake says, letting "The Art Ensemble of Chicago/take the weight . . . "

It is 1977. Ironically, after many fantasies and conversations, I am in the original Hollywood gangster city, rehearsing with two formidable musicians that I would've never dreamed of working with two years ago in that basement garage in San Francisco. I sometimes get too awestruck by formidability—something I am learning to transcend as I get older and more in love with myself. Now it is just biz-ness.

"For this last piece, I want a drone," I say, referring to my poem "Something About You," the last piece in *Dangerous Music*. "A drone . . . ," Malachi and Roscoe echo thoughtfully. "Yes," I say, "this is an elegy-type poem—I pay homage to friends, some dead and some living, and I need some kind of weird drone to give off that feeling . . ."

It is, for me, the most successful piece of the evening. When I perform it I feel a surge of pride in the coherence of our collaboration, and I am thankful for finally being in Chicago, and letting Roscoe Mitchell talk me into it.

NOTES ON THE PERFORMANCE POEM

James Schevill

The Nature of the Performance Poem

The performance poem is not written for the page and is almost impossible to notate for the page because of the physical sound and theatrical performance factors involved. In an age of overspecialization, the performance poem is a renewing link between poetry and drama. It allows the poet to break away from familiar lyrical patterns and explore new dramatic dimensions. Since the performance poem is not merely read aloud, as in most poetry readings, it must be conceived for the particular environment in which it is to be performed, and it must be adequately rehearsed. The whole aim of the performance poem is to enliven the all-too-familiar routine of the usual poetry reading in which, too often, the poet gives us a hasty, barely-to-be-heard, shortsighted reading from the page. The performance poem is not meant to displace the poem on the page. In an age of amorphous print, the performance poem is designed to help restore the physical qualities of language.

The Space

Poets read often under incredible handicaps without thinking about how their poems sound to audiences. The performance poem is intended to explore the unique relationship between poet and audience in the same way that modern theater explores unique environmental spaces. If a poet is to read in a modern auditorium, high up on a stage with an enormous gap between poet and audience, the result is often a cold, impersonal distance and an increasingly uncomfortable reading. In such an environment, Robert Frost was once heard to mutter, "The bastards are killing me." With its wide range of possible techniques, the performance poem can transform any kind of space into one appropriate for dramatic use. The scale, the tone of the performance poem, depends on the space. In a large space, large-scale effects must be created. In a small space, more intimate subtleties are essential.

Performance poems can be done with many voices in large halls, warehouses, statehouses, sports arenas, or the like. They can be performed on telephone hookups between cities and countries, in railroad stations and airports. Outdoors, they can be done in parks or plazas, can take part in familiar parades or create their own ritual processions. Or they can find intimate places—living rooms, cafes, medical waiting rooms, any small place waiting to be awakened, transformed, recognized in its daily routine.

Sound Poetry

In Europe after World War I, in such Dadaist work as that of Kurt Schwitters, and after World War II in the work of the Austrian poet Ernst Jandl, the sound poem has had a relatively strong influence. In the United States, experiments with sound poetry have remained on a more abstract, limited level. (An exception is the work of the young sound poet Dave Hazelton, who died in his twenties at the start of his career after many brave efforts to further the cause of sound poetry, particularly in the San Francisco Bay Area.) The major problem in sound poetry is to break out of the merely abstract qualities of sound and investigate the experience of linguistic sound as it relates dramatically to life. Jandl's extraordinary variations on the root sounds and meanings of *Mutter* (mother) are an example of the possibilities brought about by the linguistic revolution today. In my own work I have tried something similar with the word "woman," in a sound poem in the cycle *Origins,* printed in my book, *Violence and Glory.* How does a simple word like "woman" break down into the emotional elements of sound involved in conception, birth, the sexual act? But as I tried to notate the poem toward a syllabic indication of its sound patterns, it still remains silent on the page. It must be performed in many possible ways. It must be heard in performance to be experienced.

In many ways, every poem must be read aloud—to help clarify phrasing, metrical form, the voice that speaks the poem, or whatever techniques need to be heard. Sound poetry explores the hidden sources of sound, the roots of language involved with gesture, with animal sounds and bird-songs, with noise of every kind. Sound poetry goes beyond the traditional patterns of conventional, communicative sound into the deepest structures of physical language. In so doing, it emphasizes the mysterious, isolated sound of syllables. It jolts conventional syntax into unique arrangements. (e. e. cummings wrote some poems that must be considered anew for their sound values.) It questions the rational surface of language and exposes the emotional, often irrational roots.

Often modern composers have done more for sound poetry than poets— for example, John Cage with his investigations of Thoreau's *Journals* and their relationship to natural sounds, and Luciano Berio in such a work as *Sequenza III,* where a collage of sound fragments, historical and contemporary, haunts the protagonist's mind. Probably the future of sound poetry lies in an investigation into the close relationship between poetry and music that is becoming evidenced again after years of neglect.

The Use of Multiple Voices

Sound poetry is an important aspect of the performance poem in that it pursues, as I have indicated, the hidden, psychological sounds of language.

However, it is usually limited to one voice. Directing the Poetry Center in San Francisco in the 1960s [at San Francisco State University], growing tired of the limited possibilities of one voice, I began to experiment with performance poems that used two voices. Two voices provide the essential conflict of drama. Beyond that, there are infinite possibilities. Why not, I thought, since I was a frustrated musician, combine one voice speaking and chanting with another voice singing?—create a counterpoint, the marvelous dual exploration of music and poetry similar to the lost effects of the Greek chorus. My wife, the singer Margot Schevill, was a great help in this regard. We experimented in various ways. Perhaps the most successful of our experiments is a performance poem called "Walking and Running," which I printed in *Violence and Glory*—but, unfortunately, without the essential melodic line that I wrote for her to sing. The poem is about the difference between walking and running as ways of life. I read, very slowly and with different rhythmical syncopations, the saga of a man who walks through life, "taking a slow look at things," and resolving that "slow, slow, is the way to go." Against this plodding voyage, Margot sings the story of a woman who runs through life joyously:

> *Running, running, running*
> *Is the way to move,*
> *Open high the heart,*
> *Pump out the laziness*
> *Of spirit, cleave the air*
> *Like a fast bird, the Swift*
> *That drinks skimming over water,*
> *Picks up food and nesting straw*
> *On the wing and mates while flying!*
> *Running, running, running is the way to move . . .*

Needless to say, in a performance poem like this, timing is all important. Nor is humor to be neglected. Tone determines the poem, the differences between speaking, chanting, and singing that go to make up the comic clash of these walking and running personalities. Depending on the performer, the tone can change with every performance.

Beyond two voices, the possibilities of vocal combinations are almost infinite. The great choral traditions of oral literature should be revived. The ability to write on a large scale for choral effects is required. Perhaps the place to start is with the tape recorder, where it is relatively easy to record a large number of different voices. Then, if the poet can prove his or her effectiveness in choral poems on tape, perhaps the poet can persuade some choral group to let him or her experiment with the performance poems.

Visual Effects

In a visual age, concrete poetry has become a strong influence today. It enables visual poets to play with the appearance, the visual structures of language, rather than the sounds. The problem, in an age of specialization, is that concrete poetry caters to specialization. The advantage of experimenting with visual effects in the performance poem is that one searches in the direction of unifying rather than separating the senses. What difference does it make if one approaches the borderline theater? At some point, theater and the performance poem merge, and the distinction, like the futile argument of the difference between poetry and prose, is unimportant.

Experiment freely, then, with visual effects, bearing in mind that the primary purpose is to illuminate language, to restore poetry to its primary magic. Use film techniques or slide projections with the poet's voice or a variety of voices. Enlist artists, sculptors. Seek to restore the close relationship between poetry and art that has been confined too much to the printed page. Once I read a poem of mine about what garbage collectors find in their daily collections. A high school student had read the poem before my appearance and had gone to his local dump to collect and build a garbage sculpture. It was an amazing invention of found objects, but the principal of this particular school was aghast. How could this disgusting collection of garbage be called art? He ordered it out of the school, and another anti-school rebel was created.

The mystery of poetry must always investigate the relationship of the senses. Where the rational voice stops, the musical, the artistic, the dramatic elements with their eerie, imaginative effects, begin. Sound, color, stretch the rational syllables, give them new meaning.

Movement

Movement, I imagine the reader protesting, is definitely theatrical. If the performance poem is to permit movement, all definitions of poetry are shattered. All that is shattered is the safety of the book, the sanctuary of the passive reader who is slowly tranquilizing himself or herself to death.

Dance and poetry is another possible unity. It is nothing new. The Greeks knew the significance of this relationship. The great Asian and African dance-dramas have always known this instinctive, physical connection. The problem is that our dance and poetry experiments, like jazz and poetry, have always been self-conscious. Everyone wants to do his or her own thing. The ritual connections of poetry and dance are anonymous. Perhaps, as in sacred ritual ceremonies, we should not even know the names of the performers. The few experiments I have carried out with dancers have been of limited satisfaction, because they have usually ended as interpretations, improvisations. What is needed is fusion, the joint creation of the work from the beginning, words and movement together. But it requires the singular elimination of ego, a joint dedication to the work.

Mime is another possibility. But mime demands silence, is the immediate protest. Yes, but contemporary poetry, as in Beckett, is discovering the demands, the directions of silence. What is perhaps possible to investigate through mime and poetry is the essence of silence. Titling, as in silent films, voices coming over the radio, the television, the telephone—all are a possibility. And the silent presence of the poet speaking about the possibilities of silence to the mime—that might surprise us too.

Finally, the poet as actor. No, please, that is too much. The poet is poet, not actor. The poet is too clumsy; the poet cannot move. He or she is only the reader up there, giving us the sound of the poem. But some poets, such as Theodore Roethke, have always broken out into clumsy, exuberant dances while reading. What if a poet were to create a reading in which all of his or her poems required unusual movements? No, no, this is drama again. What does it matter? It is poetry searching for a new language of movement. Perhaps the next Poetry Festival, instead of all the familiar names, will be six poets in search of movement. If they can restrain their egos, that might surprise us with joy. God knows, we need joy, not the old defensive gestures of poetry maintaining its isolation in a materialistic society.

The Audience

My god, says the reader, he is ending with the greatest contemporary theatrical problem, the relationship between actor and audience. True, but it's also the greatest poetic problem. Shall we continue to write poetry out of some proud, defensive isolation, continuing to believe stubbornly that poetry will survive in an age when the creative initiative is largely in science? Or shall we seek again the ancient, communal responsibilities of poetry? As poets, the choice is ours. It does not mean that we all have immediately to become performance poets. It does mean that we have to learn about the possibilities and impossibilities of performance poems in this time of great transformations. The word on the page will survive only if it is capable of new dimensions. That requires a new sense of audience. Poets must stop giving readings that demonstrate either a lack of understanding of what audience involves or a real indifference, even contempt, of the audience.

Not that the audience can be attacked, shocked, as in the old days of the Dadaists and Surrealists. Such shock is difficult, if not impossible, to achieve when television has trained us how to be indifferent to violence. Audiences can be involved only with poetry that reaches out to them on all levels of the senses. Often this can be done by a simple, true reading of the poem—even better, if it is followed by a second reading. Too often poets skim from one poem to another as if they were birds in flight. Alas, the audience cannot fly. They are anchored to their seats or to the floor on which they are sitting. As in theater, there is the possibility of the poet moving the audience, inviting them to move, challenging them to hear the poem from another angle, another position.

The main thing is to involve the audience, stationary or not. If the audience becomes sympathetic to the poet's experience, half the battle is won. The audience does not have to speak, but they cannot remain passive, lost in their individual fantasies. Perhaps the final goal is for the audience to speak, not necessarily just in applause or praise, but as part of the performance poem. What might it mean if true poems were written that contain part for the audience? I have witnessed some experiments in this regard, and, again, they have been unsatisfactory, or pathetic, because they have never solved the problem of ego-display on the part of the poet or the audience. The real significance of the performance poem is that it permits us ways to experiment with the enduring communal dream, men and women as brother and sister to men and women, breaking through ironic isolations into the challenge of ancient communal rituals.

146

Talking:
Notes on Writing and Reading

Eileen Shukofsky

In June of 1975, I began working with a dancer/choreographer, Eric Trules, who was interested in using voice/speech patterns as structures for dance. I would bring in material to read. Eric would develop frameworks for movement improvisation based on the information I gave him, which usually came in two ways: the structure and content of the written piece (as it existed in print, its own character); the way I read it (my character). What follows are two sections from notes taken during/ after those work sessions.

Wednesday, June 19

We begin with my exercise:

I.

Read pages 266 to 268 from Böll's *Group Portrait with Lady,* Margaret's speech to the Au. on what happened to Schlömer, in a fairly normal, conversational, character tone;

read pages 87 to 89 from Borges' "The Man on the Threshold," the speech on making a judge of a madman, in a super-rapid, barely intelligible, very clipped tone;

read each of these, one after another, three times apiece;

during this part with Eric only listening.

II.

After a rest, read the passages again, two times each, sitting with our backs as much as possible flush to one another.

III.

Stop reading and let Eric work.

Reading and movement together.

The readings of three are exhausting. I find myself weakening a great deal by the third time around, where it becomes difficult for me to pay attention. But after a silence and a rest, we go into the second part, and I feel, to me, surprisingly strong. Perhaps it is that extra element of our backs being together, and feeling my own movements of speaking meet a resistance: another body. Something seems to be clicking somehow, the energy feeling very powerful to me. When I am done I go to sit down.

Eric begins to move. He works out the piece, which begins to develop a shape within and beyond the contexts of the content in the readings, although the relationship to the passages is strong for me.

Two distinctive kinds of movement series give the piece a basic structure: a series of slow, graceful sweeping movements that often run diagonally to and from the corners of the dance area; these movements often pause in poses or postures that grow increasingly looser/weaker as the piece progresses. Within the context of the readings there are strong ties to Margaret's speech, the postures of her words as she discusses what are such deeply personal events of her history, in such a casual, conversational manner—the interview. Beyond that, the movements suggest all those stances of body/spirit/personality that we assume as part of dealing with the world. Eric's body bends as one total reed, a long graceful line, accented with the most tender but formal of hands, gestures of ferns at a tea party, perhaps in the Garden of Flowers in Wonderland. As these gestures/postures weaken, they fold into themselves, go beyond what seems silly to what seems foolish and finally somewhat mad. A sudden wind in the garden, a summer storm. The rose petals wet together; a daisy bends its head back into its stems, a kink that cannot straighten. This confrontation with the substance of our machinations unravelling our stance, our face. It is not a question of flowery speech, but a matter of straight talk which is primarily a diversion, an evasion. This is part of what Eric dances, part of the dance.

You can learn a lot of things
  from the flowers,
Oh, especially in the month
  of June.
You can learn a lot of things
  from the flowers
All on a summer's afternoon.

—song fragment from Disney's *Alice in Wonderland*

The second series of movements is composed of abrupt, jolted, staccato feet sounding, weight and movement on one foot beating back along the diagonal, pounding fractures of sound body/weight/stage, apoplectic momentarily, rising from silence and surface calm, bullets breaking. How the force of what is true takes us beyond ourselves, that part of ourselves we prepare for public viewing. Oh yes the river will run its course, but not without whirlpools, rapids, a sudden bend where trees block the motion, the jam, the bursting, over and over again and again. Eric shakes his hands so his fingers snap—groups of snaps—that quality of force in the wrist that catches his fingers off guard and makes for sound. An attempted explanation? Fingers to mouth, tap tap, the head angled forward, the body rigid.

But a turn from the corner, sliding into grace again.

What holds these two series together is a transitory movement that Eric later says comes from Margaret's speech when a young boy, the son of her friend Leni, asks her, "Margaret, why does Harry always want to go into you so deep?" From the bottom of a sweep Eric brings both arms up, half-circled out and up at the fingers and holds—still—holds—his arms his eyes up—holding—air, space, expectation, holding. Well, has something been tossed? Has something been dropped and is it being waited for? Or is something simply being held, the upward eyes a distraction? After a time, arms curved up and back curved over

the jolted bits of movement bursting out in ever more violent shots and the second series begins.

Later we talk about how it all worked, why. It was good to see that yes something is possible from all this, that it was okay to feed off the narrative and speech/body structure/movements, but not to stop finding new ways to listen or become repetitive, or have to impose certain kinds of structures. I am asked to become critical in my watching, so slipping into known movements or patterns isn't allowed, and I will do my best.

There's a certain exhaustion and elation that is too full, so the fourth part of the exercise isn't done.

Eric and I continued to work with ways of exploring the relationships between dance (movement), speech (sound), and the written word, and a series of "dance readings," as we called them, were performed at MoMing, dance/performance center in Chicago, on two Saturday nights in October of 1975.

The process of finding, presenting and performing the material for dance readings caused me to view pieces of writing in very particular ways, and I found myself automatically "scoring" anything I might come across. This, and one other thing, started to bother me: whereas

Eric was able to improvise within specified frameworks for each piece we performed, I was limited to doing a "set" reading. As I became more fidgety with this, I also began to find ways to expand the work process, and developed my own systems for vocal improvisations.

Again, from the notebook.

Sunday, June 29

Sentences and sentence fragments from daily talk.
"If I had my way
If I had my way
If I had my way, but I do."
"If you think that's something
If you think that's something
If you think that's something, listen to this."
"Why don't'cha come over for dinner
tonight, bring yer wife."
"Oh boy oh boy oh boy."
"No, no, no; okay, okay."
I repeat these again and again until Eric develops a system of body notation for each phrase. Then we both improvise on the order and intensity of the phrases.

I am frustrated by the structure until I recall what I already knew, that speaking is music, is song. After all.

The more I worked with these sentences, the more I wanted to let loose. Sentences and words were first abstracted into sustained and rhythmic sounds, then were built again into whole and new phrases. (For example: If you think that's something, come over to dinner tonight.) I found I could make jokes. Or be melodramatic. It was delightful and difficult.

When we performed this piece, we used five other dancers (Susan Kimmelman, Donna Mandel, Kasia Mintch, Jackie Radis, Wendy Swett). The system multiplied itself in a fascinating way: Here, now, were a total of six dancers with their own set movement phrases for each of the set vocal phrases. I could say, "If you think that's something . . .," and each dancer would respond with his or her own movement vocabulary. In a kind of classical jazz fashion, we began and ended the piece with the set vocal and movement phrases, and then improvised off each other in between.

Since the October '75 performances I've done more improvisation work with dancers as well as musicians, in particular Santez (jazz saxophone), Steve Lynch (percussion and reeds), and Tom Pile (piano). The structures are always simple, and open to infinite possibilities. I usually have two or three images in mind that may hook into two or three words or perhaps a phrase. Sometimes I have a progression in mind to help me get from place to place if I need it.

Street Fair Improvisation, three dancers (Susan, Jackie, Eric), Tom Pile playing a Fender Rhodes, me with a microphone. June 1976, Chicago.

Three elements:
- call dancers in to dance space from their places at street corners, improvise on their names.
- talk/chants from jump rope, hand jive, street games (that is, one potato, two potato; fire, fire false alarm, Jackie fell into Eric's arms, how many kisses did she receive, close your eyes and you will see; it's my ball you play my way . . .). Fragment and sustain. Build into narrative fragments based on dancers' relationships and activities.
- counting chant (five, ten, fifteen, twenty, twenty-five, thirty . . . ninety-five, a hundred, five, ten . . .). Repeat in its soft, sing-song as many times as needed until piece ends.

The children watching from their seats in the street begin to sing the numbers chant, and stay with me till the end.

I'm a poet who's been doing more and more work with prose. What's come out of the vocal work, more than anything else, is, exactly, the element of performance. That between the reader and the page, something is done, happens. The process involved being that the work presents itself, and all the mystery and possibility that that involves.

Beyond that important generality is the way my performance work has caused me to be even more demanding with my written work. That I become increasingly clearer. The exhausting speed and invention of the live performances, which must articulate away from fuzziness (smudging a contour drawing in search of implied volume; a superfluous glissando), channeling to exact.

I've also learned from repetition and the anticipation of being-on-the-spot. Being there. Then there are the silences and stillnesses, but that's a whole other area.

I'm currently working with Jackie Radis, a dancer/choreographer who is concerned wtih stillness, rhythm, and image. I've been doing more movement and the accompaniment work has been not so much my voice as it has been rhythmic patterns I make by tossing a softball, or hitting a triangle. What's been more important here are the structural connections I've found—while participating in the setting of movement in time and space—to statement. To saying what I see. To a line in space or a line in time. Again, it is delightful, and difficult, and very much in process.

THREE DANCES AND NOTES

Jackson Mac Low

1st Dance:
Making Things New—6 February 1964

He makes himself comfortable
& matches parcels.

Then he makes glass boil
while having political material get in
& coming by.

Soon after, he's giving gold cushions or seeming to do so,
taking opinions,
shocking,
pointing to a fact that seems to be an error & showing it to be
      other than it seems,
& presently paining by going or having waves.

Then after doing some waiting,
he disgusts someone
& names things.

A little while later he gets out with things
& finally either rewards someone for something or goes up under
      something.

From *The Pronouns: A Collection of 40 Dances—for the Dancers*, by Jackson Mac Low.

Those make thunder though taking pigs somewhere,
but one of those says something after a minute.

Presently those get insects.

Those touch
& give enough of anything to anyone,
planting all the while.

Soon those are reacting to orange hair.

After that those spend time shutting something.

Later still each of those give the neck a knifing or all of those
    come to give a parallel meal, beautiful & shocking.

Those will themselves to be dead or come to see something
    narrow.

One of those says things as a worm would
while all of those discuss something brown.

Numbering,
each of those has an example.

At the end those are all saying things about making gardens.

40th Dance:
Giving Falsely—22 March 1964

Many begin by getting insects.

Then many make thunder though taking pigs somewhere,
& many give a simple form to a bridge
while coming against something or fearing things.

A little later, after making glass boil
& having political material get in,
many, while being in flight,
name things.

Then many have or seem to have serious holes,
& many question many;
many make payments to many,
& many seem to put examples up.

Finally many quietly chalk a strange tall bottle.

Some Remarks to the Dancers:
How the Dances Are To Be Performed
& How They Were Made

THE PRONOUNS is "A COLLECTION OF 40 DANCES"—not a *series*.
That is, despite the fact that the dances are numbered, each is a separate &
complete work in itself & may be performed on a program before or after any
or none of the other dances in the collection. Also, any number of different
realizations of one or more of the dances may succeed or follow each other
during a particular performance. For example, a program might have on it
such a succession of the dances as the following, in which each reappearance of
a dance's number stands for a different realization of that dance: 5, 7, 10, 5, 22,
40, 33, 33, 11, 7, 1, 7, 1, 1, 10, 28, 18, 6, 22, 5.

By suggesting a *succession* of realizations of dances, I do not intend to rule
out entirely the possibilities of simultaneous or overlapping performances of
various dances on a program. However, I do wish to *de-emphasize* these
possibilities (which might seem most appropriate in view of the fact that so
much of my past work—my simultaneous poems & other simultaneities—
involves the simultaneous &/or overlapping performance of separate works
that are also members of non-ordered collections, e.g., *The Numbered Asym-
metries*) in order to encourage performances in which some or all of the dances
are realized *one at a time* in various orders of succession. The important thing is
that (even in overlapping realizations or the like) the *integrity* of each dance—
its having a definite beginning, middle & end—ought to be completely clear in
every performance.

The dances require various numbers of performers. Some are obviously
solos or duets, & some will be found to require a group of a definite number
that will probably be the same in any realization, but the sizes of the groups
required in many of them are somewhat indefinite & are to be decided for each
realization by the dancers themselves by careful interpretation of the given
text.

In realizing any particular dance, the individual dancer or group of dancers
has a very large degree of freedom of interpretation. However, although they
are to interpret the successive lines of each of those poems-which-are-also-
dance-instructions as they see fit, dancers are required to find *some definite
interpretation of the meaning of every line* of the dance–poems they choose to
realize. Above all, no line or series of lines may be left uninterpreted &
unrealized simply because it seems too complicated or obscure to realize as
movement (&/or sound or speech).

In addition to finding concrete meanings as actions for every line of each
dance–poem realized, the dancers must carefully work out the time-relations
between the various actions, as indicated by their positions in the poems & by
the particular conjunctions & adverbs used to connect them together within
the sentence-length strophes, & to connect these strophes together. For
example, if a poem indicates that someone "has the chest between thick things
while they say things about making gardens," dancers may realize each of these

actions as they see fit, but they must take place simultaneously, *not* one after the other.

There is a seemingly unlimited multiplicity of possible realizations for each of these dances because the judgments of the particular dancers will determine such matters as degrees of literalness or figurativeness in interpreting & realizing instructions. Each dancer or group of dancers must decide for themselves whether, &/or to what extent, to use or avoid props, miming, &c., & whether, &/or to what extent, to be consistent in such use or avoidance—one might, for instance, within the same realization, sometimes use props & sometimes dispense with them, even in different appearances of the same action in a poem. Thus, while the text of each dance–poem is completely determinate, &, if realized, is to be realized in its entirely, the actual movements & actions constituting any particular realization are very largely unpredictable from the text of the poem of which it is a realization.

I first conceived these dance-instruction-poems as *either* being read aloud as poems (& I have read many of them at poetry readings) *or* as being realized as dances. Lately, however, I have come to agree with a number of persons who've heard me read them that the poems themselves might well be read aloud during *some* of their realizations as dances. A program might include, then, some realizations accompanied by the reading aloud of the poems & some not so accompanied.

In any case, the sounds of the reading of the poems, when they are read, &/or any other sounds used as "accompaniment" to the dances must never get in the way of the sounds produced by the dancers themselves in accordance with those instructions calling for sound or speech. It is to be emphasized that wherever a line calls for sound-production or speech, this instruction must be taken literally, at least insofar as the dancers must produce some definite sound or speak some words or other, as they find appropriate. . . .

Now, as to HOW THEY WERE MADE: Many of the actions of the 40 dances that comprise *THE PRONOUNS* were drawn by a systematic chance method (outlined below) from a "pack" of 56 filing cards, on each of which are typed one to five actions, denoted by gerunds or gerundial phrases, e.g., "jumping," "having a letter over one eye," & "giving the neck a knifing or coming to give a parallel meal, beautiful & shocking." 170 different actions are each named once in this pack of cards, & three more, "jumping," "mapping," & "questioning," are each named twice. (That is, in the 56 sets of one to five actions, there are, in all, 176 "places" filled by 173 *different* actions, three of which actions occur in two of the sets, each of the rest only in one.)

This pack of actions was composed in May 1961. At that time, these 56 sets of one to five actions were typed on another set of filing cards, on each of which one to ten single words were also typed. Both these single words & all the definite lexical words among the words & phrases denoting actions were drawn, with the help of the Rand table of a million random digits, from the 850-word Basic English Word List. In the action-naming phrases, each Basic English word was used in any desired form (i.e., as verb, adverb, adjective, or noun, in the singular or the plural, &c.; for example, if I drew the word "beautiful," "beautifully," "beauties," "beauty's," "beautifying," "beautified," &c., might be used.). Structure words (conjunctions, prepositions, pronouns, indefinite nouns, &c.) were freely used in connecting these Basic English "nuclei" into phrases. However, the number & order of succession of the Basic English "nuclei" in each action-phrase were determined by systematic chance, although their grammatical forms & connections were freely chosen by the author. [The pack of cards having both action phrases and separated words on them was titled "Nuclei for Simone Forti," and was realized by Forti in 1961 and Trisha Brown in 1963.]

The "1ST DANCE—MAKING THINGS NEW" was composed after the late Fred Herko, a marvelous dancer, saw Brown's performance of the "nuclei" and wanted to use the cards. Brown had them in California, where her class used them. I conceived the idea of using just the "56 Sets of Actions" as the source of a dance-instruction-poem for him to realize. After having written the "he" poem for Fred, it was natural that I thought of writing a "she" poem for Trisha [Simone, and other female dancers]. After that I decided to write a dance-instruction-poem for every word listed as a pronoun in the Merriam-Webster Dictionary (most linguists would now call such words as "everybody" nouns rather than pronouns, but I went by the book). After having written 40 of them, I thought I'd written enough of them, so there are no poems for some of the less-used pronouns (or pronounlike nouns). *(New paragraph added 1/4/71, revised 8/29/74 & 3/30—31/78.)*

In composing each dance, I would first shuffle the pack & then cut it & point blindly to one of the actions on the card cut to. This action became the title of the dance. Before or after determining the title, I would also choose which *pronoun* was to be the subject of all the sentences in that dance-poem. The title was then used as a "diastic index" to determine the successive actions of the dance & also, necessarily, their number. That is, the letters of the title determined the actions drawn for the dance: turning the filing cards over, one at a time, with occasional shufflings, I let the title letters "select" the successive actions from the sets of one to five actions as they showed up. For example, in the "37TH DANCE—BANDING," the "B" selected "*b*eing flies," the "A," "h*a*ving examples," the "N," "doing something co*n*sciously," the "D," "saying things about making gar*d*ens," &c. In some dances I gave myself the rule that the actions had to have the title letters not only in corresponding places in *any one* of the words (as in the example) but also in corresponding words. That is, if the 2nd word of the title had an "H" in the 2nd place (e.g., in "T*H*E"), the corresponding action-phrase had also to have an "H" in the 2nd place of the 2nd word, & so on.

As the method "selected" each action-word or -phrase, I made it, or a modified form of it, part of a sentence of which the pronoun chosen for that dance was the subject. While punctuation (& thus sentence length & the number & often the kinds of clauses in sentences) was largely determined by the punctuation already on the filing cards, the various conjunctions & adverbs used to connect the action-lines into sentence-strophes & to connect the sentence-strophes with each other were freely chosen. In short, although systematic chance determined many features of each dance, a few crucial features, such as which pronoun was to be the subject of all sentences in that dance & how the actions were to be connected—thus, incidentally, the time-relations persisting between the actions of the dance—were matters of free choice. . . .

THE PRONOUNS is *"FOR THE* DANCERS*"*—all the dancers every-where—& it is my hope that many of these dances will receive as many entirely different realizations as possible.

Previous Book Publications of *THE PRONOUNS*

THE PRONOUNS—A COLLECTION OF 40 *DANCES—FOR THE DANCERS—*3 *February–March* 1964. 30 pp., mimeographed by the author for use by the Judson Dance Workshop, with machine & materials supplied by the Judson Memorial Church. New York: Mac Low, March 1964.
————. 2nd ed., rev. & enl. Nine unbound, folded folios, with 9 full-page "images" (multicolored silk-screened graphics) by Ian Tyson, in a box (21$^{1}/_{2}$" x 26$^{1}/_{2}$" x 1$^{1}/_{4}$"). London: Tetrad Press, 1971.
————3rd ed., rev. & with additional prose sections. Barrytown, NY: Station Hill Press, 1979.

ART WITH NO NAME

Ron Silliman

Two small tape recorders are playing simultaneously, one on either side of the huge loft. The fidelity is poor, and the continual stream of diesel city buses imposes its own presence as though equally intentional to the recorders. From the Sony closest to the bulk of the audience that mills and hunkers uncertainly before this event comes the voice of Abigail Child: "Is that your daughter? Are you a Marxist? What is the line of a narrative?" From the Panasonic on the far side comes the "singing" of doves and Chinese nightingales. From a beam in the center of the loft's high ceiling hangs a thick rope, extending down to barely brush the floor with a hangman's noose. Halfway up, holding on with the ease of a trained gymnast, feet toward the ceiling, head to the ground, is Child. "Which way," she asks (and the crowd groans with the pun), "is down?"

Which is a question that could apply to a trend which has spread, prairie fire-style, over the entire spectrum of the arts in the West. Though recent, this phenomenon has already tested and discarded dozens of provisional titles. Some of these, like "happenings," "conceptual art," and "intermedia" have already become dated. These passages into art history signal the validation given to artwork whose moment is at once recognized to have been of value and to have passed. Other names—"idea art," "performance art," "installation," "environment," "fluxus," "total art," and, currently, "post-conceptual," "post-movement," and "polyart"—will also become historical signposts.

"Polyartists" (and others like them) tend to shun such critical terms, even when they are responsible for coining them. They feel the act of naming an art activity reduces it to an entry on the ever-expanding genealogical chart of Art History. Such enclosures have become, in their eyes, more than useless. They prevent, rather than aid, the viewer from seeing work freshly and directly, without a set of preconceived "aesthetic" notions.

Their work reflects this flight from definition. Art audiences in all fields are increasingly confronting work which appears antithetical to even the most fundamental preconceptions, such as the idea that poetry need use language (let alone rhyme!) or that a visual art need be visible. Because of its dynamics, this proliferating new art is a nonmovement, with no center, no monuments, and no name.

Abigail Child, at the end of her rope, is a case in point. The event is a "poetry reading" on the edge of San Francisco's financial district at Terminal Concepts, a warehouse turned into a sculpture studio and "art space." Normally, Child would be described as a filmmaker. Yet neither is any film being shown nor is anyone reading aloud from a book or manuscript. In a way, Child's progression toward an art that lies somewhere vaguely between several media is typical of the phenomenon as a whole.

After being graduated from Yale, Child directed black-and-white social documentaries for educational television, including *The Game,* a sympathetic portrait of the daily life of a Harlem pimp. Critical success led to a grant from the American Film Institute to produce and direct a feature-length color film based on her own script, entitled *tArgArden.* This development was unusual for any young director headed, apparently, straight for a Hollywood career.

Yet what Child wanted, and proceeded to explore in the film, was not the capacity of cinema as a device for fiction, nor to display her own talents therewith, but the subtle ways in which narrative, when practiced as an art, is a socially manipulative experience. The problem is simple: The story-teller gets to choose his or her questions. While some films announce their narrative quality by having an unseen voice detail the events on screen, Child went further, presenting the voiceover as a dialogue between two speakers. The story itself was that of a contemporary love relationship doomed to failure because of an insurmountable distance between private parties. One voice, having asked the other to "tell me a story" at the film's beginning, attempts to probe the seemingly inevitable plot. The second voice becomes increasingly less responsive, first circumventing the questions, then ignoring them altogether. Gradually the matter-of-fact presentation of the voiceover appears radically out of touch with the human pain and difficult choices which appear on the screen. In *tArgArden,* narrative, much like naming an art activity, is seen as an impediment to truth. This was not the sort of upbeat project calculated to further a career in mainstream American cinema. In fact, by the time the film was ready for release, Child was feeling so hostile to narrative that she never sought a distributor for this critique-by-example.

Which left her an artist without an art. It also left her considerably in debt, as the grant had covered less than half the final film costs. "I had," she has said, "nothing left but my body and my voice." She began to explore these—in dance, through a relatively new genre called contact improvisation, which grew out of (and often looks like) Eastern martial arts, particularly aikido, with some gymnastics thrown in; then in poetry, through a kind of purely vocal improvisation which sounds at first like jazz scatting used to translate contemporary philosophy. Finally, by the time of her arrival in San Francisco, Child had begun to work with film again, only now in a "structuralist" genre. Structural cinema is primarily concerned with the exploration of sight perception and often treats the rectangle of the screen in much the same way a contemporary painter might a canvas. In structuralism, there is no such thing as a plot. Now, Child's performances often involve two or more of these art media at one time.

Her piecemeal reinvention of "art" is by no means unique. In a recent, unpublished poem (which looks like an essay), called "My Poetry," poet David Bromige describes the parallel course his own work has taken:

My style seems to have fallen apart, deteriorated . . . it has therefore become problematical, not to say impossible, because if it limits itself to the traditional language & form of a literature it misses the basic truths about itself, while if it attempts to tell those truths it abolishes itself as literature.

Both the problem (naming art activities) and its solution (taking the art out of an old context, putting it into a new one) are often called "decontextualiza-tion." Child's performance at Terminal Concepts certainly was not recognizable as film. It bore only some similarity to what is normally thought of as poetry, or even as dance. Yet it just as clearly had all the surface characteristics of an art event. However vaguely, the audience knew the circumstance into which it had entered. Bromige, the other poet on the afternoon's bill, read from manuscripts. Everyone applauded and seemed pleased. It was an occasion at once both decontextualized and yet not so unfamiliar as to be uncomfortable for its audience.

Painting and sculpture undergo an even more radical decontextualization a few blocks southeast of Terminal Concepts in San Francisco's Yerba Buena area, which includes several acres of demolished buildings. Once the city's Greek district, later a ghetto for the urban elderly, block after block has lain fallow behind cyclone fences for years while developers, conservationists, and community activists struggled over the future form of the neighborhood. On one Third Street lot in 1976 an anonymous artist painted all of the scattered bricks and stones a pleasant Dayglo mauve. More recently, whole squares of cement in the area have begun to blossom in a rainbow of pastels. Soon thereafter persons on the mailing list of the La Mamelle Gallery received a flyer showing the silhouette of a person running over the altered area. The flyer, which announces "Location: Yerba Buena," giving no dates, identifies the figure as "Maura," who conceivably is the artist responsible. Even if this is the case, only a miniscule portion of the daily viewers of the work will ever receive the flyer. The work is an art without the framing mechanism of any art context, such as a gallery or museum, and almost without an identifiable artist to go with it. It is only half a step removed from the childish, equally delightful, graffiti which sometimes surrounds it. Where does a painter, having come this far, go next?

Why next? Because, for more than a century in almost all the arts, the elaboration of new techniques, styles, and genres has been a key defining mechanism for the arts. The revolutionary-era Russian Formalist critics went so far as to proclaim this development of the new to be the essence of art itself. Much recent art has attempted to decontextualize this definition as well, with the conceptualists of the late '60s, who replaced objects with "aesthetic ideas" that they talked of or wrote or performed, being particularly outspoken about their opposition to this incessant elaboration of art "fashion." Yet with conceptualism long since supplanted by "post-conceptualists" such as Eleanor Antin (the difference in the two seems to be in the greater emphasis of the post-conceptualists on the staging and acting out of the concept), it is obvious that art cannot decontextualize its artness, regardless how hard artists try.

Attempts have occurred in every art. When Lyn Hejinian, Doug Hall, and Jody Procter of the now-defunct Northern Fictions Consort stand up and talk, the applicable term is jazz, by virtue of Larry Och's saxophone and Rob Yohai's guitar, but when David Antin does likewise, it's poetry because—well, David Antin is a poet and that's what poets do. Hall and Procter, who collectively make up T. R. Uthco, once sat for six hours strapped into chairs bolted to the outside wall of San Francisco's La Mamelle Gallery, three storeys above the street, in which their simultaneous monologues were neither jazz nor poetry, but "art/performance." And when jazz musicians such as Baikida E. J. Carroll and Julius Hemphill incorporate film and theater into their music, as Jeff Balsmeyer incorporates them into his "writing," then Child's appropriation of poetry and gymnastics/dance into what began as film begins to take on a certain order of event. Terry Fox, perhaps the most widely respected of California's performance artists, once played a single note on two invented musical instruments with violin bows for ninety minutes by candlelight, concluding only when total darkness enveloped the space. Only someone with a prior knowledge of Fox's work would have recognized the theta shape of the candles as predicated upon the structure of the labyrinth at the Chartres Cathedral, although it was this element which endowed the piece with its visual orientation and content.

Misconceptions are inevitable. A prominent one, sometimes even among artists, is that this phenomenon is specifically an adjunct of the plastic arts. There is a history and a half-truth in such an idea, since the prototype for this art with no name was certainly the happenings of the '50s and early '60s. Although a number of writers, including Michael Kirby (*Happenings*, E. P. Dutton, 1965) and Martin Duberman (*Black Mountain*, Doubleday Anchor, 1973), trace the origin of the happening to a production by composer John Cage at Black Mountain College in North Carolina in 1952, in which poet Charles Olson, potter M. C. Richards, and musician David Tudor participated, it too had its forerunners in the work of futurists and dadaists such as Kurt Schwitters, a collagist and "sound poet." Others, such as William Seitz (*The Art of Assemblage*, The Museum of Modern Art, 1961) or Harriet Janis and Rudi Blesh (*Collage*, Chilton, 1962), who wish to stress the decontextualization of art more than the tendency toward performance, would trace the roots of this new art to the first cubist instances, in 1911-12, of incorporating "real" objects such as cloth and paper into paintings. But it was not until the work of Claes Oldenburg, Red Grooms, Jim Dine, and others in the late '50s New York scene acquired the name and notoriety of happenings that the phenomena received broad visibility. Yet even earlier, San Francisco poets Kenneth Rexroth, Lawrence Ferlinghetti, and others had begun performing their work in conjunction with jazz. Similar instances of what later would be known as "intermedia" can be found in most of the arts, such as the use of both theater and sculpture in the music of the late Harry Partch.

Insofar as those involved with happenings considered it to be a kind of painters' theater, as those in Kirby's anthology (Allan Kaprow, Robert Whitman, Dine, Grooms, and Oldenburg) clearly did, they had not as yet decontextualized, moving beyond the neat historical confines of either of those two categories. As so often happens with the first instances of any new genre, their scripts today seem more connected with the work which preceeded it than with the subsequent art which it largely brought into existence, such as the endless governmental proceedings that were an integral, though tedious, aspect of Christo's "Running Fence."

Then, too, the art gallery scene has proved flexible enough to accommodate a good deal of this new work. There already existed a long tradition, dating back at least to nineteenth-century Paris, of simply opening new spaces to announce and display alternative art tendencies which had previously been ignored. This relatively inexpensive option was also often available to artists not strictly involved in "visual" work, such as the deliberately repetitive "trance" music movement led by Steve Reich or the earliest work by Vito Acconci and Carl Andre, artists whose work had begun as poetry only to evolve into performance and extremely minimal sculpture (slabs of rectangular metal placed in a line on the floor). As also happened with Eleanor Antin, whose training was in the theater arts, the work of Acconci and Andre finally came to be more completely identified with that of the visual art scene.

However, even in this openness to alternative modes and places of presentation, parallels existed in the other arts. Prompted by the development of lower-cost printing techniques, the "small press" or "mimeo" revolution gave poets a realm of activity apart from, and often enough in opposition to, the already-established university and corporate publishers. Thus the work of Gary Snyder, Diane di Prima, Allen Ginsberg, and many others first became widely known through an art distribution system which had barely existed prior to World War II.

Nevertheless, the result has been that the fullest articulation of possible directions for this new art with no name, most likely to get sensitive, sympathetic feedback (always an important aspect of support), has been called, for want of better terms, visual art. Its best known practitioners, Terry Fox, Eleanor Antin, Bruce Nauman, Chris Burden, Lynn Hershman, John Baldessari, Michael Asher, and Tom Marioni, among others, are significantly connected to the California gallery scene. In addition, those journals which have given the most thought and attention to their work, such as *Vision* (Crown Point Press, Oakland) or *La Mamelle* (Contemporary Arts Press, San Francisco), are publications with direct connections to art spaces, such as the Museum of Conceptual Art (MOCA) and La Mamelle Gallery.

Even so, this new media often involves several disciplines at once, as happened with the Magic Theater production of Susan Hellmuth's and Jock Reynold's *Hospital* at San Francisco's Fort Mason. *Hospital* was theater more by default than inclination. Neither Hellmuth, a dancer, nor Reynolds, a sculptor, is a playwright. Others in the large cast included a poet, Renny Pritikin, another dancer, Deborah Slater, a performance artist, Jorge Soccaras, and Judy Moran, an "installation artist." As the performers switched roles—

involving, as is often the case in modern dance, no real characterization—none was required to "act." Pritikin was a janitor in one scene, a doctor in the next. Soccaras was a doctor, visitor, patient. Nor was there any plot to unravel: the dominant formal principle underlying the structuring of the piece was that of any hospital—routine. The order of the scenes was potentially as interchangeable as the nonactors' roles, the cyclical repetitiveness carrying over into the music derived from the recordings of Steve Reich.

According to Richard Schechner, founder and former editor of *The Drama Review,* theater is a transformational ceremony, and "drama" is that art whose subject, structure, and action is social process." Following sociologists Victor Turner and Erving Goffman, Schechner describes "the basic human plot":

Someone begins to move to a new place in the social order; this move is accomplished through ritual, or blocked; in either case a crisis arises because any change in status involves a readjustment of the entire scheme; this readjustment is effected ceremonially —that is, by means of theatre. (*Alcheringa/Ethnopoetics,* Boston University, 1976, p. 49)

Hospital was theatrical in that it, like any performance, was ceremonial. An audience gathered and sat in the dark, watching a space transformed into a place, a stage. But it was without drama because the overwhelming dominance of institutional routine drained the roles of individuation. Furthermore, in framing itself as a "play," by virtue of the Magic Theater's sponsorship, *Hospital* submerged to some extent all the art forms that were simultaneously involved.

This trend toward performance as the constituting element of decontextualization in all the arts, whether it be poetry or film, as in the case of Abigail Child, or the plastic arts in general, as with Terry Fox, is a major aspect of this new art. Some critics have dismissed this as being the inevitable result of the interfacing of any two art forms. Yet Schechner's viewpoint gives a more fundamental clue as to why performance in previously nonperforming arts has suddenly become so important. Art itself is moving to a new place in the social order.

In a sense, the new art reflects the whole of American society in this era which is post-'60s, post-Vietnam, post-Watergate and not yet anything intelligible in its own right. Yet obviously it is more than just that, since this art has in one form or another been with us since the '50s. If the role of art in a so-called primitive or tribal society is to pass on the content of the community and its myths and cultures, possibly the content of modern life is just this uncertainty and anxiety as to one's place in the larger role of things. If nobody feels very certain as to their context in life, then "decontextualization" would seem to be an inevitable consequence.

HAND Show:

An Interview with Carol Sue Thomas

Stephen Vincent

"You work *through* the mask. The spirit of the mask has to come into you. The Balinese carve their masks from trees that grow in the cemetery, because they believe that the spirits of the people there have grown up through the roots of the trees. When you put the mask on, you put on the spirit of that mask. . . . The actor really has to project all that through the mask. Maybe underneath, his face or her face is working; but the mask is inanimate. But it will still come through."—Carol Sue Thomas

On December 18, 1977, *the poet Darrell Gray hosted The 6th Actualist Convention at Terminal Concepts, a performance and reading space located on First near Mission Street in San Francisco. The event, beginning at three in the afternoon and ending at midnight, involved a huge variety of poets and performance artists. Among them was Carol Sue Thomas, who performed* Hand Show, *a piece that she and George Coates, of the Blake Street Hawkeyes, jointly created for the occasion. This interview with Thomas was held some time after the performance at her home in San Francisco.*

STEPHEN VINCENT: Why don't you describe the piece you did at the Actualist Convention? What was it called?

CAROL SUE THOMAS: *Hand Show.*

SV: How did that title happen?

CST: George Coates and I decided we wanted to work together. He is one of the Blake Street Hawkeyes, who also directed *2019* with Leonard Pitt. He agreed that he would show some of his work at the Actualist Convention.

SV: Is he language oriented?

CST: Yes, both language and movement together. I'm a street mime and street performer, and I work with people a lot. George and I both worked on sections of this piece. We would work on a section, and it would become too literal, and we would take it apart. It's George's belief that if it's literal—if it's been written before—then it's really not original and not very exciting. If you see a Tennessee Williams play, you're just seeing another version of what Tennessee Williams had written a long, long time ago. There isn't anything new to explore; there isn't anything exciting for the audience to see or experience. There isn't any place for that mind to have to go to work. They're just sitting there being fed what they're seeing. So we would take lots of sections . . .

SV: Sections . . . meaning?

CST: Sections of this piece. If you recall, sometimes something might happen, would start to happen, and the audience would say, "Oh, oh, what is this? oh, oh, I think I get what that is, oh, now I'm beginning to feel comfortable, now I'm beginning to understand it. I see it and . . . oh, wait a minute! it just changed! and now it's something completely new." The audience is never really left to relax absolutely. They are always being made to work and create in their own minds things that are happening. We took past experiences of mine; we took things that I had written—poems, letters—words that would come out of my mind, situations that would come up at rehearsals, different energies, and we would start to put together this piece. We designed and custom-made it for the Actualist Convention. There were going to be a group of poets listening to poetry readings, and it was our opinion that poets are probably the worst readers of their own material. A lot of times, the poems don't make sense because of the way they are read; there is no logic, nothing to grab ahold of. We decided out of all the things, all of the craziness that was going to go on for about ten minutes, we could stimulate our audience to a point that they could give words when I asked for the words, and they weren't necessarily words that had literal meaning, because I wasn't asking for the literal meaning of something, I was asking for " . . . a word like shoe that holds no bars; grass: give me another word for grass that doesn't send a telegram." And people would continue to give me words, and I would write the words on my arms and then went on to something else. I shot up with the words, pumped up, juiced up—whatever; got myself high; got myself excited; got myself into a frenzy. You know, climaxed, exploded, to get all the way up there, and just melted and got giddy and just floated away with all these words and got high and ridiculous and got soft and got vulnerable and got silly and got back into looking on my arm at the words that had been fed to me by the audience and read them back the poem that they had created.

SV: Let me get back to the beginning of the piece. You came out on the floor pushing milk containers . . .

CST: . . . blue plastic cases to carry milk . . .

SV: . . . and what were you saying?

CST: I was saying "Pass-the-hatters. Pass-the-hatters. Pass-the-hatters."

SV: Where did that phrase come from?

CST: I'm a "pass-the-hatter." As a mime, I'm a street artist and a pass-the-hatter. I was sure there were lots of pass-the-hatters there, and I was looking for my people.

SV: And you were pushing *empty* cases.

CST: Pushing empty cases. I was just searching out my audience. I was also setting up a field of energy for the audience to gather around.

SV: I wasn't quite sure what you were saying with "pass-the-hatters" other than it was a call. It was not clear what your intentions were with the audience; it was not completely a call, but almost a plea—something in between.

CST: Something in between. Sometimes it was a plea, sometimes I was searching, and sometimes I was just angry. "Pass-the hatters. Pass-the-hatters." [angry tone]

SV: Why were you angry?

CST: Sometimes you put out a lot of energy when you perform, and maybe you pass the hat and nothing comes in. And other times maybe you put out no energy at all, and your hat is full.

SV: So you were indicating the totality of that experience of passing the hat to others to an audience that you felt might be connected to that experience, though that wasn't required, particularly, in terms of the context of the event.

CST: Also I think a lot of times people write poetry not because they're going to be paid x amount of dollars for the poem, but something comes from deep inside of them, and they want to express it and share it, and it's creative. In essence, they're passing the hat too. Somebody else is passing the buck. And they're passing the hat.

SV: After you give your hat, you want some kind of reciprocation. And when the reciprocation doesn't come, then you're going to get disappointed or comical or whatever. But what happened?

CST: In the next part of my performance, I did a little performance which was really a bit off center. If you recall, I walked the tightrope on my boxes in pantomime and on purpose in *very poor* pantomime. It wasn't a technically perfect version of someone walking a tightrope; I was just walking across my very flat boxes, falling off and singing and making the noise of the energy that went on as if I were—what's his name? Pierre Petit, I'll call him—that's not it, he's very, very famous [and walks between buildings]. That same kind of energy.

SV: How were you dressed?

CST: I was dressed as many eccentric lady poets may be dressed. Maybe one decade a certain kind of fabric was in style, and another decade scarves on your head were in style. A lot of times artistic people are so caught up in their work that the way they are dressed really doesn't matter. There might have been lots of bracelets, so you put on lots of bracelets; you put this on and that on, and it really doesn't matter what goes together because all of them are your favorite things anyway. So you feel good.

SV: So what you wore was just an abundance of everything, like a collage.

CST: Right. A collage.

SV: You jammed all those styles together into one point in time. I remember it was impressively shaggy. So, when you were doing the tightrope, what were you trying to establish with the audience? What was going on? What brought that image to the surface?

CST: I had those boxes with me, and I was pushing my load, and I got it out there. I was structuring my boxes for something that comes later. They were my stage set, you might say. At the same time I was taking the audience on the adventure of the tightrope and falling off and "pass the hat, pass the hat" and getting back up on my tightrope and continuing to walk until I got to the end. I sat down on the end of the boxes; I then became different characters. Very deadpan. There was no acting going on—which was acting itself. It takes a lot of energy to have absolutely no energy interchange at all. So I did voices for different characters—who to me are people I have met on the street, or a conglomeration of people I have met on the street. I think the first one was a big businessman. I remember exactly who he was, in big grey suit and great big pot belly, and he was just really impressed with me, and then he went and impressed me with a card. The dialogue that came out during the *Hand Show* piece is much different from the dialogue that went on. But I meet lots of different kinds of characters on the street. And the first one was a distributor, a truck driver; he distributed lavastines.

SV: "Lavastines"? What is a "lavastine"?

CST: *Lavastine*—you know what a *lavastine* is. He also had a CB radio, by the way. The next character I did was one that was the closest to me. George Coates and I really argued about the next character. It was the one place in the piece that I got to have my way. And the dialogue was "Happy. Happeee. Haaappeeee. Don't make me happeee. Please don't make me. Please, I don't want to be happeee." [a high whiny voice] And I feel that with the whole punk rock movement and so many things that are going on today, that's what people are really saying: "I don't want to be happy. It ain't cool to be happy. Don't make me happy. I want to be miserable. I don't want to get up, and I want to be down. Down is up for me." And I just think that it's so psuedo.

SV: In terms of having an audience of poets—and, relating to that fact, the choice of characters: a businessman, a distributor, the person who doesn't want to be happy—was there any kind of intention there in terms of the audience, or was that really just stuff you were working up from yourself? How did these characters connect with the context?

CST: I just think that I come in contact with a great cross section of the world when I'm performing on the street, and I believe I had one aggressive businessman, a truckdriver, one punker, I don't want to be happy, lost generation, one gay person, *who really was very authoritative on flower pots,* like on nothing. So many people stretch things, make such a big deal out of absolutely nothing, because there's really nothing going on except what's going on inside me. [this all done in parody—a self-important affected voice] And the last person was a hooker. *Loneleee.* All of us have been lonely; all of us at one time or another have said, "Heh, man! Don't bug me. I don't want to be happy. I want to be miserable." I think all of us at one time or another have felt sort of aggressive or egotistical or big. I just think they were different characters to hit on emotions that we all feel as human beings, that are some place in each of us as people.

SV: You had four characters. What was the switch then?

CST: The switch after that, I went to the West Indies. [laughter] I know, I left you there! But I did go to the West Indies. I was in the West Indies a couple of years ago, and I had written a poem about a young black man who was going blind. He was a calypso singer on the Island of Curaçao, and he had his boys with him. He rowed out in a row boat and talked to us on the sailboat after we had docked; he had all kinds of trinkets to sell—butterflies made out of shells, and oysters that they scrape off trees—and that evening he wanted to come back with his boys and sing calypso. Calypso is a very big thing. I never realized it's a political expression. Every year at carnival time a song is chosen from all the islands and singers to be their song of the year, which has a lot of political content to it. I was very impressed with this man who was of a different culture. He was going blind, and he had this group of boys with him that played music. That night they came out to the boat, and they sang their songs for us. He sang three songs. He asked us for two out of the three—to give him an idea of what our favorite ones were because of the calypso contest that was coming up. I wrote a poem about him. His name is Sky Scraper. In his West Indian accent, which I really can't imitate or create because it is really not very close to my memory, he would say, "C'mon, boys." The boys were sitting there on the boat sleeping; they were all nodding out. He would say, "C'mon, boys, sing another song." And he would start in, and they would just come alive and awake and play the music and then go back to sleep. Then he would talk to us, and then they would play the next one. So the next line at the Actualist Convention in *Hand Show* was "C'mon, boys, commee on, boys." [repeats phrase several times at different pitches and levels] It was like yelling, "Come on, gang, come on, my people, come with me." You know, "Let's go, boys, let's get out there, let's do it." Again we're dealing with dynamics, of voice to create the energy. I believe I went from sitting on that box being a little person to standing up and being this leader of people. You know, "C'mon, boys, c'mon, boys." Then I stopped, and I noticed that I had some markings on my arms. I had moles on my arms.

S V: When you were shouting "C'mon, boys" were you directing it at the audience?

C S T: No, it was just out there, it was universal. Completely universal. Then I immediately switched back to me, Carol Sue Thomas, being Carol Sue in that room, standing up on a box, dressed in funny clothes in front of a group of poets who were celebrating that night. I talked to them just as I would sit and talk to you. "I have some nice markings on my arm."

S V: You came off this universal landscape and then you began . . . ?

C S T: All of a sudden I was right back there with the audience. I think that was the first time that I was ever really right there. Then I began talking to them. You know, "What's going on here? Who wrote 'The cigarette is a glass of milk'"? [from last year's convention] You know, "I want some answers. Answer me a question." It's not necessary that the words make literal sense, but people knew exactly what I was talking about. They knew exactly what my intentions were when I was singing sounds, instead of saying words. You know if I was going "OOEEWEE" [a skewered nose sound] while I was walking across my tightropes, people knew what that energy was; words don't really matter. It's the intention. It's the same thing as the mask that's between you and your audience; you project *through* the mask; you project through your words. You could go to another country and speak English words and they will understand you if your intention is out there.

S V: At this point you were directly addressing an audience that is aware of "The cigarette is a glass of milk"; there were a number of people familiar with that line [of the poet Dave Morice]. Anyway, you began a direct relationship with the audience. It was like an insistence on a shared space.

CST: A rapport.

SV: What did you do with it?

CST: I started asking them questions that nobody was answering. I really didn't expect them to answer because the questions were not literal. "Answer me a question."

SV: How did you arrive at that?

CST: I just said it during a rehearsal. The entire piece was improvised. Nothing was ever written down. It was working through me and who I am and where I've been and what I have experienced. In putting together a piece for somebody else . . . there was a lot of craziness. I took my audience a lot of places, a lot of abuse I gave my audience. I had a lot of reaction out of them already, at this point, even though they hadn't gone anywhere, or done anything. I had the attention of every single person in that room.

SV: And you were on the attack. "Answer me a question."

CST: So I wanted a show of hands.

SV: What did people do?

CST: Soon people showed me their hands. But I went way beyond that. What I wanted was a hand show. "Show of hands. Hand show. Hand show." I wanted a hand show. "A show hand show. A show of hands."

SV: You wanted to take "hand show" or "show of hands" further.

CST: Right. I could feel the energy I put out to them was very, very intense. I could feel that they had just about had it. They were just about at the exploding point. They had been irritated just about enough. Nothing really quite made sense to them up to this point, and they had just about had it.

SV: You were making demands that couldn't be fully answered. But you were raising the energy level so that they either had to burst one way or leave the room. So what did you do then when you got it that high?

CST: *Enough*. I told them that was EEEnough. Then everyone relaxed for an instant, and I asked them if there was a word for this, which began the audience participation. From then on, that next section was completely improvised—a very intimate time, because the performer and the audience were really one. It was really a marriage at that moment. I took out my pen and rolled up my sleeve and asked for words.

SV: You put your left arm up in the air, almost like a fist.

CST: Right. Like I was going to hit somebody. Like, "If you park that bicycle one more time in the driveway, you're going to get this knuckle pie." [voice imitates tough guy] And also I assume people would do that if they were going to shoot drugs. They would pump up. They would make their veins stand up, the same way a person's veins stand out when they're angry; it's a tension. I took words from people. They gave me words—"milk man," "grocer." I started writing them down on my arm. And then there were ways that I asked them for words that would be again had (the conversation that was going on between us had no literal meaning, but it had meaning beyond that).

SV: As I recall, you asked for opposites.

CST: I would ask for opposites but not necessarily *an* opposite. Questions

171

like, "Another word for that word. Another word for blue that does not mean color. A six-syllable word. A door that is not a door. Like a word that can't be fixed. A word that issues a premium. A word that will arrive on Friday. A word that goes against the grain. A word that fits like a brick. A word that holds no bars (bonds)."

SV: Do you remember the words you wrote now? You didn't go home and write them down after? [Carol Sue Thomas shakes her head] You mean you threw it all away?

CST: Too pure! Too pure! I remember the first one was "high high." And I remember the second one was "mailbox."

SV: I remember "Edsel." It was the opposite of something.

CST: It was great. The association to begin with makes absolutely no sense, but people still have a word association; they still have a vision. They still have something that comes out. So I took those words, and I pumped them into my veins. I pumped them into my brain. I got myself loaded, high, climaxed; washed myself warm, loving, light, just went to a place I wanted to go, euphoria, utopia.

SV: That was when your fist broke.

CST: Right.

SV: Was there a point where you reread the language? The whole thing.

CST: The last thing.

SV: So you got euphoricized.

CST: I danced. I sang. "A pretty girl is like a melody" and the rest of the words do not matter, or how I sang, or what I said [singing this; then a switch] because the action was still happening, was going on, and there was a dance, and at the same time all those boxes I had been carrying around, pushing and standing on, building with, walking across, and so on were becoming integrated into my body. I put my feet in them and walked around in them, danced in them—like snow boots. I got them on my arms and got them over my head. I became a block figure, a robot—a lady robot, because the dress was still swinging, and the voice was still singing. It was like a radio; it was also like a radar screen. There were voices coming out and energy going out into the audience.

SV: You were exploring what you could do with those boxes, and in the process you became a robot, a radar screen, snow boots, oversize boots, and all along you were singing; it was like a . . .

CST: . . . a lullaby.

SV: Almost like Ophelia's song as she floats downstream.

CST: I was floating downstream on my words. I was still high.

SV: Maybe Ophelia is a mistake. She's floating downstream singing words to a suicide. You were on a stream going up!

CST: Maybe. I was the radio. I was different radio stations. Again they were not words. They were sounds that meant words. People could fill in the words with whatever they wanted.

SV: Like how?

CST: AAAOOOOOWWEEEOOWW. [her voice does a sound swirl, like an out-of-whack radar screen] One could be a detective story, one could be romance, one could be the news—whatever.

SV: You scrambled the sounds in such a way as to indicate the tonality of each kind of program without going into the verbal specifics.

CST: Definitely. At that point I took my boxes off my arms, kept the box on my head, and said, "I would like to read to you a poem: High high/Milk box/Garage dog roared/so on and so forth"—reading it with a measure, to a beat, making it make sense. You can take any group of words and they make sense by the tone, the way you start out, and the way you punctuate the ending. It just will make sense to you.

SV: And how do you think you were making that story sound as you read it? Do you remember?

CST: It would sound like, "I got up this morning and put the water on the stove, turned it on to boil, and then I ran up to the grocery store to get the newspaper and tried to get back home in time before the water was all boiled out of the pan so I could make some coffee. But one thing—I'm not drinking coffee anymore because . . ."*

SV: In other words you were bringing the language of the poem, the words on your arm, back into a day-to-day space (that was maybe the opposite of having your arm all jacked up). Instead of having it all jacked up like you were shooting drugs, you were bringing the audience back into a space that was also maybe a sense of parody of the way some poets read. So part of the intention of the piece was to pose the frame of the normal poetry reading and go back and explore the whole, deepen it, and just go all over the place. And that was the end of the piece?

CST: Yes, that was the end.

SV: What happened when you finished?

CST: I finished and introduced myself and introduced George Coates, because I really felt that he was in there too. It was conceived and directed with him, and I was very pleased with the response.

---

* Carol Sue Thomas picked up the interviewer's gift copy of *Omens from the Flight of Birds: The First 101 Days of Jimmy Carter* (Momo's Press, 1977) and read a journal entry by Keith Abbot.

WHERE IS THE PIECE?

An Account of a Talk by David Antin

Ellen Zweig

DAVID ANTIN'S PIECE, "Figures of Speech and Figures of Thought," was performed at 80 Langton Street, San Francisco, on May 13, 1978. The talk series of which it was a part, now held at 80 Langton Street, began at Bob Perelman's loft in 1976. Originally attended by a small group of poets who call themselves "language-centered," these talks increased in popularity as the San Francisco poetry community became more aware of the activities of the "language-centered" group. In 1977 the talks moved to 80 Langton Street, an alternative art space that provided more room for the growing audience and a more public space for the talks.

David Antin's piece was significantly altered by its inclusion in the 80 Langton Street talk series. Both during the piece and after, spectators and participants, including Antin, debated the nature of the piece. In other words, the following questions seemed important: When did this piece begin and end? What was part of the piece and what wasn't? What was the nature of this piece?

"Figures of Speech and Figures of Thought" was framed as a piece in both time and space. The audience knew when it began (when to pay attention to the performance area) and when it ended (when to leave). We also knew when it changed. The piece unfolded before us—a process, an interaction between David Antin and 80 Langton. David Antin usually talks rapidly and nonstop for at least an hour. Audiences at 80 Langton Street are well-known for their aggressive interruptions of speakers in the talk series.

The piece consisted of three basic parts: David Antin talking, an improvised lecture similar to other of his pieces; a discussion that included questions and interruptions; and a metadiscussion, similar to

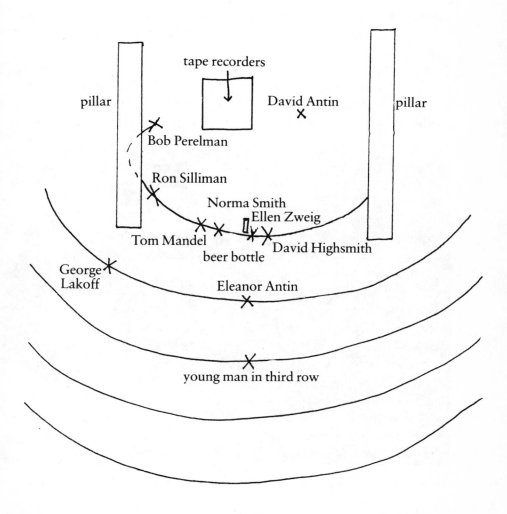

discussions that might go on in a group therapy session or in any situation involving people interested in self-reflective modes.

The dynamics of the piece, its process, its ability to change from one part to the next, depended on a struggle for control which amounted to a struggle for the attention of the audience. Antin was interrupted almost immediately by both Tom Mandel and David Highsmith when he began to discuss the title of his talk (T.M.: "Which was what?"; D.H.: "How many titles were there?") Antin ignored these first inter-ruptions. Since he didn't acknowledge these questions, he still held the floor and continued to talk.

Antin explained his interest in figures of speech and figures of thought, the Greek rhetorical categories he had been thinking about for some time. He said he thought of talking (his activity for the moment) as "a kind of model for the way we in some sense come to represent to each other our apprehension of reality. . . ." He pointed out that he sees a "communicative model" as "basic to any theory of art." Next, he gave a brief history of discourse analysis, concentrating on the Greek and Roman rhetoricians. Although the first part of Antin's talk seemed rambling and the audience wasn't always sure where he was going, it is

David Antin at 80 Langton Street, San Francisco, 1978. Photograph by Philip Galgiani

typical of Antin to begin slowly, searching around as he's talking for something to say—usually for some metaphor. He talks around his subject tentatively until he finds that metaphor.

Here he found it in a long discussion of the Greek theory of harmony which he used to describe a situation in which several people are talking to each other. Each person's voice is represented by a different tone. Antin compared this use of tone as metaphor to the Greek notion of politics, by listing types of oratory, and types of tropes, and by discussing the Greek notion of representation in which "everything has a name." Finally, he presented his improvement on the Greek categorization by dividing the figures into "traffic management" (articulations and organizations) and "handholds of the mind."

Not until Ron Silliman said "Bernadette Mayer" in response to Antin's description of "traffic management" did Antin acknowledge the interrupters with "O.k. All right. Bernadette Mayer . . . memory." Even after this acknowledgment Antin held the floor for some time, further defining his categories. "Traffic management" was described as a kind of surface manipulation of ideas, while "handholds of the mind" was something deeper.

The only other interchange that Antin acknowledged was a strange interchange with Tom Mandel. Antin had been describing metaphor and mentioned that George Lakoff, Ron Silliman, and a number of others were to do a talk/performance about metaphor. When it became clear to Antin that Tom was one of the others, he asked him his last name. Tom replied "Seven" in response to the "*number* of others" in Antin's description of the participants. Antin then called Tom, "Tom Seven." Those who understood the joke—those in the audience who knew Tom's real last name and who understood that Antin had slighted Tom by not knowing that he was the third member of the future performance team—laughed. Our rather uneasy laughter probably indicated to at least some of the people who didn't know the situation that there was something odd about it. In any case, this interchange was elicited by Antin, and, although Tom's joke could be seen as a power move, not until later did Tom really become part of the piece.

Antin's acknowledgment of Ron opened the way for further interruptions, and eventually the piece took its first turn from Antin talk to 80 Langton discussion. The change was gradual. At first, short discussions interrupted Antin, but he regained the floor each time. The discussions usually consisted of questions asked of Antin (two-person interchanges, with one of these people being Antin) and short interchanges between Tom Mandel, Ron Silliman, David Highsmith, and Norma Smith. At one point, Antin tried to regain the floor by saying, "I didn't finish my set." At another point, he regained control by telling the story of Laurie, through which he hoped to further explain his term "hand-holds of the mind."

Laurie, a young woman who stopped eating, was diagnosed as having *anorexia nervosa*. Antin chose to see her not as sick but as an athlete. Although her competition with herself to be ever thinner might (and did, although Antin never got to say this) result in her death, she perfected the skills of not-eating in a culture that encourages us to eat and consume.

Bob Perelman interrupted the story to complain that " . . . in the story you [Antin] know what happened, the audience doesn't. . . . " This is an obvious attribute of a story (although sometimes some of the listeners know the story already), and Antin clearly used the story as a device to keep our attention for an extended period of time.

After the Laurie story, the piece moved more strongly into the discussion mode. Bob Perelman tried to bring the piece back to Antin by saying that he'd like to get back to figures of thought. This move focused our attention on Antin, again by focusing on his subject (the discussion had gotten rather rambling). At this point, Antin was able to talk for an extended period of time, on discourse as a way of learning.

The piece could be seen as vacillating between talk and discussion more profitably than it could be seen in a linear sequence from talk *to* discussion. Inevitably, since the pattern had been set, the piece was interrupted again, this time by Ron Silliman. Ron used a powerful move. He began a metadiscussion of the piece: "I was thinking of the way you structured the beginning of the talk tonight in which you set forth a topic and then proceeded . . . to immediately move to a ground that was essentially foreign to a large part of the audience . . . the audience here was in a situation of waiting for 20-odd minutes or so to see what the point was going to be before anybody felt any kind of permission to then proceed to speak. . . . " Silliman referred to Antin's comment from a previous talk that poetry was "uninterruptible discourse," and implied that Antin's talking is just as "uninterruptible."

By taking the discussion to the metalevel, Ron pointed out the intersection of the Antin talking mode and the 80 Langton mode. He later pointed out that in his opinion " . . . what we've seen is a transition from one form to another form in the course of the past hour or so." By interpreting what went on and by implying that he'd been a powerful force in changing the form, Ron gained momentary control in the power game of the piece.

Although Ron actually began the metadiscussion, it didn't become the main mode of the piece until a young man in the third row[1] interrupted. For a short while we saw an alternation of discussion and metadiscussion.

When the young man in the third row raised the piece to the metalevel, it never reverted back to any other level. Because he took the piece to an emotional level, this powerless person in a powerless position was able to gain control of the whole piece. He essentially guilt-tripped the participants who had to respond in order not to appear as bad people in the eyes of the audience.

The young man's interruption began politely: "I don't know if this is the appropriate time to say this, . . ." and moved from this tentative beginning to a description of strong personal feelings. "For the first hour or so, I've felt upset with the situation. . . ." He pointed out that the arrangement of seats presented a problem in communication, since all of the participants were in the first row with their backs toward the rest of the audience. He also agreed that the "possibility for interruption in your discourse is important," but the actual presence of interruption seemed to him to be bad for the piece.

This metadiscussion was furthered by Eleanor Antin, who seconded the young man in the third row with a powerful performance. Her anger, expressed in terms of feminist political rhetoric ("We're all prisoners of them. It's about five men. . . . This is a very macho situation") and in terms of her expectations ("I came here to hear art") incensed almost everyone in the room. For one thing, her interpretation of the situation as "macho" was generally seen as off-base both by the threatened men and by many of the women in the room. People were willing to concede that the seating arrangement had made a bad situation; the speakers were all in the front row, and anyone in the back rows hadn't been able to see their faces and consequently had felt alienated. However, very few could agree that this situation was caused by male dominance (even though the primary speakers had all been male).

In spite of the general disagreement with her specifics, Ellie's dra-

---

[1]I'm sorry to say that I never found out his name, but have always thought of him fondly as the "young man in the third row."

matic entrance into the metadiscussion was catalytic, more powerful and controversial than that of the young man who had merely served as an example. Powerless people were suddenly asserting their right to speak. In t-groups and other therapy groups, this catalytic role is common. Someone with the ability to express herself or himself powerfully will take on all of the emotions (especially the repressed hostilities) of the group and will burst out with a diatribe that is generally seen as completely off-base by the group participants. This outburst helps to free the other members of the group to express their emotions and to sort them out into an acceptable interpretation of the interactions. The young man and Ellie Antin moved the metadiscussion from a discussion of the formal qualities of the piece (which essentially was the discussion that Ron initiated) to a discussion of the emotions of the participants and of the nonparticipants.

David Antin, eager to gain control of these interpretations (after all it would be remembered as his piece), insisted that he wasn't upset by the interruptions; in fact, he had expected them and had been interested in seeing what would happen when David Antin met 80 Langton. After he regained control in this way, it was possible for him to bring the piece to an end.

The Time Frame

The struggle for control of the piece made it difficult, at the time of the piece, for the observers and the participants to determine exactly what was the piece and what wasn't. Everyone agreed on one thing: There was something called "the piece." In the end, there was only one way to find that piece.

Every piece in performance has a formal beginning and end. This formal frame, like the frame around a picture,[2] is usually clear. Someone announces the performance, or the performer, who is known by most of the audience, simply walks onto the stage and begins. Sometimes a curtain will go up; sometimes either the announcer or performer will say something like "O.k. Ready? Let's begin." The end is also formal. The performer will say "thank you," the announcer will reappear with some announcements about next week, and the curtain will go down.

---

[2]See Erving Goffman's *Frame Analysis* (Harper and Row, New York, 1974) for a more extensive analysis of the phenomenon of frame. The term is also used widely in discussions of art theory, since the obvious metaphor of the picture frame readily comes to mind.

In the case of David Antin's piece, the situation seemed to be more complex. But it was really very simple. At a certain point, Bob Perelman said, "Take it away," which signalled the formal beginning. At the end, it was again Bob who gave the formal ending: "Well, listen, thanks a lot. I enjoyed it." Everything within this frame can be considered part of the piece. Later, we'll see that only those things that the audience is directed to pay attention to within the frame are part of the piece.

The beginning and end of a piece are probably not as clear cut as I've first portrayed them. For example, the preframe events that surrounded the David Antin piece consisted of general milling around and a great deal of fiddling with tape recorders. The milling around is common to most performances as the audience trickles in. This is a social occasion, so friends find and greet each other; everyone finds a seat. The tape recorders were also preframe, yet they inhabited an ambiguous area. David Antin had arrived and was fiddling with his own tape recorder. There were at least six other recorders on a table in the performance area, and their owners were adjusting tapes. The audience, already seated and ready for the piece, became interested in this fiddling which was going on in the spatial frame if not the temporal frame of the piece. Furthermore, as soon as Bob said, "Take it away," Antin called attention to the tape recorders: "This is going to be fun when everyone has to turn it over." Ron Silliman was still having trouble with his, and, when he finally sat down, Antin said, "Now that Ron's recorder is working we're capable of doing it." It could be argued that this comment by Antin is the true formal beginning of the piece.

Only two people in the room could have started and stopped the piece. One was David Antin, who was the performer; the other was Bob Perelman, the organizer of the talk series and the announcer for the evening. In some sense, both Perelman and Antin gave a formal beginning to the piece.

Both of them also ended the piece. Strangely enough, the end began with a reference to the tape recorders and to a frame. The young man in the third row stated that the tape recorders made the audience aware of the social situation of the piece. Antin said he didn't understand this, and the young man tried to explain: "It demands that you step outside of the frame of the situation. It's sort of a negative frame." Antin and the audience still seemed to be puzzled by this analysis, and someone asked if we could hear the end of the story about Laurie (which had been interrupted). Antin replied that we'd have to hear it in print, and ended the piece by saying: "Anyway, I'm sorry. I enjoyed it, and I realize all the problems that developed, but I think the problems . . . are partly generic problems. . . ." Notice that he's already talking about the piece in the past tense, referring to "it" as though it were over. Again, we enter an ambiguous area. Antin continued to talk, explaining what he meant by "generic problems." He ended again by saying: "I enjoyed it. It's not like my other works. It's sort of like my other works." Again, he explained that, when he wrote it, he would make it look different. We may have the impression that, although Antin was ending the piece, he might have gone on ending it for a long time. Bob Perelman came to the rescue by echoing one of Antin's phrases: "Well, listen, thanks a lot. I enjoyed it."

The piece was clearly over. The members of the audience stood up, started talking to each other in small groups, and began putting away the chairs.

The Spatial Frame

In addition to the time frame, the piece had a spatial frame. The chairs were arranged in wide rows. Antin stood between two pillars which framed him almost as though he were on a proscenium arch stage. The table with the tape recorders was also between the pillars. As the piece changed from lecture to discussion to metadiscussion, the spatial frame moved out into the audience, breaking the "fourth wall" (a theatrical term used to indicate the invisible wall between the actors and the audience in a proscenium arch stage).[3] During the discussion, all of the interrupters were located in the first row; the spatial frame moved out to them. During the metadiscussion, the frame slowly moved to cover all of the audience. At first, it covered only the third row, then the second row, then all of the rows. At no time did the piece move out of the spatial frame of Antin, pillars, and audience in rows. If someone left the room, he or she was no longer in the piece. If someone moved to stand by the door (which was far across the room from the chairs), they probably did this in order to remove themselves from the spatial frame, to become audience again. No one participated from outside this spatial frame.

I have said that everything within the temporal and spatial frame of the piece is by definition part of the piece. Although the temporal frame is a wide instead of a narrow band of time, and the spatial frame shifted

---

[3]See Margaret Croyden's *Lunatics, Lovers, and Poets; The Contemporary Experimental Theatre* (McGraw Hill, New York, 1974) for a discussion of some attempts to break through this "fourth wall," a term widely used in dramatic theory.

at least twice during the performance, a description of the boundaries of these frames helps determine the boundaries of the piece itself.

Then is everything inside these frames part of the piece? Did anything happen during the time and in the space of the piece that wasn't in the piece? Since both David Antin, as the performer of the piece, and Bob Perelman, as the organizer of the series, had the power to begin and end the piece, they also had the power to declare what was or wasn't in the piece. In the course of the piece other participants vied for this power, although, strangely enough, no one else tried to declare the piece's beginning or end. Theoretically they could have done so as soon as they became part of the piece. And several participants analyzed the piece as ending at a certain point. During the metadiscussion a woman said, "I'm not familiar with the structure of these talks, but to me it stopped when people started raising objections to people responding." Eleanor Antin pointed out to David that he stopped taping when the discussion format took over. Nevertheless, these interpretations were incorrect by consensus. If they had been correct, everyone would have left their seats and eventually left the building. The audience knew intuitively when the piece was over, and an observer could determine when the piece was over, because the audience left and eventually the room was empty.

Focused Attention

The piece itself can be seen as a conglomerate of moments of focused attention.[4] The audience's attention was mainly focused by David Antin, secondarily by Bob Perelman. Perelman focused attention on Antin, both by the fact that he'd organized and publicized the talk and by pointing to Antin ("Take it away," he said *to* Antin) when he arrived and when the tape recorders seemed to be ready. Attention was also focused on Antin by the performance space, the pillar frame, the chairs all pointing in one direction with Antin standing in front facing them. In addition, attention was focused on Antin because he began and continued talking. At first, the expectations of the audience were fulfilled; they were hearing David Antin talk.

David Antin, in turn, focused the audience's attention on his subject matter, by talking about it, and on his talking, also by talking about it. The piece began in a self-reflective mode, with Antin describing his

[4]Livia Polanyi first suggested I consider "attention" and gave me the term "focused attention."

talking pieces: "Since they end at some time and begin at some time, I call them pieces: That is, they are not in any sense infinitely extensive ... they seem to connect with each other by fragmentary means, so there are pieces. ..." Or when he began to discuss his subject, figures of speech and figures of thought: "The reason I began to consider the issue was that I thought of talking ... as a kind of paradigmatic situation, a kind of model for the way we in some sense come to represent to each other our apprehension of reality. ..."

Antin also focused our attention on several people and objects that later became the center of the piece. Although Antin probably didn't intend these entities to become the center—in his words, he uses what's "handy"—he did contribute to their ability to enter the situation by pointing to them earlier in the piece. He discussed the tape recorders, Ron Silliman's in particular, at the very beginning of his talk and again about half-way through the piece when all of the tapes needed to be turned. This opened the way for the young man in the third row, who made a big point about the effect that noticing the tape recorders had had on the piece. Although he had by the time he mentioned them earned the right to direct our attention by instigating the metadiscussion, his use of the tape recorder example was buttressed by Antin's earlier references to the recorders.

Antin also mentioned several of the people in the audience early on in the piece, and these people—Ron Silliman, George Lakoff, Tom Mandel, Bob Perelman, Eleanor Antin—all became important participants in the later stages of the piece. Kathleen Fraser, to whom Antin referred in this same early group, was the one exception; she didn't participate. People participated who weren't mentioned by Antin, but, for the most part, they participated after that brave young man in the third row pointed out that they weren't included.

We see that the hierarchy of control which existed at the Antin talk may exist in any performance situation in which the boundaries between the performers and the audience, and even the boundaries between the piece and the not-piece (art and life), are not immediately clear. The hierarchy could be seen as:

1. David Antin (as performer)
2. Bob Perelman (as organizer of series, and as one of the people mentioned by Antin)
3. Ron Silliman (person in the front row who speaks and is mentioned by Antin)

184

4. Tom Mandel (person in the front row who speaks and is mentioned by Antin, although at first Antin doesn't know his last name or, in fact, that this person in the front row is Tom Mandel). (Both Ron and Tom can be seen to have changed the course of the piece.)
5. The young man in the third row (who spoke out and changed the course of the piece, the hero of the powerless)
6. Eleanor Antin (who was mentioned by David, and who reacted strongly to the young man in the third row and to the situation of the piece)
7. George Lakoff (who was mentioned early on by Antin, who made a rather dramatic entrance, and who spoke once during the discussion and again during the metadiscussion after Ellie mentioned him)
8. David Highsmith and Norma Smith (who both spoke during the discussion but who weren't mentioned by Antin, although they were acknowledged by Antin during the discussion. Both sat in the front row.)
9. All those who spoke up during the metadiscussion (and were in some way mentioned by the young man in the third row since he noticed their silence)
10. All those who never spoke during the piece and remained audience; the powerless. These people were all potentially powerful after the heroism of the young man in the third row.

This hierarchy depended not only on the spatial position of the participants but also on the fact that they were mentioned by someone or acknowledged by someone in a higher position in the hierarchy. In other words, our attention was focused at least for a time on each of them. Only the young man in the third row focused our attention on himself without the help of any other participant or of a position in the front row, and with only the negative argument that he was in the third row and not in the first. However, his position was immediately encouraged by Eleanor Antin and by David Antin's attention to the particular issues that the young man brought up. In addition, the young man in the third row was helped to gain attention in the situation because he jumped to a metalevel. Perhaps he felt himself to be in a double-bind.[5] He disliked the interruptions that he was witnessing and didn't want to be one of the interrupters. He equally disliked his powerless position—silent, in the third row. In order to get out of his powerless position and at the same time avoid doing the very thing he was about to criticize, he had to turn our attention to the discussion itself. By doing this he couldn't be ignored, since he had called to question the very activity of the piece.

Many events took place during the piece that weren't part of the

---

[5]See Gregory Bateson, "Toward a Theory of Schizophrenia," *Steps to an Ecology of Mind* (Ballantine, New York, 1972).

piece. I remember only one because it happened near my feet and because I can hear it on my tape. Someone knocked over a beer bottle. Since Antin uses what's handy, he easily could have used that beer bottle. Any event could have been brought to our attention as part of the piece, or one of the other participants could have used it. However, the beer bottle went unnoticed, an event outside the domain of this particular piece.

David Antin's piece, "Figures of Speech and Figures of Thought," was a framed and focused work of art eventually created by several people. It did resemble life in one important way. The performer and the audience engaged in a power game for control of the making of the piece and for the attention of the audience. Only in the beginning and the ending of the piece was the original authority of David Antin and Bob Perelman respected.

Even the last word in *this* piece will go to Antin. He wrote me in a letter thanking me for the copies I'd sent him of the tapes I'd made of "Figures of Speech and Figures of Thought":

My own machine did not get much beyond the rap (interrupted and continued) that I did. It only picked up that part of the floor talk that I more or less deliberately allowed to penetrate the piece, or prepared or provoked, by loosening my narrative hold or the tautness of a particular analysis. . . . I'm looking forward to hearing what went on. . . . [6]

---

[6]In a letter dated August 21, 1978.

A RESPONSE TO ELLEN ZWEIG

David Antin

ABOUT YOUR PIECE. I enjoyed reading it, but I have a couple of suggestions which I think might help you. First, I think you overemphasize the notion of a power struggle, which, no doubt, you may have experienced, but . . . it seems to me you tend to disregard completely the socially encoded system of courtesy which mitigated in this situation, and in most other noncrisis situations, any competition for control.

Let me elaborate a little. I was an invited guest, invited to speak—invited speakers are usually accorded the courtesy of being listened to, especially by the inviting hosts, who have a bond of acquaintance and hospitality, which sets up constraints on their behavior. Now 80 Langton had a tradition of discussion with its invited speakers, but the difference between listening and discussing is a matter of degree. Or, rather, there was in this case an uncertain terrain between my normal "piece" and 80 Langton's habits, which were themselves somewhat variable.

I was aware of the character of the discussions at 80 Langton. But I was even more aware of the special intentions of Ron Silliman and Bob Perelman in relation to my work, because Ron and I had been exchanging letters for some time before I accepted an invitation to talk there. In the most recent letter before the invitation, Ron referred to a talk of mine that he had heard about, which had taken place in New York, and which was an abrasive commentary on Marxist rhetoric, among other things, and suggested that I had sensed a formal problem in my talk pieces—their monologue structure, which had gone about as far as it could—and that, knowingly or not, I was seeking a kind of "catastrophe" by provoking the audience to enter the piece, perhaps to liberate me from my formal *cul de sac*.

Since Ron and I hold rather different views of the significance of "formal issues" in art, I was not enormously impressed with his analysis here, but I took the invitation to perform at Bob Perelman's loft, which was made in this letter, to be a kind of amiable challenge to my "form"—the single-voiced talk piece (I do not call it a monologue, since I assume that I am always probing the audience concerns in the talk). Now it would have been extremely obtuse of me not to have considered the likelihood that my acquaintances among the "language-centered poets" would try to enter the piece. But I also assumed they would have to do this within some kind of acceptable way—a way that reflected the sense of their own obligations to courtesy, based on the invitation and on the history of their interest in my work. Our relation was not one of hostility.

If you consider this, you will note that all the interruptions that take place are more in the nature of proposals that conform to a social etiquette. Interruptions are more or less relevant, or at least they are made to appear so. Nobody tries to shout me down. When a speaker rises to make a suggestion, it is in the nature of a challenge to my interpretation of something within my talk, or an attempt to divert it in a slightly different direction. Consider [Tom] Mandel's questioning of my model of stock car driving and its relevance or value for an inter-pretation of what is usually called *anorexia*. This interruption conforms very closely to the demand for relevancy in interruptions.

This brings up another point—the issue of the material of my talk. That was not improvised at all. I knew I was going to talk about figures of speech and figures of the mind—for the very good reason that I am convinced of the triviality of what is called formalist analysis, and I was specifically proposing a critique of previous stylistic analyses. In sug-gesting the distinctions between "decorations," "traffic management," and "handholds for the mind," I was proposing a nonformalist analysis of the modes of proceeding through language—which I suspect lies fairly far from what the language-centered poets have considered. They have generally considered the possibility of breaking discourse and representation and attempting to construct new synecdochical systems of meaning with the fragments of language left, after they have broken up its syntax and more or less commonplace semantic structure. This piece was done precisely for them. All that was improvised was what I was precisely going to say in relation to my own concerns with rhetoric and theirs.

Apparently, I also moved improvisatorily into the issues of the Greek theory of harmony—which is fundamentally political and is conceived in terms of the competition of voices seeking to be heard and which considered democracy a form of cacophony (not harmonically ordered). This, apparently, since I have never done this before except in a class on Greek critical theory, must have been my response to the fantasy of participatory or democratic poetry (art) that Ron seemed to be proposing. I have never been impressed with the idea of democracy, and the idea of democracy in the domain of the arts or of the mind is fundamentally preposterous. And I was prefiguring the comedy that was to follow, when the main figures of 80 Langton tried to perforate the piece, politely but didactically, as I proceeded.

You see, we are all—Ron and Bob Perelman and, perhaps, Mandel, whom I know much less well, and myself—all didactic artists. I was trying to demonstrate to them, by letting them try to enter my piece, the triviality of the outcome they would attain. They were trying to demonstrate to me the productiveness of the participatory mode of 80 Langton. But all of this was to be done within the etiquette of collegial disagreement. After all, we are all artists, and respect each other, no doubt in varying degrees. But none of us considers the other an idiot, or an academic, or even hopelessly out of the ballgame.

So . . . the scene that was set by the main participants of 80 Langton and myself was of friendly disagreement. And not even openly stated disagreement. So the competition had to be governed within the terrain of something like art making. Meanwhile, for the others at 80 Langton, not committed to a special mode of modernism—to formalist stylistics or participatory stylistics—the situation was somewhat different. They were coming to hear a performance. This gave me something of an edge. The outsiders—"the people," so to speak—not having any particular issue to debate with me, would find the interruptions by the aristocratic party (equivalent to the barons who claimed the rights of the Magna Carta for themselves, not the people) to be greatly interfering with their lives . . . the performance they had expected to hear and wanted to hear. You will note that the outsiders, or seeming outsiders—the young man in the third row, George Lakoff, Ellie, etc.—found the 80 Langton poets mainly interfering with the performance, though this ceased to be the issue during the later stages of the metadiscussion. But you should also observe that as long as I withheld the story's completion, everyone outside of the aristocratic party felt somewhat deprived.

As the speaker (in the royal role), I could manipulate this to my own amusement, as long as I wanted or cared. You see, I would never have had the slightest difficulty in shutting everybody out of the talk, if I had wanted to build up the intensity of the narrative. Virtually nothing can stop an experienced and skillful narrator who has a real story to tell and an audience interested in its outcome. On the other hand, I didn't know how much I wanted to do that. I was at 80 Langton in an exploratory mood, and I wanted to know if the significance of my rap would sufficiently pique the intellectual interest of my friends to cause them to let go of their theoretical interest in participating. And I didn't want to push them too hard toward the story, because it would have felt a little bit like cheating. I was enjoying their entries, which turned out, as is always the case in this kind of situation, to take us over no especially new or valuable ground—in spite of the considerable intelligence and education of the participants.

I'm afraid I am a rather playful combatant—if that word applies to my role. I like to think of myself as a bit more like Buster Keaton than the crowd that forms the melee as he passes through.

The only thing I would wish to add to this emphasis on the relation between the "content" of the piece and the behavior of the actors is that the issues of etiquette were paramount for virtually everyone who spoke—including the young man in the third row. Though you didn't know this, he was not a stranger to me. He's a young musician and artist with whom I had discussed the possibility of his coming to San Diego some time before I arrived at 80 Langton. We had spoken on the phone twice, and at length, so that he could claim acquaintance with me. This gave him the right to enter, though he didn't announce that he had this right. But nobody else did either.

The people who entered the piece before the entry of the young man all felt they had the right to entry through a kind of social intimacy as acquaintances or recognized colleagues. Because nobody assumed the young man in the third row had a special acquaintance right, his entry threw open the doors to everyone else, though they did not come in until Ellie's energetic entry blew the scene wide open. But this, too, has special etiquette attached to it. Ellie didn't enter earlier—because of her close relation to me. It was not till "the integrity of the piece" was defended, or its violation objected to, by a "stranger" (she didn't know him), that she felt the right to enter. From here on in, I think you have most of the piece under control.

So, as you see, what I object to most is your failure to deal with the relationship between the material of the piece and behavior of the participants. Secondly, I think you misjudge the degree of improvisation, by supposing I am groping around as much as all that. I knew what I wanted to address quite well; I had some notion of the terms I was going to address it in, and what I was looking for was *the way*. As for the story . . . it appeared as I spoke, but here is the most curious problem for anyone writing on it. You can say I knew the ending—but only if you are sure it's a true story, or that I couldn't tell a true story in somewhat peculiar, fanciful, or deceitful way. . . .

VISITORS

Henry David Thoreau

I HAD THREE CHAIRS in my house; one for solitude, two for friendship, three for society. When visitors came in larger and unexpected numbers there was but the third chair for them all, but they generally economized the room by standing up. It is surprising how many great men and women a small house will contain. I have had twenty-five or thirty souls, with their bodies, at once under my roof, and yet we often parted without being aware that we had come very near to one another . . .

One inconvenience I sometimes experienced in so small a house, the difficulty of getting to a sufficient distance from my guest when we began to utter the big thoughts in big words. You want room for your thoughts to get into sailing trim and run a course or two before they make their port. The bullet of your thought must have overcome its lateral and ricochet motion and fallen into its last and steady course before it reaches the ear of the hearer, else it may plow out again through the side of his head. Also, our sentences wanted room to hold and form their columns in the interval. Individuals, like nations, must have suitable broad and natural boundaries, even a considerable neutral ground, between them. I have found it a singular luxury to talk across the pond to a companion on the opposite side. In my house we were so near that we could not begin to hear,—we could not speak low enough to be heard; as when you throw two stones into calm water so near that they break each other's undulations. If we were not merely loquacious and loud talkers, then we can afford to stand very near together, cheek by jowl, and feel each other's breath; but if we speak reservedly and thoughtfully, we want to be further apart, that all animal heat and moisture may have a chance to evaporate. (If we would enjoy the most intimate society with that in each of us which is without, or above, being spoken to, we must not only be silent, but commonly so far apart bodily that we cannot possibly hear each other's voice in any case. Referred to this standard, speech is for the convenience of those who are hard of hearing; but there are many fine things which we cannot say if we have to shout.) As the conversation began to assume a loftier and grander tone, we gradually shoved our chairs farther apart till they touched the wall in opposite corners, and then commonly there was not room enough.

From "Visitors" in *Walden,* by Henry David Thoreau.

READING *KETJAK*

Ron Silliman

The Text

Lines 1; 3; & 5 of a twelve-line work:

Revolving door.

Revolving door. Fountains of the financial district. Houseboats beached at the point of low tide, only to float again when the sunset is reflected in the water. A sequence of objects which to him appears to be a caravan of fellaheen, a circus, camels pulling wagons of bear cages, tamed ostriches in toy hats, begins a slow migration to the right vanishing point on the horizon line.

Revolving door. Earth science. Fountains of the financial district spout soft water in a hard wind. How the heel rises and the ankle bends to carry the body from one stair to the next. She was a unit in a bum space, she was a damaged child. The fishermen's cormorants wear rings around their necks to keep them from swallowing, to force them to surrender the catch. Dark brown houseboats beached at the point of low tide—men atop their cabin roofs, idle, play a dobro, a jaw's harp, a 12-string guitar—only to float again when the sunset is reflected in the water. Silverfish, potatobugs. What I want is the gray-blue grain of western summer. The nurse, by a subtle shift of weight, moves in front of the student in order to more rapidly board the bus. A cardboard box of wool sweaters on top of the book case to indicate Home. A day of rain in the middle of June. A sequence of objects, silhouettes, which to him appears to be a caravan of fellaheen, a circus, dromedaries pulling wagons bearing tiger cages, tamed ostriches in toy hats, begins a slow migration to the right vanishing point on the horizon line. We ate them.

In the This Press edition, the final line of the poem is 45 pages long, containing more than 10,000 words.

The Act

On Saturday, September 16, 1978, between noon & 4:30 pm, I read, without amplification or intermission, the entirety of *Ketjak*, at the corner of Powell & Market streets in San Francisco.

The Site

Powell & Market is a public ceremonial locale devoted primarily to the tourist boarding of cable cars. More than any other spot in the City, it is frequented by street musicians, evangelists of varying persuasions, & others in search of a largely random audience. I stood at the base of the steps of 1 Powell Street, the original headquarters of the Bank of America. Across Powell is a large, tourist-oriented Woolworth's in the ground-floor level of the Flood Building, an ornate, old office structure that once housed the administrative offices of most of the railroad industry on the West Coast. Next to the Flood Building on Market is Samuel's Jewelers, where for years Dashiell Hammett had been employed to write advertising copy. Immediately to the southwest of 1 Powell is Halladie Plaza, named for the inventor of the cable car & site of the Powell Bart Station, where, on September 16th, a Hawaiian drum chorus was playing. Beyond the Plaza is the Tenderloin, where I had just completed a year's work on a multi-disciplinary ethnography project.

Reading Function

To give a typical poetry reading, a normal presentation of a text of unusual length. This required enabling (empowering) the audience to move freely, even to come & go, without disrupting the event. The architectural tradition of such readings tends toward enclosed sites of intimate dimensions. While this might be ideal for most readings, it nevertheless imposes limitations which have nothing to do with the text itself. Like the so-called little magazine, most reading spaces militate for the short poem, the eminently discrete (& disposable) affective experience.

Audience Function

Parallel to the problem of time posed by such sites as the coffee house, the art gallery, the church, the rear-of-the-bookstore & the room-on-the-campus is the way in which such spaces limit the possibility of audience, again quite like publication in a specifically literary magazine. The social tradition of these institutions functions as a screen, & not merely to keep the boisterous drunks at bay either. Having, in February, 1976, given identical readings at Folsom State Prison & the University of California at San Diego, I already had some grounds for a further investigation of the presentation of aesthetic material beyond the traditional bracketing mechanisms available to most poets. A nonaesthetic audience receives such information without the enveloping codes most listeners bring to a "reading," & therefore experience it as language first. Necessarily, they too will hypothesize a social code in order to place their experience within a context, without which its meaning would remain opaque & foreign, but this is, both in time & importance, a secondary occurrence.

Performance Functions

The elaboration in the past three decades of performance art has taken place at the margins of pre-existing forms: poetry (particularly readings), sculpture, dance, theater, film, and so on. This much was to have been expected—no art lacks precedent—but it carries within this fact an inherent danger, that of rendering performance a new mode of mere modernism, embarking on a path whose various dead-ends have already been all too adequately demonstrated in every medium. Because performance is based on (sometimes several) prior codes, specifically aesthetic ones, the usual practice of this new form has often been to import heretofore "nonaesthetic" information into the territory of whichever frame is being used. The new content, be it the animal movements of Simone Forti or the monologic discourse of David Antin, enters the new realm as a type of ready-made. Instead of being investigated in any rigorous or useful sense, it simply is subjected to the shaping imposed by the importing code. This neither explores new dimensions nor calls into question the structuring of the aesthetic codes themselves (which, at the present historical moment, would be the primary subject of a truthfully political art). Such performance is, in fact, a kind of aesthetic colonialism, making the whole world of meaning artfully the property of a certain few. My decision was to invert this, to give an "ordinary reading" in all aspects save length at a busy streetcorner in the middle of the day. The aesthetic code was subjected to the larger & noisier ones of everyday life.

Language Functions

There presently exist several binary divisions of language &/or content in general: (1) paradigm/syntagm (Saussure), (2) condensation/displacement (Freud), (3) denotative/connotative (Barthes), (4) metaphor/metonymy (Lacan), & (5) discursive/constative (Beneviste). To which I would add *citation/representation,* meaning that every sentence either seeks to represent reality (whether imagistically, conceptually or discursively), or else is a (more or less) direct citation from that reality, such as quotation &, in some instances, allusion. *Ketjak* plays extensively with all of these, & particularly the last. Consider the first two sentences of the 5th line, previously quoted. *Revolving door* is simultaneously syntagmatic, a displacement, a particularly connotative denotation, a metaphor, constative &, at once, citational & representative. *Earth science* is paradigmatic, a condensation, purely connotative, metonymic, constative & representational. Three differences account for this: (1) *Revolving door* is much more readily recognized as a name for a specific object than *Earth science* (which could refer to the study of soil, geology proper, geography & perhaps others), which is less familiar; (2) *Revolving door* is a metaphor for the reading function of re-entering the content in each line (much as the caravan sentence is a metaphor for the progress of the sentence itself); (3) this is the fifth occurrence of *Revolving door,* & the first for the second sentence. While *Revolving door* is representational of, first, a type of entrance &, second, the act of reading, it is also a quotation from the earlier paragraphs. Also, the fact of its familiarity foregrounds the adjectival function of *Revolving,* while the laxer specificity of *Earth science* should push the reading mind to search out definitions before syntax. In *Ketjak,* these affective levels of understanding occur within a form aimed at stressing their presence prior to that of any suprasentence content. Repetition has the advantage of blocking the possibility of narrative or discourse, without the need to defer the signifieds toward a collective nonreferentiality, such as one finds in the work of Coolidge or Andrews (or even, elsewhere, in my own). Because of the rapidity of occurrence of sentences (emphasized on the page by the use of the paragraph form), these understandings do not take place at the level of analytical consciousness. Nor should they require either training in linguistics or an education in recent poetics: They should be tangible, at some level, to any reasonably knowledge-able speaker of the language. The presumption, made by some antago-nists of what they call language poetry, that it is obscure or otherwise "difficult," is precisely a presumption that such work can only be comprehended through an extensive level of specialized education. Under the right conditions (& the competent writers will see to it that conditions are "right"), that presumption is nonsense, a mere expres-sion of some people of their own unwillingness to let go of their own aesthetic encoding long enough to look at what is in front of them. Reading *Ketjak* was a test in my own belief in my work, but one undertaken in confidence.

Practical Considerations

In college I had supported myself by reading to blind graduate & law students, sometimes as much as eleven hours on a single day near finals, so I knew that four & one-half hours were within easy reach.

I know also that I had to limit my water intake, during the course of the reading.

Regardless of First Amendment protections, there are conditions under which such a performance could be subjected to the whimsical application of municipal statute (street artist without a license, obstruc-tion of the sidewalk, noise abatement). A lawyer was "on call" through-out the event.

A lesson I'd learned from a year's work in the Tenderloin, which served well during the reading, is that psychotics & most street alco-holics respect an aggressive assertion of presence. Only one person tried to jam a toothbrush down my mouth as I read.

I did want the presence of some support, not only for such con-tingencies as that & to combat the general alienation of any streetcorner speaker (I after all was hardly to see anything beyond the borders of my page), but because I intended the event as a communication to other poets, concerning their work as well as mine. I sent out a flyer & listed the reading in *Poetry Flash*.

Lessons, If Any

Volume strains the voice, & volume was necessary given the drum chorus, the hare krishna people & street musicians. This had at least three consequences I had not anticipated:

1) my physical movements became more pronounced;
2) after the 60th page, I began to spit blood onto the pages of the text;
3) six hours after the reading, I lost my voice entirely, & did not get it back for three days.

Ron Silliman reading *Ketjak* at the corner of Powell & Market, San Francisco, 1978. Photograph by Alan Bernheimer

MITCHELL'S DEATH

Linda Montano

ON AUGUST 19, 1977, my ex-husband Mitchell Payne died at 33, very suddenly and tragically in Kansas City. I mourned his death in my work and performed "Mitchell's Death" at the Center for Music Experiment in San Diego on April 23, 1978.

Performers: Linda Montano, Pauline Oliveros, Al Rossi.

Structure: The event was structured in the form of a cross.
Horizontal:
  1. A TV monitor with images of my face as acupuncture needles were placed in it.
  2. Pauline Oliveros, sitting, playing a Japanese bowl gong, chanting (Buddhism).
  3. Men, chanting, acupuncture needles in my face (Catholicism).
  4. Al Rossi, chanting and playing a *sruti* box (Hinduism).
Vertical:
  1. Light was projected in back of me from the light on the lectern.
  2. Sound was amplified and delayed three times and projected in front of me.

The Event: I entered the space after Pauline and Al, turned on the TV, then the light, and stood at the lectern. I wore a black dress (one my grandmother had given to me twenty years earlier). I began chanting (Gregorian chant: martyr, Saint Sebastian, guilt, grief) for 25 minutes the story of Mitchell's death from the minute that I heard about it to the time that I saw his body in the mortuary. The sound was amplified and delayed three times and projected out into the audience.

All of my Catholic imagery came together in this piece—Saint, Martyr, Cross, Religion, Stations of the Cross, Death, Lent, Crucifixion. The piece blended Nun, Singer, Ex-wife, Ex-widow, Sinner, Saint. FRIDAY A.M., August 19th, I wake at 7 or so, look at the clock. I wish that chicken would stop crowing. Preacher man running around the yard echoing himself into the adjacent meadow. Pauline goes out to find him, comes back. I tell her my dream. A new one. Instead of being bothered by the baby, I throw sand at it when it throws sand at me. Pauline says something about her dream. A dead foetus and bloody clothes. She then goes outside and tries to catch the chicken. At 10:30 I ask Pauline's advice about selling a tape recorder that belonged to Mitchell and me. Things from my past. Then the phone rings. It's 11 A.M. It's Joe Gregg from K.C. I have some very shocking news for you. Mitchell is dead. Mitchell is dead from a gun accident. I scream, start to faint. Call Pauline, Pauline Mitchell is dead. He shot himself. Joe says no it was an accident. He didn't shoot himself. I then ask why did he have guns. Who was he going hunting with, becoming very accusative and angry. Blaming. Joe said we were going skeet shooting. I said when. Wanting to place blame. Covering over my sorrow with blame and anger. I thank Joe. He says if there is anything you need let me know. We hang up. Not much information about anything. Pauline is holding me. I collapse in her arms. Jillene is there, looks on. Pauline's visitors are at the door. She leaves. Is open and effusive with them, then tells them about Mitchell. Comes back into the bedroom pulled between two emotions . . . joy at seeing her friends and sorrow. Sweat is pouring from her face which is filled with disbelief and pain. She looks down at me and I say what shall I do. She says I feel like calling my mother. Then I begin a series of phone calls which don't end. Which go on and on and on. I call everyone. First Mildred. Not home. Then Henry. The phone rings for about 5 minutes in the shoe store which means that they are busy. Dad I have some bad news. Mitchell is dead. He died from a gun accident. Henry says he should know better than to fool around with guns. He doesn't know anything about them. Whatever he said released as whole big lump . . . it presented the other side. Laughter. Honesty. No emotion in his voice. Another perspective. I call Chris. Don't want to hang up. We talk and talk and talk. Won't hang up. She cries. We repeat it over and over so we can both believe it. Then Bill in Alaska. Steven. I

201

think of everyone. Minnette is in Greece. Thornley in Children's Hospital. Mildred calls back again talking about it. Repeating. Wanting her here. Somehow the words make it real and not real. Make it credible. Mitchell's image in my mind. Pictures begin. I try to picture where he was shot . . . face? heart? Did he suffer? Died instantly? Did his face get blown off? Images, I see the room where it happened. See it clearly. Talking. Pauline brings in some tuna salad and brown bread. Can't eat then eat. So hungry but not hungry at all. Feels paradoxical. Eating and mourning, tears and tuna fish. Pauline's friends visit. We all drink champagne. His brother committed suicide in a closet in Canada. Did Mitchell? Guilt. Did I do it? My fault? Was he despondent? Lonely? Miss me too much? I remember my feelings when he moved to K.C. I was very apprehensive, anxious. Preknowledge? I felt his trip across the country. Saw him in K.C. living in his grandmother's house. Dark. Lonely. I felt concerned. It was a tremendously big trip, breaking from S.F. His insistence on the move, on that pilgrimage, lasted three or more years. He had to go back. Why? Then our last phone call two weeks before. I called needing to talk . . . my life had large questions. I needed his help. Mitchell all I want to do is meditate. Meditate he said. You know how you like to do that. No Rose, your life seems right now. Don't worry. You're not being selfish. Don't worry Rose. His last words. He tells me about his new house. 100 years old. Asked the people living there if they wanted to sell. Mitchell so impetuous. What he wanted he somehow managed to get. Energy to make things happen, always that way. Then he would be upset because he had too many wants, too many needs. His friend Luther Jensen, 76 years old. A bromoil photographer. I am relieved. He's found somebody to work with. There was always a very old person in Mitchell's life . . . his grandmother, Del, Papa. Mitchell's charm and grace attracted almost everyone. Then his trip to the Art Institute that day. He hesitates to tell me about changing his clothes there at the office and then coming back to work, changing his clothes, going to work. Is it because I made him shop at thrift stores and now he's buying expensive suits and shirts? Mitchell we're friends. Tell me. We don't live in the same house any more but there is love. You can tell me about your new life style. Rose, there's an old woman here in Kansas who writes country western music and she's 90 or so and I'm going to see her. She has a small toy piano and she gets up in the night because it's real quiet then and she writes songs. I ask are you going to record her? I don't know what he answered. He's eager to go to lunch, to the Art Institute. I have your Christmas present here from last year . . . I'll send it. Good and put some food in it. Bye Mitch. Bye Rose. I love you. We hang up. //////////////Images. His face then does he have a face now? Is it blown off? Is he dead? I should go to Kansas immediately. I call Kansas. Laura Pearson answers. Informative. Mitch was getting a serial number from a gun for Jojo. He was in the kitchen. Joe came over to put some crab meat in the icebox which wouldn't fit in theirs. Then Mitch invited Joe for breakfast. I wonder, was he really lonely needing some friends around? Joe said no he had to go be with his new baby. That brought up the thought that Mitch really wanted children and I didn't. Joe put together a shotgun and they were to go skeet shooting on Saturday. He warned Mitchell don't put any bullets in it or be careful or something like that . . . it's an old gun and then 1/2 hour later Margaret, the maid, warm, generous Margaret found Mitchell with a towel around his waist lying between the kitchen and dining room, dead. She screamed, ran out, across the street. They were supposed to have lunch that day. He drove her to the bus stop the night before then went to Safeway. Probably his last act before going home. The doctor from across saw that he was dead. Then 2 ambulances, police, detectives, people to clean up. Laura I want to come to Kansas. I have to go there. I must see him. I have to go. Pauline in and out comforting and caring. Feeling everything with me. Vitamins every few hours. Then food, sleep, vitamins, foot massage. Pauline, lighting candles. I lie in bed with phone books, phone numbers, memories . . . his recent throat infection and sick for two weeks. Thought that he had his father's throat cancer and would die. Called me that day and talked with Pauline. Then cut his mound of Venus on his hand. Stitches, distressed. Was he depressed? He died by the phone. Was that a metaphor for wanting to call somebody? But Laura said that he had made popcorn that morning. He always made it when he was happy. Family questions. Clues. Little sleep. Up at 5 A.M. Phone Dr. Mishra, Ellen Swartz. Giotto. Giotto calls back. You've had a hard year haven't you. I cry more for myself than for Mitchell. Don't feel guilty Linda. That's like telling a fish not to swim. But Pauline, Giotto, Chris, Mill, friends say don't feel guilty. Guilt is one of the first emotions to come with death . . . then anger, shock, disbelief . . . not in that order. Finally acceptance. But being the ex-wife and Mitchell's death possibly being suicide . . . accentuated and accelerated the natural grief. Pauline continued to counsel and prepare me. Reading from books, talking about her grandmother's death. That first night Moira came over and we all drink . . . do whatever you want. Shout, scream, cry. Moira giving permission and advice. Go to the funeral. Yes, you must complete that cycle. You must do that ritual. I am sick from drinking, from shock. Sleep in Paul's room with the phone. Pauline ministering and talking. Sunday A.M. I fly to Kansas. August 21. Where is Mitchell's body? I hadn't asked anyone. Mort and Barb called on Sunday and said could stay with them. Feel welcome. We want you here Linda. Come ahead. Pauline drives Jillene and me to the airport. 6:30 A.M. And then waits in line with me. I am sinking fast. She had packed a food package for me, high protein bars, fruit. She steers me to the plane. My body shakes. I'm weak. She seems to get even stronger than she already is. Is it the adrenalin that comes at the time of crisis? The plane ride to Dallas seems interminable, long, without end. Dallas. I call Sue Thornley. Good call. Supportive. Come and see me and spend time in San Francisco. I feel bolstered. Hang up, eat two bananas. Get on the plane and sit next to a man who looks exactly like Mitchell. I also see him all over the Dallas airport. Thirley, what's happening to me? I keep seeing Mitchell all over the Dallas airport. I saw you all over San Francisco when you left Rose. O.K. It's just loss I guess. I sneak looks at the man next to me. Can he see me looking at him? I'm spying. Mitchell's neck, hair, eyes, face. Older. I talk to him. Want him to be Mitchell. Read Elizabeth Kubler Ross. It's not the quantity but the quality of life that we're interested in. That helps. The quality of Mitchell's life was very incredible. He loved light. Pups look at the light in this room. Rose looks at this man and the light on his face. Lying in bed for hours surrounded with photo books . . . looking at light, people in light, rooms in light. My eyes are open very wide and have been since Friday at 11 when I heard the news. I arrive in K.C. Laura meets me. I talk and am hoarse. Can't talk loudly. We go to Mill and Net's for supper. The walk into the house that I was sure that I would never enter again. He died there at home. He died there. I walk in shaking. No life left in me. I walk past the phone. Stand on the spot where he died. I'm glued and can't move. People pour out of rooms, doors. It looks like a party but we all have the same thought . . . Mitchell is dead. We're from different classes, races, backgrounds, states, and countries, but unified in death. I hug Millie who walks around the kitchen, using the phone, greeting me on the spot where he died. I walk into the front room, hug Net. Jim and I cry. Warmth coming out of him. Net Jr. seems tired. Everyone there. Where's Grandmother Alice? I go

204

upstairs. She is on her way down. No words Alice. We're gripping each other's hands. I have no words. The vulnerability of grief is a language. It was an honor knowing you Linda. I'm surprised at her words. You have contributed to my life. Millie walks up. If you two want to talk go into the front room. Millie begins to cry. Recognition. Dinner a party atmosphere. Millie talks about donating Mitchell's eyes so now two people can see out of them. I'm surprised at her bravery. His corneas. His kidneys were not able to be used but they tried giving them away also. No talk of where he is . . . the funeral . . . and a feeling that no questions are to be asked. Closed. I walk between rooms and want to stand on the spot where he died. Monday I wake up wanting to see Mitchell's body. Wanting to see Mitchell. Where is he? Nobody mentions him. He is missed. It's as if he's there but he isn't. Or is he? I want to see him. Am desperate. I must tell Barbara. She calls the funeral home immediately and we make plans to go. I start pacing, restless. Not able to believe it. Wanting it, not wanting it. The drive interminable. We arrive. I run in and ask where he is. A somber sad man says you just missed the body. The casket is closed anyway. The body is at the crematorium. We go away and I can hardly walk yet adrenalin is high. Paradox. Drive back again. I must see him. Call the crematorium. Go over. I expect to see smoke stacks but it's just like another funeral home. Large. I run in. Wait ½ hour. I am breathing with difficulty. Internal combustion. Insides searing. Eyes wide open. Like a drug experience . . . seeing, hearing all. At high intensity. Highly motivated. A man of about 30 midwestern coloring and hair comes into the room. Signals. I charge out of my seat, energy propelling me. I hear him say that he's lying on a table sheets over him . . . etc. I run in. The room is 20 ft. x 50 ft. Mitchell's body is lying on a hospital table which is chrome, silver, antiseptic, institutional. Not in a slick coffin. Not in a suit but is lying on a table covered with a sheet. He is so available. Not dressed. I can get close. I can't believe what I am seeing. His face bloated a bit, certainly distorted. A hole the size of a silver dollar on his right cheek. His face intact but so changed. A pink putty fills the hole. Little pieces of it in his hair. His eyebrows ruffled not neat. Everything impassive, not mobile. Like sleep but too still for sleep. Are you asleep Mitchell? I touch his arm. Feel it cold and hard through the sheet. Must touch him. Eyes not there but donated so two people have his corneas. Somehow I would like to meet them. Lips tight. Nose funny. Left ear destroyed. The bullet still in his head? I pull the sheet down. Shocked by black stitches.

Autopsy. Reminded of the hospital pictures. His preparation for death in Rochester. Remembering days when he would come home from the hospital pale and silent . . . talking about corpses and the Sears clippers used to cut ribs. I remember the description and look at him and see it all mirrored in his body. I talk with him in whispers, wanting more time alone with him. Ask him how he is. How did it happen? Why? What happened Pups?? Shock, disbelief. Wanting to stay with him. Hold him. No repulsion. No fear. His nipples erect. Feet cold and nonresponsive even when I massage them. Blood stains on his toes. I arrange his hair. It's clean but needs fluffing. Then I remember the Tibetan Book of the Dead and whisper in his ear. Don't be afraid Mitchell. It's O.K. Pups. Go on. Don't be scared. Surrender. Whatever fears you are experiencing are only illusions. Go on and don't fear. Don't worry. No more worry. I whisper and tears fall on the sheet. I blow my nose on it not caring about the smell, the decay setting in. A strange smell . . . not his. Hard to identify. Wanting to lift the whole sheet . . . I can't get my eyes off of him . . . a blend of curiosity and love . . . wanting to be close. Wanting to participate in some way so that it can be tactile and real to me. I know best by touch, by contact, by closeness. Morton and I stand there. Holding hands. So glad for Morton. Right there. He and Barb were very responsive and kind. Morton leaves. More time alone. Then Tim says we're leaving. I go reluctantly, unwillingly. Pulling myself away. After that there began a whole series of events.

RITUAL IN BLACK AND WHITE:
Montano's Ritual and Oliveros's Response

Ellen Zweig

L inda Montano's piece, "Mitchell's Death," was the second-to-last piece in the three-day performance festival, "What's Cooking II," held April 21-23, 1978, at the Center for Music Experiment in San Diego. It had been three days of excellent music, dance, theater, performance art—and this last evening was no exception.

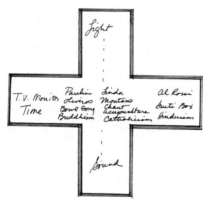

We had just seen Norma Jean Deak's "Jane Danger"; Y. L. Wong in a startling dance, "Call of Ancient Voices"; David Antin talking and rapidly changing clothes in one of the funniest performances I've ever seen him do. The mood of the evening was humor: Jane Danger learning to be a spy under the tutelage of Deak's dry wit; Wong's dance ending as she tore up a head of lettuce and threw it at the audience; David Antin exploring figures of speech by dressing in motorcycle leathers and rapidly changing hats and shirts, talking nonstop through it all. We were unprepared for the seriousness of Linda Montano's piece. She entered a dark performance area.

Clothed in black, her face was clown-white, and from her cheeks and forehead thin needles hanging from the skin shook and, shining, formed a precarious mask. She turned on a videotape and walked to a lectern which hid her—all but her white-masked face. She turned on a bright light that shone on the paper she would read, and behind her it lit the otherwise empty wall.

This was the ritual. Visuals: Linda Montano on videotape applying the make-up she was wearing in the performance. First, slowly she puts on the white face; then, even more slowly, she inserts long thin needles into the skin of her face. It doesn't look painful; there's no blood—only the slow needles which I later found out were being placed carefully in certain acupuncture points of the face. Next to the television set, seated cross-legged on a cushion, was Pauline Oliveros, with a Japanese bowl gong; next to her, Linda behind the lectern; and finally Al Rossi, cross-legged on another cushion, with a South Indian *sruti* box. Everyone wore black. Sound: The videotape was Linda's voice reading a journal, a description of the death of her ex-husband, a description made from precise detail. She read in a drone. Because of the tape delay, there was a feeling of echo and depth. Musical accompaniment came from Pauline Oliveros's voice singing "ooooh" (as in "blue"), an occasional hit of the Japanese gong, and the drone of Al Rossi's bellows.

The mood of the evening had changed quite suddenly; we were caught in the emotions of a mourning ritual. Eleanor Antin and Melvin Freilicher were sobbing in front of me; I was stunned. When the piece ended, Linda turned off the videotape and left the room. We sat in our seats. I had no idea how I'd ever leave that room or ever shake off that sense of deep mourning. And, although I felt that the piece must have been a cleansing for Linda as chief mourner, I had nowhere to go but further into that deep mourning that the details of "Mitchell's Death" had brought me to.

I didn't leave my seat, couldn't leave. I waited for the last piece on my program, which promised to be by Pauline Oliveros, untitled except by a picture of a spiral:

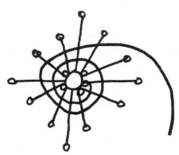

Oliveros's piece was also a ritual. Everyone was dressed in white. In the center of the spiral, the performers hit a large drum; others at the points of the design played clarinets. Still others played the rims of crystal glasses filled with water. Coryl Crane played a large glass bowl, rubbing her fingers around the rim; water shimmered a clear reflection to her whiteness. Ellen Band entered, two fluorescent green sticks hanging from her arms; she chanted a Hebrew chant which she had chosen herself, a tribute to the power of the word. She walked the spiral, slowly, almost painfully slowly. The music was a kind of drone, an otherwordly song, something wholly spiritual, something to lift us out of our bodies, to purify us.

As I sat, entranced by the ethereal sounds of Pauline Oliveros's music, I knew that I had witnessed the work of a true community. This piece had been planned carefully and with love to give us something in place of mourning. I was witnessing perhaps for the first time a community of artists who loved each other and who could bring that love to an audience of friends and strangers. And I was involved in a series of rituals performed by a group of people who knew the true power of ritual, knew how to use that power for the good of the individual (Linda, as chief mourner) and of the community. We left, perhaps as the audiences had left the Greek theater of the past, cleansed and brought together in the cleansing.

Pauline Oliveros, Linda Montano, and Al Rossi at the Center for Music Experiment, San Diego, 1978. Photograph by Robert Gross

Video

THE VIDEO-POETRY WORK-SHOP / LAKE PLACID

Stephen Vincent

FROM 1975 TO 1977, Don Grabau, Allan King, and Barbara Kristaponis developed and sustained the Video-Poetry Performing Workshop on the edge of Lake Placid. During the summers of those years, courtesy of grants from the New York Arts Council and others, they were able to invite a number of video-artists and poets to work together to create poem-centered performance pieces. Usually the artist and the poet in company with students in the program would work together night and day for a week to pull together a Saturday night public performance.

I was invited to perform during the summer of 1976. My project would be to work with the staff and students to create a piece around my poem *The Ballad of Artie Bremer*. (Bremer, as you might remember, was the young constantly smiling man who tried to assassinate George Wallace). The poem had been published as a small book with crow-quill

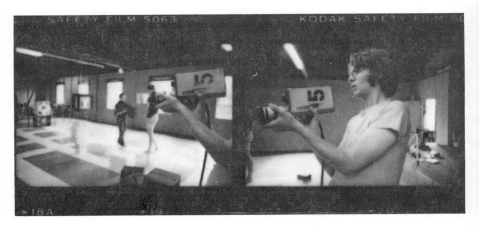

pen drawings of Bremer and his various artifacts by Michael Myers. And this would be my opportunity to take the poem and the conception of the book out into a larger space and world.

At Lake Placid, instead of just preparing to read the poem from behind a podium on a stage, I found myself with what seemed an incredible set of resources usually not easily accessible to the institutionally unaffiliated poet in the City. The workshop was located in an abandoned community hall among some trees on a cliff near the edge of the lake. Inside were at least twenty tv monitors, a room of editing tables, a stage, and an open performance space that could be used in almost any way. Across the middle rafter of the room, which was about one hundred feet long, an elaborate rope jitney held three monitors in wooden cages. One was able to slide back and forth, high and parallel to the rafter, and the other two hung parallel, fifteen feet apart, able to move either up or down on the vertical as the top set moved horizontally.

Video was integral to the work. During the week, as we developed the performance space, we would take the camera out on the street. The idea was to get footage that would amplify the performed character of

poem. We spent three hours in front of a dime store asking people if they remembered: "Who was Artie Bremer?" Many would make imaginative guesses (*a dancer, a new rock star*) but the only black person we saw that day, slightly embarrassed at the question, remembered. "Wasn't he the man who shot Wallace?" We made footage of pinball machines and the game of pong, the bell and *ping* sounds working to the edge of Bremer's psychosis. Back at the studio, I would do a thirty-minute tape, facing my face in the video while doing an obsessed rendering of episodes from Bremer's *Diary* from memory. (As he missed a try at Nixon in Toronto from a gas station because Nixon's limousine went by too fast, or tried to lose his virginity in a massage parlor in New York City).

The tapes would all become part of a master tape that would be orchestrated into the performance, which we were also working on. The audience would sit on pillows on the stage and below. The rest of the

room became a cage with black-and-white crepe-paper bars hooked from rafter to floor. The floor itself was patterned with crossing bars, lines of black-and-white construction paper, upon which, in turn, were stacked about a dozen cardboard boxes covered with either black or white paper. In addition to the three monitors on the jitney that faced the audience from the other end of the cage, stacks of video monitors stood in each remaining corner and in the space on the side directly behind where I would read the poem from within the "cage."

Besides myself, during the performance two dancers, a man and a woman, would move across the paper bars on the floor. The two would intersect at the corners, or in the actual row, where they would exchange and build precarious structures with the black-and-white boxes. On the night of the performance, besides the moving dancers, one of the camera people would also move while recording the action, and the

images would be transmitted into several of the monitors—the ones not transmitting the edited master tape of the street materials and the Bremer monologue. My actual reading of the poem, instead of being seven or eight minutes, was expanded to the half-hour. Long pauses in my reading would allow more focus to be put on the dancers at various points, and on the tapes at others. At times I would improvise off the monologue, getting into echo repetitions with the microphone, and then repeating various elements of the text. In effect the work was a combination of a whole variety of informations, many of them colliding against each other, or finding resonance or harmony, in order to create an expanded whole.

The ritual of pulling together the performance, collecting the street footage, interviewing the personae of the poem, pulling together the set, working with the dancers, making the master tape, creating the whole Bremerish world, I found to be an incredible expansion of the original poem. And then doing the performance, feeling the arrival of that. And, as final act, going with the audience, tearing down the set, kicking it out the door—all the crepe paper and boxes, going to the edge of the lake to burn the set down, including a copy of the book in the fire, purging the air of Bremer, the crippled assassin—it became an enormous event.

It was a definite turn away from the conventional use of video to record poetry readings. I always had been turned off by that dull process of pointing the camera at the poet and letting it roll for the reading, with

maybe a few angle and hand shots, an odd approach to archives. I could never imagine sitting through a replay of most of that stuff. An audio-tape à la radio would be just fine; it would let the imagination move. The fact, as at the Workshop, that the cameras and tapes could not only diversify space but that video could bring information into the poem; work as ambiguity, juxtaposition; act as a way of amplifying the line and content of the poem in multiple ways, was very attractive and a courageous and imaginative effort on the parts of Don, Allan, and Barbara.

Unfortunately, for various reasons and lack of fuller support, the workshop had to close down in the winter of 1977. What follows are other accounts by the poet Faye Kicknosway and Don Grabau, a poet and a coordinator. The photos are by Barbara Kristaponis and the graphics are by Allan King.

FROM 2ND CHANCE MAN:
The Cigarette Poem

Faye Kicknosway

Part II: Donald

"—somehow the impressions of a living mind are absorbed and stored by the environment. They remain dormant until someone who is telepathically responsive to them arrives on the scene. Then they set off the hallucinatory process in that person's mind and somebody sees a ghost."—James Raymond Wolfe*

place.
especially another place. The solidity of bone and muscle kept isolated from the distance moving around the ear, the cameras in the room
i come to
two-dimensional—flattening; and this a bowl, an inversion, a place of the spirit overlooked by a mountain named white face and white-faced with clouds.
here.
lake placid, saranac lake.
i have come to a sacred place. a meeting place with my friends. invited here, entered through the rocks and mountains. lakes. and donald and i have been talking. he about the yucatan and this place, somehow related. and the video room, the tvs all around. and the equipment. everything focussed on the two-dimensional.
and what you see isnt real. your eye has the habit of the pictures and fills in. holes. black and white holes. not real at all. not even in your eye.
the habit of vision, of thinking you see. but you remember. re/member reality. over and over. a system. habit.
warned at watertown: "you travellun alone?" chawing on his donut, old grisly man. "you got another 3hrs ta go." and a slow, menacing grin. "would keep to the main roads if i was you."
going 65. curves and up and down. remembering pieces of indian songs from

---

* In "Can Mental Telepathy Trigger a Haunting?" *Occult Magazine,* vol. 5, no. 1, April 1974, p. 68.

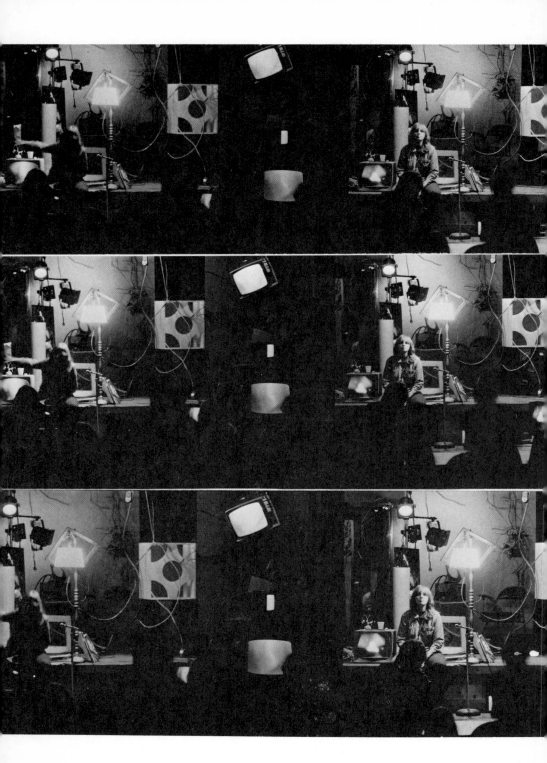

my early pow wow days. singing them. unstrung to any songs, not even
together in any part, except that memory breaking loose—maybe it the cow-
boy from the trees, maybe it the bandit with the dimmed perception of
wholeness, the slicked hair, the china-cold eye, the "reelity" i carry. indian
songs, broken and scattered in the car. maybe the bodies of the collective
people singing, one window open, thin voices from the rock, time caught in
these roads. the place of the 6 nations. and its sioux i remember. sioux, here, in
this place so different from their country, their razor grass, badland country. i
know them cowboys, them tag playing, greaser-cowboys. i always been their
indian. "hey, compadres, nishnobs; help."
no wonder im in a video place, to watch the flat get flatter. water held until its
dust. white spots/black
spots. the eye completing from a set/habit what it does not see. what it
supposes. poses. the eye. misconnection to the other organs. cones imbalanced.
ritual blinking. subliminal. the eye is prisoner of garbage: 20 minutes is 20
years long. mothers frequency jams inner-ear balance of child. color red
demands spirits pass through it to the unseen vibrations. child, electric blip in
video tape, skin-oil distortions. useless channel out. mother vertical hold.
ulcers a habit of the eye, of the landscape coded, repeated. inversion happens
when the landscape is a bowl. fills with spirit.
mountain talks spirit as moisture. spirit moves down the highway. the living
are asleep, operatives of the spirit. perfect place for "reelity." cameras. vision
dont see; vision penetrates. plugs hang from ceiling. floral: stamens moving.
connections of spirit. video sucks the energy out. i sat, watched hrs of it. could
hardly move. has to be exorcism, as way ghosts speak. tv set is reindeer mask,
cave shaman speaks through it.
mystic place. and donald my good companion. and allen. and barbara. and
janice. we talk of the water and the mountains, of opposites, of the conjoining
of elements, of hands and feet, left and right, of moving as vision in this visual
place.
visual. visceral. the mountain names are body parts: white face, elbow, knee.
the landscape turned human, us walking on it, in it.
the event of what seems to be real, is reel only.
to look ahead at the image being taped, you look behind, at the tv screen where
the image is happening.
medusa. the spots your eye connects as a deliberate way of not seeing. "these
dots make this picture."
the eye stays asleep.
swallowed by spirit, singing me through the open window.
"come out," i say to it. "come out."
and it does.
the dead breathe; the mountain white with their breath. spooky place, being
cooked in the mountains belly. lying flat, crawling to the sacred chamber where
the stored images secure reality. "this bison, I want him dead outside." crawl
out and find him dead.
for exorcism you go to high ground. frequency quick here. you gather teeth
from the air, put them through ghost images. they get strong, catch in video

tubes, radio bands of woman at sink, child at lunch, man at newspaper, shoes off, look sidewize, something passing through the room—air; "close that window, willya?" crazy, in-the-spots-between-the-picture 11 o'clock news, not think "banana" or "beer," think "bear," think pine tar in hair, legs bristle, have to blink—"whaddya put in that stew?"—shamans in mountains—lake placid—play the sound of each chakra, a noise peculiar to the livng room happens, a passion, raw, opens.
lines break. forces. the genitals rear back in their skins.
"donald, you bring me to a sacred place," i say. we sit in howard johnsons. "scary place. poetry can get visible here. its been dark, waiting. its been words, landscape painting, no need for sound in it, all these years, can be free of that. poetry psychic breathing. here can reel, as in music, dance, can reel, as in drunken or ecstatic. poetry not secular, not pruned of its nails, its knees, not pages in front of the face or shirted, lifebuoy/sweat smelling po-ets. garden, re-entry to the eye as magic, you say "yes" to what inhabits you, get friendly with it, it gives you the shape of bear or hedge. a poetry of no words, of visuals and sound combined/combining different always because metabolic level changes, breathing different in human/earth thing always. poetry. breathing." bowl. belly-bowl. lake placid. gestation with ghost images. i am brought back into my parent, but it is my male parent. and i will be born again. his legs spread toward the west. his fingers knot in his belly. i will eat his intestines, his liver, his stomach. i will birth slow. i will chew the hair of his scrotum, his legs, let him know what it is to birth a flesh-spirit. let him roll and wonder what horrible thing he ate to shit me.

VIDEO POETRY
In the Adirondacks

Don Grabau and Al King,
with photographs by Barbara Kristaponis

Video. The image: fire
over water. So much space from here to there. In
between. Ghosts moving from mountain
to mountain. Tamalpais looking eastward
to Whiteface: enthusiasm. A name missing, Wahopartenie, Tahawus, he
splits the sky; thunder
rolls out of the earth. The image: television on the mountain,
video-poetry. Proceed with
caution: who is where? I take warning from the ghost of
the electric monk:

> *"Geography is in trouble all over*
> *Lograire."*

Begin here. Again. When we began to combine poetry with video we did not
know how to do it or where to begin. Janice wrote a poem: short & simple:

> *I wake up*
> *and see you. You*
> *are walking toward me*
> *smiling, talking.*
> *And behind you*
> *I see you. You are walking*
> *toward me*
> *smiling, talking.*
>
> *O god, that is horror.*
> *I push the button:*
> *Cynic*

We used it as a script. Janice lay down on a patterned purple, red, & blue
spread. I held a Porta-Pak camera (wide-angle lens) very close to her face, left
side up: profile. Filled the tv screen with that image. Al & Keith put another
camera on a tripod, pointed it at Al. White background. Both cameras fed into
a mixer. We switched Al into negative; he became a white silhouette. We
superimposed the images. Added music. Worked and reworked it. Timing. The
tape begins: gray screen, music with voice of woman, distant & humming
low . . . the image fades up: an arabesque pattern on screen left moving into

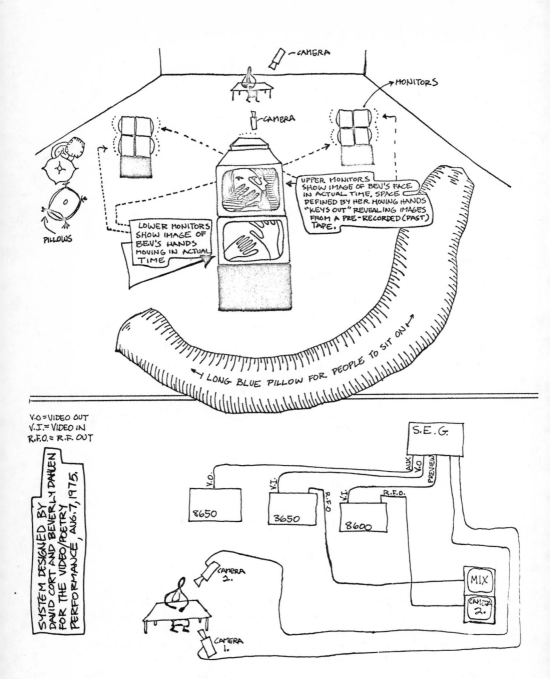

CAMERA

MONITORS

CAMERA

UPPER MONITORS SHOW IMAGE OF BEV'S FACE IN ACTUAL TIME. SPACE DEFINED BY HER MOVING HANDS "KEYS OUT" REVEALING IMAGES FROM A PRE-RECORDED (PAST) TAPE.

LOWER MONITORS SHOW IMAGE OF BEV'S HANDS MOVING IN ACTUAL TIME

PILLOWS

1 LONG BLUE PILLOW FOR PEOPLE TO SIT ON

V.O = VIDEO OUT
V.I. = VIDEO IN
R.F.O. = R.F. OUT

SYSTEM DESIGNED BY DAVID CORT AND BEVERLY DAHLEN FOR THE VIDEO/POETRY PERFORMANCE, AUG. 7, 1975.

S.E.G.

AUX
V.O
PREVIEW

V.O

V.I.

R.F.O

V.I.

R.F.O.

8650

3650

8600

CAMERA 2.

MIX

CAMERA 2.

CAMERA 1.

222

— TIME DELAY SYSTEMS —

① VISUAL DELAY

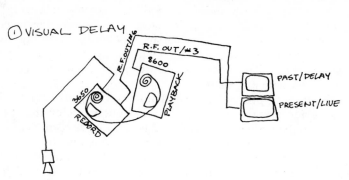

R.F. OUT/#6
R.F. OUT/#3
8600
PLAYBACK
3650
RECORD

PAST/DELAY

PRESENT/LIVE

② AUDIO AND VISUAL DELAY

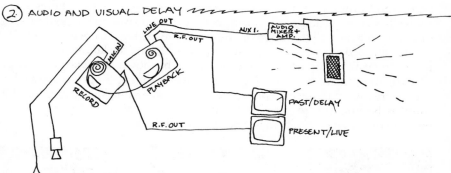

LINE OUT
AUX 1.
AUDIO MIXER + AMP.
R.F. OUT
MIC IN
RECORD
PLAYBACK
R.F. OUT
PAST/DELAY
PRESENT/LIVE

③ MIXED VISUALS AND AUDIO DELAY

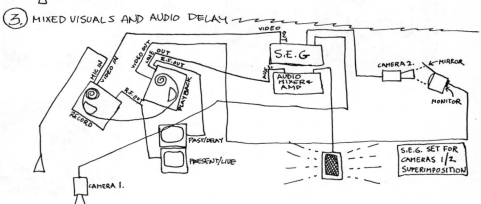

VIDEO
VIDEO OUT
LINE OUT
R.F. OUT
S.E.G
AUX
AUDIO MIXER + AMP
CAMERA 2.
MIRROR
MIC IN
VIDEO IN
R.F. OUT
PLAYBACK
RECORD
MONITOR
PAST/DELAY
PRESENT/LIVE
CAMERA 1.
S.E.G. SET FOR CAMERAS 1/2 SUPERIMPOSITION

[IN EACH SYSTEM, A LINE FROM VIDEO OUT TO VIDEO IN CONNECTS THE 2 DECKS USED.]
[THIS PRODUCES A GREATER STABILITY IN THE 2 IMAGES]

Janice's face screen right. Stillness. Her eyes open. A white figure moves out of screen left, and walks toward her, enters her face, & disappears. Same figure re-enters, same pattern repeated. At the word "god" her face goes negative; I move my camera closer until only her eye is left large on the screen. She never speaks the last word; it appears in her face when she says "button"; it is liquid & constantly changing in motion. It grows larger with her eye & dominates the screen; you see her eye thru it. The process is called keying; the poem/tape ends there. And that is how/where we began.

We stayed with this basic process for several months. Using prewritten poems as scripts and video as a means of visually acting out or interpreting the words. Change occurred mostly in the form of additions: dance & mime, cracked mirrors, slide projections. The emphasis was on video-poetry as a group process: four to ten people working together with the poet trying to develop a shared sense of the rhythm—meaning—breathing/voice of the poem. During this process the poet was not always or only *on camera* but present centrally as the speaker of the poem, as the person providing the rhythm—mood from which all other activity radiated outward: poet/poem as Seed.

But this process was still geared toward producing the famous end result, the WORKOFART, a tape. Something that would be shown to an audience. And it was apparent to everyone involved in the process that it, *the process,* was the active, creative, sharing experience from which something new emerged. The problem became how to extend this activity to "the audience." So we began to invite people to participate in live performances.

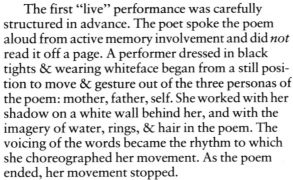

The first "live" performance was carefully structured in advance. The poet spoke the poem aloud from active memory involvement and did *not* read it off a page. A performer dressed in black tights & wearing whiteface began from a still position to move & gesture out of the three personas of the poem: mother, father, self. She worked with her shadow on a white wall behind her, and with the imagery of water, rings, & hair in the poem. The voicing of the words became the rhythm to which she choreographed her movement. As the poem ended, her movement stopped.

That was the event as seen live in the room, but the addition of video extended it to three tv screens placed around the room. What was happening in each of those screens was something else again;

three people from the audience, each with a camera, were selecting and combining elements of the event to create three new & simultaneous ones. And they too were choreographing the poem according to the rhythm they felt in the voice. How they moved with the camera, whether they showed the real performer or the shadow on the wall, whether they filled the screen with only a hand or a b&w abstract form in or out of focus effected the final experience of the event as video-poem.

After a performance like this feedback can be very good. You can replay each tape & talk about it; sometimes people want to repeat the event so they can tighten up their conception—change this or that aspect of their camera work or ask the performer or poet to modify the words, gestures, or rhythm. After this particular event, for instance, a woman urges us to add her humming to the reading; someone else added a loud, shrill scream at a particular word as the poet spoke. A man noticed a doll's head in the room and wanted to bring it into the picture . . . & there is talk, talk, talk all around this. As people alternately use the cameras & equipment they become increasingly involved. There are usually enough goof-ups that the mood becomes relaxed and feelings flow.

All this can have a bizarre effect on the poet. His/her work becomes public property, in a sense, and s/he must let go of it—watch it go thru changes. That experience can reveal to you aspects of your work that you've never seen or dealt with before. Why does that word occurring at that moment in the poem make someone want to scream? Don't ask; let them scream, & experience it yourself. let the man put the doll's head in the act; if it doesn't work for you, tell him why. Take up a camera yourself & tape as you speak the poem; ask someone else present to act out or mime to the poem. Form sound groups: a rhythm set, an echo set. Play.

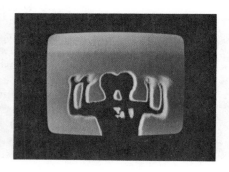

The unique contribution of video to this kind of performance is its immediacy. You see what you are taping as you tape it; tv sets placed around the room display whatever you are framing in your camera. Everyone present sees it; you see it. So you don't have to hide behind your camera with your eye glued to the viewfinder. You can watch what you're doing in the tv sets along with everyone else. And that connects you to the process—there is no delay, as in film. The flow is not stopped but loops back on itself. Instant feedback. Change: room/space—tv/space & in between them both, outside is VIDEOSPACE.

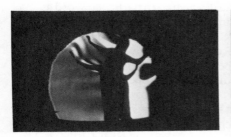

Videospace: outside/inside; like opening the *I Ching* and walking into it—the Land of Oz. Its effect on a poet is intense—where is the poem? Is it what you thought you were going to speak, is it on a page in front of you, or is it happening here/now? What is going on in those tv screens? Should you concentrate on your poem & speak it to the "real" people present in this "real" room or play inside the *fantasy(?)* of the screen? Look how your arm melts into light! If you are not fighting yourself, if you are not caught up in a schizy perception of two realities at once, you move instantly into Videospace . . . a very nice place to be. Haptic. Proprioceptive. Anything goes. And there goes your old poem you thought you were so interested in. So? Play, improvise. There are no mistakes; mistakes become discovery.

But that is a total challenge. And I have yet to experience any poet fully accepting it.

There is too much dazzle; too many incredible tricks . . . one of those "technicians" is keying you, another one has turned his camera into the screen . . . long lines of you extend into god knows where: keying; feedback. You yourself want to move your hand back & forth because you can see it on the tv screen, and when you move it this way there is a hole in it, and in the hole there is your eye, and doesn't this remind you of that old poem you wrote. And so on.

It seems to me there are three possible solutions to this dilemma:

1. make the *prewritten poem* central, use it as a script, and use video with it in a "filmic" sense;

2. use the prewritten poem to *improvise* with, experiment with the video as pure video, & combine/ choreograph the two, selecting & controlling all effects; or

3. saturate yourself with Videospace, use no prewritten poem, but create, speak, voice, sing *in that moment*.

In the summer of 1976 we tried all three. all three.

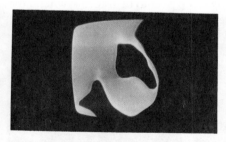

The Center for Music, Drama and Art in Lake Placid, New York, which sponsors the Video Center, gave us additional funds & support so that we could invite guest artists from the fields of video & poetry to work with us last summer in a special Video-Poetry Workshop. With their help, and funds from Poets & Writers, Inc., and the New York State Council on the Arts, we were able to explore further the concept of video-poetry, and to offer free performances to the public.

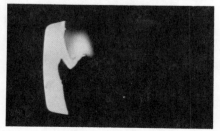

227

We invited two poets—Faye Kicknosway and Beverly Dahlen—and one video artist—David Cort—to participate in the workshop. All of us were familiar with their work: David is exploring video & poetry in a number of video systems he has designed which give the poet understanding & a good measure of control over how & when her/his image will be effected; Faye & Beverly are two poets whose styles and methods of reading are extraordinarily varied & who are open to experimentation. The workshop was an exciting, frustrating, & sometimes hectic success.

Faye arrived toward the end of June, observed that the area is a geographical bowl, gave homage to the Mountain, Wahopartenie, with her *Grandfather* poem, & set to work. She agreed to structure the video-poetry performance around the idea of the poet as Shaman and the problem of the proscenium stage.

Performance

8:00 p.m. light outside. light in-
side. people begin to come in; the stage
hung with wires, broken mirrors, tv sets
all over the theater—hanging upside
down & crooked on the stage. people on
their screens saying poetry o yeah, sure.
when is it, where? me come o no, i read
Longfellow when i need it. street inter-
views playing back. everyone settles in.
darkness. faye's voice over the speaker
system, pre-recorded:

    All these voices; whose house am I?

the voice continues developing a theme: karma, inheritance, the past, old things, clutter. the stage fills with blue light. no poet to be seen. anywhere. the voice of the past with no body. the tv screens begin to light up and an image occurs: long shot of a foot . . . the camera zooms in/slow: the voice begins again:

the cat
approaches and my life
discharges small green islands of meat
and blood, small blue faces knit
from the rags feeling can not absorb. the cat
approaches, licking the tiny pockets
of its grief. the cat
approaches, its winter arms burning,
its soft flesh burning. the cat
approaches and it is windows and photographs,
it is dwarves
coming loose from paintings, skin
coming loose from the heart. the cat
approaches and its fur is stiff and spiney and
it chews its whiskers with its leather
teeth. the cat

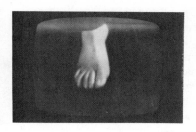

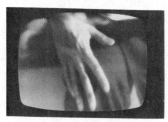

approaches and its red hooves
dig my heart open. the cat
approaches and it is dust
rising from the nest of the universe
and i sleep
between its claws, blind
as salt, blind
as wood. the cat
approaches and its razor tongue
kisses the moon awake, kisses stars
loose from heaven. the cat
approaches and the earth, and the things of
the earth
yammer and yowl and drown in the thick sea
of its throat. the cat
approaches and the wind digs its hands into the mud
of my legs,
my feet
and i escape down
into the earth as roots and clay. the cat
approaches and dreams climb the chemic moisture
of its fur. the cat
approaches and its hearts noise, its wings
noise fits my body and my hands sweat,
my belly sweats and i

am the cat, moving
through the window of your dream, moving
through the earth of your dream,
the fire of your dream,
as blossoms and fingers,
as seaweed and hair,
as gemstones and apples; i

am the cat and i
move as moonlight,
as firelight,
as lamplight through
the thin red branches of your lips, the thick green branches of your eyes.

O.K. So that was a prerecorded tape playing on fifteen tv sets placed around the theater. It is an example of a controlled & structured "filmic" video tape. Two cameras rhythmically exploring the body language of the poet reading. It begins from a distance, moves in closer to the foot, and gradually climbs up thru the hands to the face of the poet who is revealed directly, openly at the end.

At which point the actual poet present moves out of the blue light of the mirrored stage & comes toward the audience. The Mystery is being dropped and Faye feels good—you can hear it in her voice: "i wake, my friend, i/wake. and my eyes stun/you. and my voice shakes/you. i wake, and look/for you, look at/you . . ."

Faye arrives at the foot of the stage, sits down & finishes the poem. There is laughter & applause. She talks a bit about what we think we are doing, reads more poems (no video), and we all take a coffee break.

The second half was performed in a video system using four cameras looped thru a mixer. One camera fixed on a tripod showing a portrait of Beethoven; another tripod camera fixed on Faye & keyed so that she & Beethoven were imagistically mixed; Keith hand-held a third camera pointing angularly into a tv screen for pulsing feedback patterns; and the final camera passed from hand to hand thru the audience so that we could all mix our faces & blend into the process. Faye read poem-letters to B/ven & her voice was mixed with the piano version of HIS FIFTH. Organized madness. Who is who? What is art? Us.

The final event was a combination of live & prerecorded work: we began by playing an earlier group tape on which Faye read a long mantra/poem, "Blue China Plates" . . . the images on it of all of us playing, dancing, wearing cups on our heads, running in & out of the camera eye & Faye orchestrating the entire happening with this impossible, crazy poem . . . "blue, blue, blue china plates . . ." about ten lines into the taped poem. At the refrain, Faye began to read *live* with/against herself thru the same piece: "blue china plates come in envelopes from europe/you are in the middle of them dressed/like harpo marx. . . ." Thru use of a gen-lock we moved back & forth in time from video images of the past to the present . . . ourselves & our voices mingling over & over in rondo form . . . "blue, blue, blue china plates wearing stockings & short skirts/not blinking, photographed as refrigerators, with deep/voices, announcing the weather over the radio . . ."

The driving, angry/happy chantlike rhythm of the poem mixed with itself thru the sound system had an incredible effect on all of us. Faye ended it completely exhausted & throwing her arms up into the air crying: "And *that* was just for fun!"

The performance ended right there on a note of celebration.

The energy released by that performance was startling. Poet; image boxes; audience—a genuine circuit of interplay. Video. An extension of the nervous system; poet/audience . . . synapses woven together one to another. Hook in/up; wires run like arteries all over the area. Free cameras; we can pick them up & feed into each other: gestures, movements, sounds, a group ritual. All our selves reflected back to us. We move in a physical space—thru the wires, lenses, and electricity we move into Videospace . . . a ritual space where gravity, cause–effect, time can be transcended. We create or rediscover a new breathing: videopoetry.

With the arrival of Bev and David in August we were ready for a new go at it. And after much reading & discussion of Bev's work we decided on an approach . . . David would design a video system that would plunge Bev headfirst into Videospace. There would be no hocus-pocus about it; the system would be totally visible—no darkness or air of magick about it. Together they would work out a detailed performance of six or seven poems that fused the visual & the verbal & revealed itself as video-poetry, & we would repeat that work at the performance and then open up the system to the audience for participation. The system was designed to incorporate aux tapes that could be mixed with the poet's live reading; several of us prepared tapes exploring the tree, water, rock imagery of the poems. The second stage of the event was centered in a time-delay/feedback system . . . a pure expression of video where the poet can work with a kind of image echo & decay—you can watch yourself repeat the same gesture, listen to yourself say the same words, see/feel/ hear them literally recede into oblivion; & all the while new gestures, images, sounds take their place. Bev found *the* poem that seemed written for just such an experience: "I don't understand this light these/burns which finding them go all the way/back to what/not single event/ though I can't be sure/I can't remember . . . " Each word echoing on the other while image after image of Bev speaking dissolved in the light.

Performance

Bright light; tv sets, cables, mikes—everything visible. Bev and David talk about the system: how it works, what it feels like. There are three columns of four tvs (each) arranged in a semi-circular pattern; six are facing inward toward the poet & six outward to the audience . . . the poet centered in "the ring of bone"

—Lew Welch's famous description of Videospace.

Beverly takes her seat and begins to speak the first poem: it is designed as a two-channel work . . . in each column one tv set (lower) shows Bev's hands folded, another (upper) shows her face from waist up:

It is a gesture I do
that grew
out of my mother
in me.

As she speaks the lines she moves her hands; they are keyed & thru them you begin to catch glimpses of her face close-up, fingers to her lips. It is a beautifully complex image displayed on the top tv set in each column: Bev's real-time face, a prerecorded face with fingers to lips, and a moving "cut-out" of her hands that blends one facial image with the other . . . "I am trying to remember/what she/was afraid to say/all those/years, fingers folded/against her mouth,/head turned away."

This same care & precision marked the performance of each poem. It is something that is perhaps hard to appreciate unless you have experienced the difficulty firsthand of trying to fuse video & poetry . . . the subtle, layered imagery of a poem can get lost if you opt for a too-literal approach. You don't necessarily want to look at an apple on twelve screens every time you hear apple.

At the conclusion of this set of prepared pieces we opened the system to the audience. . . . Some people came up and read their own poems in the system & others worked with Bev & their individual prerecorded tapes. After an initial apprehensive air . . . what can I do in there? The mood relaxed & people began to just play in the system. . . . What happened shortly after that was a pure treat: "The Lady in the Chinese Tomb."

was buried in 20 layers of silk
in three locked boxes
2100 years ago.

I see her coffins in a dream
one above another
hovering.

It is part of the puzzle: who she was
in her great death provided for
so many years

rises now the perfected
object of all those labors.

Her pots of food.   Her tea-sets.   Her
comb.   Her brass mirror.

It is all we have: this dug-up
stuff.   This leather corpse.

They say she was a very great lady.

In China
now
they are digging up the great ladies
and looking hard at them.

You couldn't call "The Chinese Lady" an accident; David had very carefully prepared a system, Beverly had already written the poem. But it was one of those fortuitous, synchronistic events that elated all of us as it happened. Lydie was massaging her face in Videospace; Barbara, Janice, and Karen were passing their hands over her eyes; Keith & I were inserting feedback and tearing the key; and Mike was wandering around with a Porta-Pak and caught the whole thing off the screen.

When the image of Lydie's face began to split & bubble with pulses of light everyone cried out "poem! poem!" and Bev brought "The Chinese Lady" into the world . . . video-poetry: a feeling that melded us all with ooh's and aah's into one united creative effort.

And the performance ended after at least an hour of everyone present playing in time-delay.

And where do we go from there? Winter is here now; snow all over Whiteface. Mountain shadow. Tahawus . . . lots of cold & silence.

We are concentrating on community documentaries & teaching basic video. And we are continuing to experiment with video-poetry: Al has just set up a two-channel mirror-image matrix that promises hours of fun & discovery,

& poetry is falling out all over the place in the form of snow. We are up to our ears in it & looking forward to the summer when we hope to move into color and deeper exploration of video-poetry as live & improvised performances shared free with the public. We are committed to the belief that videotape is not a WORKOFART, but merely a catalyst for the art process . . . and to quote David Ross even further:

If video art tends to blur the line between art and life and make less of the difference between artist and viewer, perhaps it is because, as Gregory Bateson notes in Steps to an Ecology of Mind, *we are approaching a culture where we, like the Balinese, can have no art, but rather do everything well.*

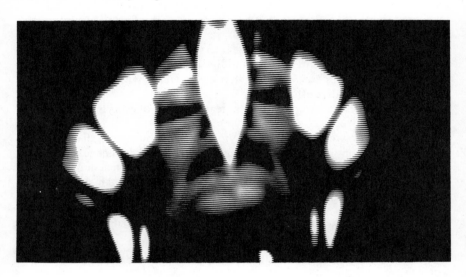

Disc & Cassette

From "The Aesthetics of Silence"

Susan Sontag

. . . another use for silence: furnishing or aiding speech to attain its maximum integrity or seriousness. Everyone has experienced how, when punctuated by long silences, words weigh more; they become almost palpable. Or how, when one talks less, one begins feeling more fully one's physical presence in a given space. Silence undermines "bad speech," by which I mean dissociated speech—speech dissociated from the body (and, therefore, from feeling), speech not organically informed by the sensuous presence and concrete particularity of the speaker and by the individual occasion for using language. Unmoored from the body, speech deteriorates. It becomes false, inane, ignoble, weightless. Silence can inhibit or counter-act this tendency, providing a kind of ballast, monitoring and even correcting language when it becomes inauthentic.

From "The Aesthetics of Silence," in *Styles of Radical Will* by Susan Sontag, Farrar, Straus and Giroux, 1969, p. 20.

Speech: as It Falls: Is Poetry

More Notes on Oral Poetry

Cid Corman

*A word is dead
When it is said,
Some say.*

*I say it just
begins to live
That day.*

—Emily Dickinson (1872?)

MUCH TOO SLOW is it dawning on some that hearing is far more acute in man than seeing. As a poet friend today remarked on hearing me say this—of his newborn baby—Already we draw meaning from each cry and grunt and breath.

The spoken word—if it is unrehearsed—if it is given, as it usually is, to event, to occasion—is and must be poetry. It is of an economy of force that is operative with a constancy that no other form of human address has to offer. And it doesnt—that is the essence of its economy

Reprinted from *Word for Word/Essays on the Arts of Language,* vol. 1, Santa Barbara: Black Sparrow Press, 1977, pp. 83–87. Originally published in *Origin,* 3rd series, no. 11, October 1968.

precisely—negate the other senses, but rather evokes them more. A little reflection tells us that we see more with hearing/saying than with our eyes alone and at a depth of vision that sight alone cannot procure. Indeed, we have to turn to the finest painting and sculpture and architecture to approach equal possibility.

But speech is of an overwhelming immediacy. And it penetrates with a more coherent intimacy than even music, for we know the faces of speech better than we know musical combinations.

In fact, speech is not only OF body, it is our most intimate form of relation. But, and this is a point that warrants stressing, it is neither separate from the body, nor does it transcend the body.

I

---

in 1954, in Paris, with a wire-recorder lent me by the American Fulbright Commission—all that they had at that time, I recorded my first improvised poems. (My first essays on ORAL POETRY date from that experience and that, without any prompting on my part, they should suddenly be referred to by younger people, when they went unnoticed almost completely at the time, is an omen I can hardly ignore.)

It may be worth being explicit about what I mean by "improvised poems." The poems are immediate: they are not planned in advance and there is absolutely no text. Naturally, I am thinking of poems all the time and the improvisations are likely to open from some already well-mulled base. But the moment the machine is in motion there is no time to reflect—except WITHIN event. And I must be prepared to accommodate the accidental—whatever chance sounds may enter or visual recognitions, etc. I usually project—not too many or I may forget and have, as a matter of fact, in longer sequences. And, of course, if I should feel so prompted, I could exceed the stated limit. But I take the limitation as an extra tension and ground: it compels a more acute concentration.

The poems have, as it happens, NOT been revised in ANY way and NONE, as it happens, have been erased. For, in such poems, there can be no "mistake": error is an active component here. It is always likely and always pertinent.

Those poems, again as it happens, made in Paris, for one reason or another, remained unheard by me until a month ago. Perhaps the extended interval, during which my work had undergone considerable metamorphosis, was salutary. In any case, it meant "distance" for cooler judgment. (At the time when they were made, my initial impression was one of startled elation—for I felt that something decisive had occurred, accidentally on purpose, you might say.)

The re-hearing after so many years, was far more startling and elating, for the poems had not lost any of their original force, but in addition they carried for me a total recall of the scene—to textures, smells, physical space, and psychic condition. Certainly the most vivid recall experience of my life.

It reminded me of my first aural shock. At the end of World War II a brief recording made by a childhood friend who was killed during the war was played by a mutual friend. The voice was of such stunning accuracy and intimacy that I could hardly breathe: the effect was almost TOO MUCH. The vivacity of the boy was wholly present again and his absence took on such relief as to make me wonder what "spirit" might be.

2
_____

As a result of hearing the old recording—rerecorded some years ago by a friend onto tape—I have started again at improvising poems, but with the chance of greater extension—with my own equipment and with more time for it—I mean to push it along the solitary vocal arc as far as possible—without any technical trickery.

Then—when I feel I have reached the limit, my limits, of working alone and "straight"—I want to improvise with a small audience—a few friends or maybe just one other person. And this can be done also, to some extent, with distances between. Then with large audiences. Then various technical possibilities can be brought into play—but with very careful consideration of what each "device" means or may mean in terms of the event.

It may be realized, even by those of you who are unfamiliar with the experience, that to improvise poems alone in the face of the machine is, in a sense, THE human situation par excellence. The machine, going, imposes a TIME that is no longer that of the clock though it is strictly sequential, serial (if you will). And the time is one of psychic tensions, geared both by the going machine and the human capacity of expression.

It may seem sometimes like "acting," for it is clearly a PERFORM-ANCE, but it is "theatre" of such painful intimacy that it moves well beyond that "theatre of cruelty" Artaud envisaged.

For the listener it is as if his own heart were become articulate: the meaning of what man is is brought home with an accuracy that cannot be evaded.

3

Whether the poems I have made would be paralleled by others improvising I cannot know—but I would suppose not. My improvisations are bound to reflect the nature of my own poetic preoccupations and the modes that are their expressive outs. The grace is that a man is suddenly allowed the opportunity to address others from his own most intimate depths without any drapery and in the fulness of his intelligence WITHIN OCCASION.

No improvisation can ever be repeated. It is ONCE essentially and vitally. The words can be copied onto paper and annotations of the voicing provided: I have tried this and published—in 1955—some of what was possible. But there is no annotation either fine enough or economical enough to state the event—assuming it were worth the effort. I did what I did, then, since it was such a novel experience and some sort of projection of it was necessary, if others were to get an idea of what it was all about. Even so, the little response I had—indicated my failure to get the experience across. With the much larger circulation of recording units and the increased interest in such media, the sense of what is involved is likely now to spread more rapidly. And be more understood. And—hopefully—realized.

Obviously the thing can be FAKED and the tape can be used merely as a device to catch spill from drug experiences or as a psychiatric extension of confession, etc. But the act of poetry remains constant: a sense of the other is inherent in it. Not as one to be impressed, but as one to be MET at the most profound level possible—that is, from the fulness of my being to the fulness of his.

4

The voice is an extraordinary instrument. And it is one that is intrinsic to human excellence. Every human sound has meaning for us. Music is relatively vague in comparison with ANY language and that vagueness is a very active component of its attractiveness and power—for it mutes judgment. Speech, in any of its forms, engages us with an almost terrible precision; it is so strictly provocative.

As chidren we had plenty of occasion to turn to the jingle:

Sticks and stones
Can break my bones—
But names will
  never harm me!

But the very need to resort to the jingle, as a taunting comeback, tells how much deeper than bone words wound. Or a poet's young son in Montreal, when I was once walking him to school and two classmate girls went by and made teasing cracks about the size of his ears, which turned a healthy crimson, muttered to me: They dont mean anything to me, such words—but why (he pleaded with me!) do they keep ringing in my head?

Why indeed!

Language is our medium. And it is weapon, instrument, plume and rapier, bomb and caress. It is the soul and spirit that we extol ourselves by. It is the exaltation and exultation man has provided himself out of his physical being. It is a bond.

5

The voice of the poet, the genius of language, he for whom words are substantive and always renewable and renewing, his nourishment to receive and to offer, as it finds its way out immediately onto tape, out of the depths of the plight in which it finds itself in him, cannot fail to touch at once every listening heart. It evokes the man of man. It says—with love—we are inextricably a single soul.

If my suffering and my joy cannot contain yours, then I am too small for even your smallness. The larger breath awaits to close upon us all.

I say listen, mean speak.

We share one silence.

Continuing Oral Poetry

Cid Corman

DURING MY JOURNEY to America (from October of 1970 to March of 1971) recently I had my first opportunity to present my oral poetry to a wider circle of people than heretofore, to people who didnt know me or my work. And for the first time, and perhaps last, to a large gathering.

The experience was, needless to say, educational. For me at least.

I had made a cassette copy of my last two oral poetry tapes, so as to be easier to handle. One evening at the University of California, San Diego, in La Jolla, late in October of last year, I played the cassette recordings to about 35–40 students and faculty members assembled in a lounge.

The tapes take about an hour altogether. I provided a brief history of my work in this new medium and admitted it was all tentative as yet, since few had been exposed to it and it was hard for me via friends or myself alone to evaluate the material adequately.

The audience was attentive and quiet throughout.

At the end there were a variety of questions, laments, and comments. The following day a number of those present came to me individually and added more private responses.

Several clear points came out.

First, the oral poem is—in my practice of it—a highly intimate occasion and a number of listeners were embarrassed to be in the same room at that moment with so many others and in so well lit a room. There was the feeling that the voice, so personally directed, should be heard in a room that was darkened enough so as not to be distracting and that there should be no more than a friend or two present, if anyone else at all.

Second, not everyone is prepared to listen. This may be true of even a prepared text, of course, especially if the work is being heard for the first time. Many of the older listeners, the faculty members in particular from the literature department, felt a need for a text in hand, so as to be able to follow, and, no doubt, check back by. However, one listener, a

Reprinted from *Word for Word / Essays on the Arts of Language*, vol. 1, Santa Barbara: Black Sparrow Press, 1977, pp. 95–98.

young woman in her 30s, in special graduate studies, was able, shortly after the playing to quote many sections verbatim. She told me privately, to my astonishment, that she had been deaf for nearly all of her life—since childhood, in fact—and had had her hearing restored, by new surgical procedures, only a few years before. She was far and away the most acute listener and since many of the poems dealt with listening, she felt peculiarly addressed by them.

One critic thought that I sounded like I WAS reading from a text and NOT improvising. This response was not in accord with any other, but it suggests that the slow thoughtful pace in much of the improvisation could suggest—in its reaching—a reading. Of course, in actuality the pace varied a good deal in the pieces.

Again, I felt moved myself by what I was hearing. And since my own experience, having heard the tapes a number of times now, exceeds that of any other listener, it became all the more striking that the words and voicing continued to hold fire, to remain fundamentally "new"; that is, there was STILL an uncertainty involved as to whether the poems would find resolution.

Inasmuch as the poems are none of them resolved by some imposed conventional frame, or have any regular rhyme disposition, or any fixed meter, or indeed any clear predisposition, beyond that of communicating at depth and with extreme economy, this uncertainty may not be surprising. Even tho I know that the pieces all ARE resolved in one way or another.

This has brought me to the realization that the situation involved, the involvement in utterance, remains central. Utterance bound by consequential serial "time."

René Guénon has quite accurately shown that "time" need not be read in merely quantitative terms and in music and poetry, for example, it becomes evident that "time" has at least three dimensions and is highly qualitative. And what is operating most profoundly is what is least open to quantifiable research.

Someone also felt that McClure's improvised verbal responses to animals at a zoo were more nearly the ideal of such an oral poetry. I doubt it. Oral poetry can be rather too easily turned into clever patter, humorous exclamatory matter or deliberate nonsense.

My effort—and it is not to be taken as as final paradigm either for me or anyone else—happens to be at this time, and from the start in 1954, predicated on a poetry that addresses itself to each other at the

245

most naked and penetrating possible level. This is not a question of being confessional or shocking—which would be irrelevant—but of addressing myself from center to center.

Naturally enough, the way I phrase words, my rhythms, the words themselves, the themes, images, are always likely to be closely related to where I am at when I make the tape and that is, at least in recent years, likely to be very close to my written work.

Actually the earliest oral poems were far in advance of anything I was writing then. And I have often had the urge to write down some of my recent oral pieces and see if I can, by revision, improve them. But I have given up the task, since I have ample opportunity to write as much as anyone could wish and a good deal more, I suspect.

The third and final point that came through to me at this open session was when a number of the younger people, privately, said that they were dismayed when questions were fired at me immediately after the tape stopped. They had longed for a period of silence, even a few minutes.

I'm not sure of what this means, but I am sure it reflects an involvement that had thoughtful repercussions in them.

The oral poem is not a test for vocal interpretation; the vocalization and the poem are one and the same event.

Some people were disturbed and others gratified by the numbers that divided the poems, the numbers spoken in a rather flat manner. And finally someone asked how I REMEMBERED them—since the poems exceeded a dozen in each tape. I confessed that I had written them down at the time, for I wouldnt normally be able to remember them in my concentration.

How memorable the oral poem is is hard to say, impossible, in fact, as yet. For it would need many listenings. And whether listeners would care to undergo the experience frequently is another story.

The oral poem may be of interest for peripheral reasons, in terms of the poet's written work, in terms of how the voicing enters as part of a formal development of ideas/feelings.

I doubt if more sustained voicings of feeling-thought exist as yet.

In any event the event remains for me an open one and a place where one may speak to any other one with a directness that baffles understanding.

UTANO
23 June 1971

THE BLACK BOX SERIES/
SOME REMARKS

Alan Austin

THIS IS *Black Box*. It has a pair of cassettes inside. . . . Rather obviously we have a bias in favor of work which moves beyond the conventions of written poetry. We are interested in work which takes the largest possible risk, whether in terms of psychic exposure by the poet, in terms of social statement, or in terms of performance technique. When we find a rare piece that manages to do all three of those things in one work, it goes into the next issue.

. . . Why are we doing it? How did it come about? I think that it is worth doing. In the late '60s, I got a few random impressions of the literary scene in which I'd been working for ten years that began to puzzle me, and I didn't quite know what to do with them. The first was a fluke. From 1962 to 1969 I was literary editor of a magazine called *Motive*. *Motive* was a middle-sized, professionally-staffed monthly—political commentary, cultural analysis, the arts—and I was responsible for the poetry, the fiction, and the back of the book, the reviews. Because of a conflict . . . between the staff and the publisher, we had a couple of professional readership studies done. It was partly to establish what our real audience was. We found that with a paid circulation of 46,000 we had an actual audited readership of 135,000. More interestingly, we found that the only thing in the magazine which absolutely every reader read was the poetry. This was unheard of. I was very pleased, but I didn't know what to make of it; so I filed it away in the back of my head, in my personal pride file, and continued to brood on it.

The second thing I observed was that the audience for poetry

Reprinted from *The Publication of Poetry and Fiction: A Conference*, Washington: Library of Congress, 1977. The conference was held October 20–21, 1975, at the Library of Congress.

readings had grown enormously in the late '60s and had undoubtedly come to exceed the audience for written poetry by a factor of ten or twenty or even one hundred. That came to me in an epiphany. I was in Iowa City. Robert Creeley was reading and had been booked into a hall that was much too small, so they had to move the reading to a very much larger auditorium. And I found myself running, with at least a thousand people, down a street in Iowa City to hear a poet read. And I looked around and I said, "My God, this is not the way I've been editing poetry. Something is going on here that's been unexamined."

The third observation came out of my own period of intense political activity in the late '60s. . . . I came away from a three-year period of deep political involvement. I came back to my writing and to literary editing with a very depressing sense of the innocence of most of the poets and writers whom I knew and some anger, even, at the facility with which poets had been able to take those phenomena which we call racism, and imperialism, and sexism, and all those unpoetic words, and make them material for their work without coming to terms with the way those things affected the way they lived, the way they published their work, and the categories into which their work was divided and subdivided. To put it bluntly, it seemed to me that at that time the literary scene was less progressive and far less self-critical than the churches. And that's about the most damning thing I can think of to say.

Now, I carried those observations around in my head. I was also studying—by dumb luck, at the Institute for Policy Studies—new developments in the mass media, and I was beginning to write poetry again for the first time in several years. I came up with four hypotheses that I wanted to test. First was a literary hypothesis that the major new development, cutting across all lines of race, class, sex, or educational background, was an intense concern among poets for their own *real* voice and, as a consequence, for their relationship to their audience. Second was a social hypothesis, and that was that the audience for poetry was now much more interested in readings, much more interested in hearing poetry than in reading it in print. Third was a technological hyothesis—which was solved very easily by getting some cost estimates—that audio-tape technology was a mature technology, generally available throughout the society, that it was growing more popular, and it was also growing less expensive year by year, so that it seemed a feasible way to do a magazine. Fourth was an economic hypothesis that if new technology was adopted first and on a nonprofit basis by poets and by friends of poets, it might become a possible source of income for poets as well as a way of reaching very much larger audiences.

Now those are the hypotheses. We have been testing them through six issues, for three years, and it's time to make a report. . . . I have some good news and some bad news. First the good news. The literary and social hypotheses are, I think, unarguably true; they've been true beyond our wildest expectations. We have about 500 paid subscribers for *Black Box*, and, based on informal surveys, each of them shares their tapes around with at least nine friends. That means an audience of at least minimally 50,000 people for the tapes directly. Furthermore, we've succeeded in making agreements with over forty radio stations to broadcast the tapes, provided we have time to re-edit them into half-hour radio programs. Assuming a conservative average of 2,000 listeners on each station, which is very conservative, that is another 80,000 listeners. That means our minimum total audience, at this point, is 130,000 people. And it doesn't count sales of back issues, which also continue to sell very well.

Now, the technological hypothesis is partly correct. The cost of tape equipment has decreased, and the production cost per copy has gone down spectacularly—it has gone down nearly 40 percent since our first issue. But it takes far more editorial time and expense and overhead than we ever thought it would. So I think our original estimates remain correct; the figures have shifted to different lines.

Now the bad news. Even with that large audience, we haven't found any acceptable mechanism to lift money from anyone but the five hundred people who buy the tapes, and, to put it bluntly, if we don't find a new source of subsidy or a new formula for devising our budget or a commercial distributor, we're going to be bankrupt by next June. We've got a rather lively tiger by the tail and we need help, if anyone has any ideas.

Now, what's to be learned by what we've done? [We've heard a lot at this conference] about the life of the imagination and how that life is so ill served in America in the present economic and cultural conditions. The real question which has emerged from this conference, I think, and the question which we've sought to answer with *Black Box*, is, Why is the life of the imagination served so unimaginatively by editors and by publishers? We surely all know by now that audiences are made not born, and that you have to spend money and time and skill putting audiences together. Why don't we develop them? Why don't we discuss the strange phenomena of poets who are actually afraid of having audiences? Why don't we understand the trap we're all caught in and which came up [at this conference] at the small-press panel, where we substitute sales figures for real discussions of who our audiences are and how we relate to them? And, well, there's more. But these are the kinds of questions, I think, that form the literary agenda as a practical matter for the next ten to twelve years. And I'll leave it there.

Black Box: A Critique

Norma Smith

Black Box IS A PERIODICAL of the Audial Arts. It is published quarterly, by Alan Austin and a score of associate editors, on tape. Each issue consists of two cassettes neatly and attractively packaged in cardboard with graphics on the outside and program notes on the inside with the poetry/music/whatever.

The magazine—I'll call it that, because I like the sense here of ammunition storage—began in 1973, after Austin discovered that the audience for poetry had grown mightily during the late '60s, and, further, he came to believe that even greater numbers of people would go to live readings than would pick up poetry and read it off the page. At the same time, Austin observed that poets and other writers were writing about racism, sexism, imperialism, but were not coming to terms with the ways in which these phenomena affected their own lives as writers.

What have we here?

We have a periodical of poetry and some other arts that overlap, with sound as their common medium. The contents of this publication reflect the editors' concern to present artists from diverse portions of the American population. That is to say, in particular, artists from those portions that are rarely evident in (white) American "popular" culture —women, prisoners, non-Anglos, and artists who regard individuals belonging to these groups as having a part in American culture. Some of the presentations in *Black Box* are straightforward readings of poems, some are readings of plays or prose pieces, and some are combinings of word poetry with more instrumental music.

The artists published in *Black Box* are also diverse in the kinds of work they do and in the degree of recognition their names elicit. Denise Levertov, Etheridge Knight, Allen Ginsberg, Audre Lorde, Marge Piercy, Muriel Rukeyser, alongside serious and accomplished performers whose work is not generally well known, or may not have been published at all previously.

So, we have in *Black Box* several different things. First and most thoroughly, we have an archive of major contemporary American poets reading their own work and of younger or less-well-known artists performing their early works; we have a field for experimentation in the realm of sound and poetry, for both established literary poets and people starting out as primarily sound artists; and we have a socially, politically, economically responsible magazine of high artistic quality. *Black Box* is publishing all this, making it, theoretically, available to us, the writers, and readers/listeners out here, providing the link between artist and audience. The one dimension that *Black Box* provides that literary periodicals cannot is the sound of the poet's own voice, recorded, so that it's accessible in a way that a book does not provide.

Now for the bad news. I would like to go back to Austin's original hypothesis, that many more people would go to poetry readings than would read poetry, and, *following from that,* the proposition that the same hordes he has described as anxiously waiting outside a large hall or trampling each other to hear Robert Creeley read would as soon and as attentively sit beside a black box for 30 to 120 minutes, listening. I'm afraid not. Poetry readings are and, especially as Austin observed them in the late '60s, were social/cultural occurrences, themselves multimedia events, as the saying now goes. There was sight, smell, taste, touch, and *vibes* going on there, as well as sound. And even now, I say, we attend poetry readings for distinctly social, as well as literary, reasons.

A tape is not equivalent to a live reading, and I think that Austin is on the wrong track when he proposes that the audience for poetry would *rather* listen to a tape than read a book, or that the poet's "real" voice is, necessarily, any more palpable on tape than on the page.

Considering the medium in space, I have to trust that there are some individuals, perhaps a large number of them, who are at ease getting their poetry off a tape recorder. I personally find it distracting to push buttons, while I love to look at and see a well-made book. I find it much easier to skim in a book than on tape, to send my eyes or my hands and eyes back or forward; I find it irritating to go through button-pushing, listening, and more button-pushing to find what I'm listening for. I've talked to poets, musicians, high school English teachers, laymen, and radio programmers about this, and haven't found one who can imagine sitting and listening to a tape of poetry as they have sat and read a book of poems.

On the other hand, perhaps this argument only demonstrates, redundantly, that *Black Box* is not a book. A periodical of poetry published on tape instead of in print relieves us of the distraction of turning pages; if we can sit still and listen, it gives us the sound, the sound of the poem, which, reading, we must supply for ourselves—but *can* supply. I say this, acknowledging that one of the explorations *Black Box* carries on is exactly that exploration of the connection of a particular poem to its particular author's voice.

So. I find myself ambivalent about the form. No doubt there's still some resistance to the forms advanced technology takes, just because they are the forms of Advanced Technology; this is the resistance that Austin is trying to overcome or, at least, put into a different perspective.

I remain skeptical of the hypotheses that generated the magazine's existence. A major difficulty I find with *Black Box* is that the quality of the subscriber's experience is greatly dependent upon the quality of equipment the tape is played on. Some of the music/word pieces especially that I heard on a small portable machine sounded like mush, but I've been assured by people who've heard them on a good sound system that the same tapes are well produced and audially satisfactory. This discrepancy makes me think finally that the magazine is really designed for mass audiences, radio or classroom or library audiences, and not so much for the individual subscriber. That is perhaps in the nature of the advanced technology that Austin originally wanted to tap into. This possibility brings up further social and philosophical questions that I'm sure the editors will want to consider, or have considered.

In sum *Black Box* is a sound record of contemporary American poetry and poets and of some of the directions and possibilities advanced technology is bringing to American arts. *Black Box* is not a book, and it's not a live reading. As the first periodical of poetry in tape-cassette form, it's been an important innovative influence in arts publication and should continue to be an invaluable source of information and pleasure in libraries, classrooms, and over the radio waves, for writers, teachers, and students, for radio audiences, and for individual listeners who are privileged to have access to fine technological equipment.

NEW WILDERNESS AUDIOGRAPHICS:
A Perspective

Ellen Zweig

A mong the twenty-four cassettes issued by the New Wilderness Founda-
tion as part of its New Wilderness Audiographics series are three
cassettes recorded by Richard Schechner and Joan MacIntosh in New
Guinea. In the guise of recording anything that looked interesting during their
1972 trip to the highlands of eastern Papua–New Guinea and up the Sepik
River on the northern coast, Schechner and MacIntosh have created for the
listener a unique experience.

As I sat in my room listening to the tapes, I was there, witnessing the rituals
of New Guinea. I witnessed the famous pig feast with Schechner narrating like
a sportscaster. First, he describes the procession, clothes, musical instruments,
dancing. He gropes for the precise words—how to describe the kind of up-and-
down movement that makes this dance. He's a kind of naive observer (I'd be
like him if I were there) speculating that his watching some kind of mock battle.
Then he moves to the center of the village and suddenly sees—"O, wow!
hundreds of tons of meat, look at that. . . . " He's talking to Joan MacIntosh,
and I don't feel a bit frustrated; I can see the meat as he points it out to her, feel
his surprise as he counts the cows, horses, and pigs. MacIntosh says to him,
"I'm glad you're here to verify this story. No one would believe me." Mean-
while, I hear the sounds of a crowd of people, sometimes singing, sometimes
talking as though they're at a big party—about 2,000 people Schechner
estimates. Just as I'm wondering what it feels like to be standing in the middle
of this alien crowd of warriors brandishing bows and arrows and spears,
Schechner explains that it's "very impressive, but not frightening. The people
appear gentle."

Another lovely moment is Schechner's recording of a men's ritual with
flutes and water drums. After Schechner describes the scene, I hear the drums
filling with water and then the beautiful slosh of it as the drums accompany a
kind of yelp-chant that is both surprising and exquisite.

Other tape sections include singing and music. After some songs Schechner,
with the help of a translator, asks questions such as "when do you sing that
song?" or "what's that song about?" Once, the translator replies that it's sung

255

when human meat is eaten. Schechner then asks, "When was the last time that happened?" After some talk in a language I can't understand, the translator replies "100 years." The New Guinea tapes are full of surprises like that and an intense sense of being there. These tapes feel like a discovery, a new form emerging.

The New Wilderness cassettes are only one product of the New Wilderness Foundation. Foundation activities include, in addition to the Audiographics series and a performance series in New York, other semi-autonomous projects: the *New Wilderness Letter*, edited by Jerome Rothenberg; *Ear Magazine* (a new music literary journal), and a forthcoming poetics series (edited by Rothenberg) that will include as its first two volumes the life and works of the Mazatec shamanness, Maria Sabina, and selected work of Jackson Mac Low (for Ross-Erikson Publishers in Santa Barbara).

The publications, performances, and activities of the Foundation indicate the work of a whole generation of artists exploring what Rothenberg has called the "new wilderness." As he puts it, the activities reflect the "juxtaposition of new performance works with traditional 'transformational art' in order to make both sides reveal themselves in unexpected ways . . . towards a clarification of underlying issues of language & performance." Thus, in the pages of the *New Wilderness Letter* we find Maria Sabina next to Ernst Jandl, the Viennese concrete poet; or Nina Yankowitz, a contemporary painter whose work is meant to be "scanned" like some mysterious writing system, next to a traditional Navaho alphabetic blanket; or a Roman "horse calligram" next to Apollinaire's "Horse Calligram." In the Audiographics series, we hear our contemporaries: Jackson Mac Low, Spencer Holst, Annea Lockwood, Philip Corner, Charlie Morrow, Armand Schwerner, Hannah Weiner; others interpreting and translating older poetries: Armand Schwerner, Jerome Rothenberg, Leonard Crow Dog (singing nontraditional songs); others in complex relationships with older traditional rituals and poetries: Richard Schechner in New Guinea recording traditional ritual with commentary; the Crow Dogs singing traditional peyote songs to those of us who've used peyote in the tradition of the '60s.

This "new/old configuration," as Rothenberg calls it, isn't new. Tzara translated African chants and performed them at the Cabaret Voltaire; Rothenberg's own *Technicians of the Sacred* was the classic attempt at bringing together old and new poetries. Recently, Rothenberg joined a collective, international enterprise called SET (*sens et transformation*, Jean Pierre Faye's term) which consists of the *New Wilderness Letter*, the French publication *Change*, *Chemin de Ronde* (Marseille), *Breches* (Montreal), the Greek *Khnari* (Athens), the British *Curtains*, and *Ponto du contacto* (New York). These publications have so far produced a joint issue of *Change* on the oral (Fall, 1978). This linking is one way that ethnopoetics does what Rothenberg proposes: It "bridges multiple performance worlds." Another way is in the new/old configuration represented by *Musics* (England; eds. David Troop and Paul Burwell), *Canal* (Paris); Pauline Oliveros' Center for Music Experiment (at the

University of California at San Diego), and the New Wilderness Audiographics series.

Charlie Morrow, director of the New Wilderness Foundation and co-producer with Ondina Fiore of the Audiographics series, explains that when he conceived of the series (with Rothenberg and others), he chose to record the work of people he knew who worked from what Morrow calls a "gut or feeling" place. Each artist, says Morrow, chose the work he or she most wanted to record. Morrow sees all of the artists on the New Wilderness cassettes as sharing an interest in "transformational art." His own emphasis is on the exploration of deep feeling which will lead us into the "new wilderness."

The tapes represent an important social entity: a group of avant-garde artists who know each other, show up at the same parties, go to each other's performances, and sometimes work together. If the tapes capture even a few minutes of the cross-influences of this group they will have been worth recording.

That's the story from the inside. From the outside the tapes explore the art of performance. RoseLee Goldberg, in her book *Performance: Live Art 1909 to the Present,* explains that "live gestures have constantly been used as a weapon against the conventions of established art." The avant-garde nature of the tapes and their spontaneity confirms this theory. The tapes are recordings of art that has gone beyond the boundaries of the arts.

The spontaneity that pervades the New Guinea tapes often saves other tapes from the just-another-reading category. Jackson Mac Low's "Homage to Leona Bleiweiss" is interrupted by a flash-crashing thunderstorm; on another tape, Mac Low and Pauline Oliveros pause, and Mac Low asks, "Shall we lapse into Sluggishness or shall we do Repeopled?" Hannah Weiner's *Clairvoyant Journal* reading by Weiner, Sharon Mattlin, and Margaret De Coursey is interrupted when someone reads the word "dungarees," and everyone breaks out giggling. These moments help to raise the tapes from documentation devices to recordings that come close to the experience of live performance. The real world interruption of the thunderstorm, the eye-witness account of New Guinea ritual, even those moments when the artists discuss what to do next or giggle at what they're so seriously in the midst of doing, give the listener the feeling of being there with the performers. We, as listeners, are witnesses, participants in the process of making art.

We have Morrow's intuition that the feeling center should be explored to thank for those moments and for what seems like a new aesthetic that the New Wilderness tapes share with the new Dial-a-Poem-Poets' record *Big Ego:* Our attention is directed to the off moment, the moment that isn't quite art or that isn't consciously art, that moment where art and life are mingling.

More traditional pleasures and surprises are contained in the New Wilderness tapes. Annea Lockwood's exploration of environmental and vocal sounds in "Tiger Balm" caught me in its repetitions—tiger roars and breathing—waking me from the trance of repetition (like the one that Gertrude Stein made with words) in the middle of a woman's orgasm much like my own. Repetition and pulse play a different role in "Woman Murder" in which Lockwood records the words of women who've been beaten by men. And she's recorded all the rivers of the world for "World Rhythms."

"Breath Chant" is a virtuoso performance by Charlie Morrow of the possibilities of breath. Morrow's *Hour of Changes* is experiential; its highly basic structure consists of Catherine Shull counting the minutes by number and Charlie Morrow chanting and changing every minute on the basic tracks, with overdubs of Annea Lockwood chanting and changing every two minutes and Morrow changing every three minutes.

Repetition and pulse combined with counting makes the listener intensely aware of time, of the one hour it takes to listen, of every minute of that hour as it is counted, and ultimately of the part that counting plays in music. I played the tape while waiting for a friend to drop by; it was the longest hour I ever spent. Time is stretched in an odd way; the voice says "one," and I am already thinking "two"; at about "thirty-three" when I'm thinking "thirty-four," I forget whether she's said "thirty-four" or whether I'm thinking ahead to it.

Armand Schwerner's excellent tapes include a reading of the later *Tablets* and newer poems. A Schwerner reading is always a surprise because of the small improvisations that come from translating the written text, often visually conceived (as in the . . . . . . and + + + + + + of *Tablets*), to an oral text. Another surprise is Schwerner as an actor in his own translation of *Philoctetes;* he's especially brilliant *kvetching* and screaming through Philoctetes' pain.

In the reworking of Jerome Rothenberg's translations of Navaho Horse Songs in a multi-track version, the voice-on-voice texture approximates the complex performance situation of group singing by translating that group experience into a contemporary musical equivalent.

The Horse Songs are one culmination of Rothenberg's philosophy of the "new wilderness." We who were first struck with the vision of *Technicians of the Sacred* have followed the progress of these translations from "War God's Horse Song I and II," collected by Rothenberg through the concept of "total translation" (of non-sense or distorted phonemes, music, performance style) in the 17 *Horse Songs of Frank Mitchell* (two of which appear in Rothenberg's anthology *Shaking the Pumpkin*), to the Songs as performed by Rothenberg in this multi-track version.

Rothenberg's translation from a group event to a multi-track tape is a satisfying stage in the progress of total translation. As Rothenberg describes the original performance situation in *Shaking the Pumpkin:*

The typical Navaho performance pattern calls for each person present to follow the singer to whatever degree he can. Thus group singing is highly individualized . . . & leads to an actual indeterminacy of performance. Those who can't follow the words at all may make up their own vocal sounds—anything, in fact, for the sake of participation.

The translation of this experience onto tape was done in the following manner:

Track 1: A clean recording of the lead voice.
Track 2: A voice responsive to the first but showing less word distortion & occasional free departures from the text.
Track 3: A voice similar to that on the second track with significantly less information —i.e. recorded without written text to a playback of the first two voices at a

barely audible level.

Track 4: A voice limited to pure sound improvisations on the meaningless elements in the text, recorded under circumstances like those for the third voice.

These tracks were balanced and mixed onto a single monaural tape, with important technical assistance from Charlie Morrow.

Spencer Holst, in collaboration with Tui St. George Tucker, picks up a bunch of discarded beginnings in a wastebasket and reads them as a continuous piece, each beginning interrupted by the recorders of St. George Tucker. The piece has the effect of beginning and beginning, although certain closings occur even in the beginnings. Some of the beginnings seem complete in themselves—small aphoristic pieces that begin and end at the same time; others leave us waiting for more and are completed only by music and the next try at a beginning.

I have my favorite stories on the other tapes, like "The Typewriter Repairman," who finds that "Borges is better," and "The Case of the Giant Rat of Sumatra," in which we discover the "secret of literature."

The cassette as a recording device allows a fairly cheap distribution of work that up until now was heard only in New York, San Francisco, Los Angeles, San Diego, Chicago. Many of the New Wilderness Audiographics artists are virtually unknown outside of a small circle of other artists who've heard their work live. Yet their work has been important and influential for those working at the boundaries of their arts and at the boundary of that new wilderness called performance.

What happens to the revolutionary nature of live art when it is confronted with the tape recorder or the video camera? We have a new form: live art preserved on tape. The new form will have a new aesthetics; critics will argue about the technical quality of the tape or whether the tape captures the spontaneity of the performance at the expense of technical perfection. Live art, transient and disposable, will still be around to break through all this talk.

DISCOGRAPHY AND OTHER MATTERS

Robert Peters

A fascinating spin-off of public poetry readings is the recording of poets on tape, video cassettes, and records. Most tapes and records I've heard so far are big bores—either ego trips for the poets involved or a drizzling effort to enrich our culture-archives with the voices of deceased writers. The earliest of all, I guess, is a scratchy brief recording of Alfred Lord Tennyson reading "Come into the Garden, Maud." Now that one is valuable: Hearing it even in its gravelly state one can sense well how Tennyson's magnificent voice managed to keep Queen Victoria awake during the reading of all 133 parts of *In Memoriam*. So I have contradicted myself; the occasional stunning record has been made—Ralph Bellamay reading *The Rubaiyat of Omar Kayyam*, Dylan Thomas reading anything. For the most part, though, unless you are interested in having your ears tickled by voice-hairs from the past, ignore the recordings, and let your own brain *hear* the poems as you *read* them on the page.

The Giorno Sound-System recordings are different. I have listened through them—all five albums, all twenty sides. I have even forced that full bladder to wait for a side to be played through. This is not to say that I am never vexed, insulted, or irritated by some of these cuts. But many of them are flaky and outrageous. Poetry becomes an event rather than something embalmed for the school marms and masters. The Giorno pieces are almost always *performances*—and this is what a good poetry reading should be.

As most poetry readings go in this country, they are bastard art forms. You may hit a true performance, and you may hit some vapid, stumbling, mumbling, minesterial intoning. You may experience something unforgettable; you may find yourself in such misery that boils on your ass burst out of boredom and vexation. Have you ever had the guts, dear reader, to walk out of a poetry reading? Years later you'll get your come-uppance if you do, via some shaft of a review, some fang in your jugular, placed by the walkoutee (as distinct from the outwalker). Be advised. I rarely see anyone walk out of a reading—most poets are such terrible cowards.

Those poets who give a lot of public readings—I've probably given three hundred or so in the past twelve years—do so out of many motives. We may hope to get our books *heard*. If we publish with small presses, distribution generally stinks, and the reading is a way of distributing ourselves. Some of us like the Celebrity Trip—and no matter how minor the stir we have made in the poetry world there is always apt to be some lovely, innocent, sweet young thing in the audience who will treat us as if we were W. S. Merwin, Gerard Malanga, Anne Waldman, or Galway Kinnell. There's an Instant Fame, then—or at least the illusion of it. Some of us hope eventually to find ourselves on records and video tapes. So we keep on reading, accepting any and all invitations to stand up there and amaze the world.

I

The Giorno records do work well and include an amazing range of poets (I'll give a sampling shortly). Most of them cluster about St. Mark's Church and the reading program there. A second center is the Naropa Institute in Colorado, the poetry center nestled-over by Ginsberg and Waldman. Occasionally, someone not of these nubs will wander through the wax—Merwin, Charles Olson, Frank O'Hara, Gary Snyder. The series also includes a good spread of sound and language poets. John Giorno himself is generously represented in performances of a tripartite Giorno voice, thanks to tape recordings. Folk from the former Andy Warhol crowd get in and funky-up—Jackie Curtis and Taylor Mead. Some punk stuff appears—Patti Smith. Much William Burroughs—one album of four sides is a recording of the famous Burrough's *Nova Convention*. The engineering on all these albums is impeccable, and the prices, thanks to assistance from the National Endowment for the Arts and the New York State Arts Council, are cheap these days, less than you would expect to pay for an album by your favorite punk rock star. And the cuts are never boring!

A few of the high points on these albums are mentioned in this abbreviated list. Peter Orlovsky yodels the joys of his compost pile and rhubarb patch. Jim Carroll hustles a homosexual in a public john and is turned on. Trungpa Rimpoche intones "teeth" and breathes heavily. Giorno performs a "Suicide Sutra," and almost takes you in; he also subdues demons in America, and wipes his wrists in "blood, shit, brains, and pus." Spicer reads from *Billy the Kid* and *The Holy Grail*. Ginsberg, accompanied by Bob Dylan and other musicians, sings a wonderful ballad to New York City newsboy Jimmy Berman; later he recites "Please Master," allowing the sado-masochism to exude deliciously. Michael McClure reads a bit of beast language for lions. Frank O'Hara eats a pair of *Lunch Poems*, endures Marilyn's death, and helps the Film Industry in its time of crisis. Tom Clark licks not-too-celestial assholes with hash on his lips. Paul Blackburn does "The Once-Over" woman. Joe Brainard tells us that he shoots big loads. Ron Padgett asks for a lot of pity —even his pen weeps black ink; he feels "totally fucked." Waldman is a "Fast-Speaking Woman," Diane di Prima is "Loba," Diane Wakoski devastates a man and then exorcises his presence in her life. Gregory Corso rips through marriage and obscene honeymoons. Robert Creeley, Charles Olson, William Carlos Williams, John Cage, John Wieners, and Denise Levertov appear among the daddies and mommies of poetry. More delicious than almost any other reader is Helen Adam reciting her grisly "apartment-on-twin-peaks" poem, and her "Junkie" ballad. Charles Bukowski is on cloud nine wearing two horse-collars and lamenting the closing of topless and bottomless bars. Sylvia Plath licks daddy all over and then eats him. William Burroughs tells us he never wanted to be president. Jackie Curtis wishes herself/himself a Merry Xmas, evokes his/her lucky star, and takes off after Betty Hutton. Jerome Rothenberg is a Navajo chanting a horse-song. Joanne Kyger is full of French ideals, a little bruised, but nicely mellow. Bill Knott murders poetry in a plate of beans. Denby examines boys' shoulders, wrinkled crotches, smokeless moments in Manhattan, and the cranky woman inside him. Robert Duncan articulates "the progress of the syllables." Gary Snyder sings his wild mushroom song, celebrates dharma as an avocado, finds aluminium foil inside a ground squirrel, eulogizes the Queen of Crete and other bare-breasted, bare-footed folk who wouldn't be served in today's restaurants. Kenward Elmslie sings "Woolworth." Ed Sanders tells us what Lesbian dwarfs are like and what cocaine suppositories do. And on and on, for about 12 hours of listening.

This quick run-through is meant to celebrate these fine recordings. Young poets in all the writing programs around America should listen to them. When they put themselves together afterwards they will probably be better poets. The abundance of poets and cuts invites us to make our own anthology for playing as part of an evening, for our own enjoyment, and for exposing the fledgling poet as well as your basic stick-in-the-mud conservative poet to special vibrations of life, outrageousness, beauty, and variety in much current (and recent) poetry.

Sound

Sound Poetry:
AN INTRODUCTION

Ellen Zweig

SOUND POETS experiment with the human voice. Their art is one that contains many contradictions. Some sound poets improvise; others read from text or compose on tape. Some go to the body or consider how sounds are formed in the mouth; others manipulate the voice electronically so that it becomes unrecognizable.

Sound poetry explores the voice as human. Sound poets take apart language to see how it works. They are obsessed with phonetics. They make all of the sounds that they can with their bodies. The poet becomes close to the animal, close to the child.

Sound poetry explores the voice as other. Sound poets record and manipulate the voice. (Sten Hanson is trying to find the limits of the human voice as a recognizable entity. When do the sounds on the tapes stop sounding human?) They cut the voice into pieces, reverse it, change its speed, make it digital. The voice becomes electronic, a strange machine whining toward communication with other planets.

Sound poetry finds an interface between the body and the mind; the human and the machine. Sound poets chant, moving with the voice of the body toward trance, toward changing consciousness. They perform live, sending the voice through a synthesizer or other electronic device to change it. We hear it as both things as once: the human and the other.

Only a small selection of the works of sound poets is included in this book. But contained in their work is a microcosm of most of the ways that sound poets work. Charles Amirkhanian and Larry Wendt do mostly tape pieces. Amirkhanian's are percussive, often derived from live performance; Wendt's are technically innovative. He's presently

266

working on computer-generated and manipulated voices. Stephen Ruppenthal works with tapes, synthesizer, and live performance. His "Totemic Illusions" series is electronic, while his "Improvisation for Voice" is acoustic, physical, somewhat like scat. Charlie Morrow is a chanter. His pieces are made of breath and vision. They are concerned with the body as origin of the voice and with the voice as healer.

The scores in this section are only traces of the pieces. Amirkhanian provides some instructions for performance; Ruppenthal's scores are visually beautiful; Wendt's are mysterious.

Although sound poetry has been a flourishing form in Europe for a long time, all of the artists presented are young Americans. Amirkhanian's history and Wendt's survey of the Toronto Sound Poetry Festival give an idea of the international range of these experiments. Most of the work is esoteric, although some has entered popular culture. The Talking Heads, a punk group, do a version of Hugo Ball's "Gadji Beri Bimba" on their album *Fear of Music*. The art of sound poetry is very much alive: a festival was held in 1980 in New York City. Sound poets continue to experiment, these days with computers and interspecies communication. The whales sing. Who will answer? Wolves, crows, or a man on the beach with pebbles in his mouth?

Sound Poetry:
A Short History

Charles Amirkhanian

This article was written [in 1974] for inclusion in the LP 10 + 2: 12 American Text-Sound Pieces. It was rejected by the album's executive producer, Robert Leverant of 1750 Arch Records, as being too specialized for the general LP buyer. This is its first publication, incorporating some suggestions offered generously by Richard Kostelanetz. The reader is referred also to notes on the inner liner of the LP, which specifically treat the artists whose work is contained on the album: Clark Coolidge, John Cage, John Giorno, Anthony Gnazzo, Charles Dodge, Robert Ashley, Beth Anderson, Brion Gysin, Liam O'Gallagher, Aram Saroyan, and Charles Amirkhanian. The LP is available from 1750 Arch Records, 1750 Arch Street, Berkeley, California 94709. The album number is S-1752.

Sound poems, or text-sound compositions, are basically a cross-fertilization of the traditional arts of music and poetry. When just after World War I, Raoul Hausmann and Kurt Schwitters, two visual artists, began to present public reading of their abstract and nonsensical poems, an entirely new area of art activity was stimulated. Like the introduction of the collage in visual art, this merging of pure sound with language continues today, not so much as a "school" of art activity (Dada, surrealism, pop art) but as a very particular intermedium (like kinetic sculpture, acrylic painting, electronic music, event art) which has grown out of previous activity in the larger, formerly distinct forms (music, poetry, painting, sculpture, theater, dance). Artists as various as composers, painters, poets, sculptors, dancers, happeners, conceptualists, computer programmers, meteorologists, and mathematicians have made text-sound compositions because certain artists from all of these areas have commonly shared a fascination for language and its artistic possibilities in sound.

What might have been a short-lived art form was given tremendous impetus by technology. The availability to artists and the general public of the magnetic tape recorder (about 1950), and then of electronic devices to modulate natural sound sources including the voice (about 1955), has widened the range of creative possibilities and fostered the participation of artists from

268

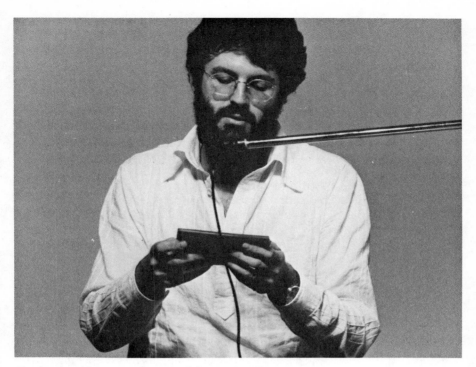

Charles Amirkhanian   Photograph by Stephen Ruppenthal

many different disciplines. Today computers are being investigated by artists, and possibilities which up until recently have been applied only to linguistic research are being used now to create synthetic speech sounds to astound us and refresh our appreciation of language as a musical material.

Poetry in its earliest forms was a sound medium. Before they were written on the page, poems were handed from generation to generation by word of mouth. This oral tradition survives today in the form of poetry readings, and "straight" poets continue to give them. But for the most part, we know a poet's poetry by the words he or she puts to print.

What distinguishes a text-sound piece (or *poesie sonore, verbosonie,* sound poetry, and so on—there are many names for the medium) from a reading by William Carlos Williams of one of his poems? Williams' poem can exist effectively in either a written form or as a recited poem. But the *Ursonate* of Kurt Schwitters, John Cage's 62 *Mesostics Re Merce Cunningham,* or *Mr. Smith in Rhodesia* by the Swedish writer Aøke Hodell exists ultimately as a sound object. There may be written notations available which give instructions for a realization of the work, much like a score for a piece of music, but the work does not exist until, like a musical work, it *is* sound.

The twentieth century has witnessed a tremendous flowering of activity in the non-syntactic, non-semantic use of language (constituting much of the work of sound poets), just as the abstract use of visual imagery has dominated painting and sculpture. The emancipation of dissonance in music between about 1900 and 1910 was paralleled by the early attempts by Lewis Carroll and Christian Morgenstern to construct artificial languages.

Although they were not primarily concerned with performance poetry, James Joyce, e. e. cummings, Abraham Lincoln Gillespie, and Gertrude Stein, as well as numerous other writers, contributed to an atmosphere which spawned the wildly experimental language-sound pieces of Tristan Tzara, Hugo Ball, Kurt Schwitters, Raoul Hausmann, and other Dadaists, including the Czechoslovakian composer and theater artist František Burian, who formed a Dada voice band. The musical analogues of this work by Burian were investigated in the form of speech choruses by Darius Milhaud (as early as 1918), Ernst Toch (1930), and Carl Orff, among others. There also were the musically naive solo and choral pieces chanted in rather inhibited rhythms by the French *Lettriste* group (begun in 1946 and still active today in France), whose primary figures are Maurice Lemaitre and Isidore Isou.

The advent of the tape recorder inspired the early investigations in France of its application to language and vocal sounds. One artist in this vein was Gil J. Wolman, whose four-minute *Vous ne poures rien pour l'homme seul* was taped in 1950. The major figures to emerge from this period are Henri Chopin, François Dufrêne, and Bernard Heidsieck.

Chopin (born in 1920), the publisher of *OU Magazine* (containing in each issue a record of sound poems from artists of many different countries), has been a leading force in the investigation of the medium. His work often explores the microscopic particles of language—phonemes, rather than syllables. These he will record over one another and at different recording speeds to create textures of animalistic howls and clucks which might represent how we humans once used our vocal cords before we became a more "civilized" species.

François Dufrêne (born in 1930), originally associated with the Letterists, also began to break language down to its smallest elements and work with spontaneous and virtuosic variations of vocal sounds sometimes recorded on tape but very often performed live with a hand-held microphone on a long cable before audiences in night-club-like settings. His presence as a performer is very strong, and he wows sound poetry audiences with his technical facility the way pianist David Tudor often did music audiences in the 1950s.

Bernard Heidsieck (born in 1928) has, since 1955, produced an extensive *oeuvre* in the tape medium. This original and exciting poet combines ambient sounds and voices of friends and passers-by on Paris street corners with an uncanny sense of drama, split-second tape editing, and fast-paced timing to create furioso fantasies, partly narrative and partly abstract, which leave the listener awed by his craft and inventiveness. A high emotional content often marks Heidsieck's work.

Musicians too have explored the tape realm and added their concerns with electronic and live-electronic manipulation to the developing tradition. Karlheinz Stockhausen's 1955-56 tape piece, *Gesang der Junglinge,* falls into this category. Most of the sounds are made by children's voices speaking and singing. These are collaged into the fabric of the piece in either their natural state or in an electronically-modified state.

Influenced by Stockhausen's *Gesang,* Luciano Berio, the Italian avant-gardist, took excerpts from James Joyce's *Ulysses,* vocalized by his then-wife singer Cathy Berberian, and manipulated these sounds into the fantastic tape music, *Omaggio a Joyce* (1958). For Steve Reich, Berio's *Omaggio* legitimized the spoken word for musical purposes and inspired Reich's well-known phase pattern works *It's Gonna Rain* (1965) and *Come Out* (1966). All of these works have been available on commercial recordings of "electronic music" and have had a great impact on subsequent audio-language pieces.

In most every country in the world now since the mid-1960s, groups of artists have been making and presenting new voice pieces with great regularity. In England, the names Bob Cobbing, Neil Mills, dom sylvester houedard, Nicolas Zurbrugg, and Lily Greenham are well known. In Sweden, the Fylkingen Group has sponsored an annual April festival of "text-sound compositions" (their term) in conjunction with the Swedish Radio: The pioneers here are Lars-Gunnar Bodin, Bengt-Emil Johnson, Sten Hanson, °Ake Hodell, and Ilmar Laaban. In Holland, the producer of Dutch literary programs at NCRV Radio, Ab van Eyck, has encouraged the participation in sound poetry (called there *verbonsonie*) of engineer Cor Doesberg, Dutch poet Herman Damen, and Belgian poet-historian Paul de Vree, as well as a talented young woman who is known primarily as a composer, Tera de Marez Oyens.

In West Germany, the major figures include Ernst Jandl, Franz Mon, Ferdinand Kriwet, Klaus Bremer, Helmut Heissenbüttel, and Nicolaus Einhorn. Gerhard Rühm, the Austrian poet and musician (who studied with Johann Mathias Hauer), is one of the most original and interesting European sound poets now active. The Italians Arrigo Lora-Totino, Luciano Ori, Mimmo Rotella, Sarenco, Lucian Marcucci, and Eugenio Miccini have produced sound poems somewhat in the tradition of Filippo Marinetti and his colleagues in the post-World War I Futurist movement.

Countless others could be named, including Ladislav Novak and Jiri Valoch of Czechoslovakia, Seiji Nikuni and Kuniharu Akiyama (the latter made sound poems as early as 1951) of Japan, Ilse and Pierre Garnier and Jean-Louis Brau of France, and numerous other younger artists whose work is just now coming to international attention and who are unknown (even to those of us who make it a point to locate such people) simply because publications and recordings are presently so sparse.

The U.S. scene has followed relatively late. In the mid-1960s Americans began to work consciously in the text-sound area. Earlier, John Cage did pioneering work with his *Williams Mix* (1952). Also, his lectures, scored as performance pieces by strictly indeterminate means, were delivered in music performance situations. In 1958 he composed *Aria* for Cathy Berberian in which the singer is called upon to speak, sing, shout, and otherwise vocalize in unusual ways and in various languages. Lately his output has included texts printed in visually pleasing arrangements made with many different styles of instant lettering, and these are chanted in ways which obscure the original words, emphasizing individual syllables and letters.

As far as the other artists represented on 10 + 2: 12 *American Text-Sound Pieces,* Clark Coolidge, John Giorno, and Aram Saroyan have approached sound poems from their activities as poets; Anthony Gnazzo, Charles Dodge, Beth Anderson, Robert Ashley, and Charles Amirkhanian began as composers; Liam O'Gallagher and Brion Gysin were initially known as painters. As one listens to the pieces on this LP, it is interesting to take note of the use by each artist of elements of music and poetry in individual works. Some pieces in this intermedium tend more toward pure music; others toward pure poetry. Others fall more nearly in the center. And often the tendencies of a piece are a reflection of the traditional single discipline from which the artist approached sound poetry.

Many other Americans have contributed important text-sound pieces. Jackson Mac Low has long performed chance-derived poetry texts in theatrical or "reading" situations, both in solo and ensemble versions. Composer Kenneth Gaburo has developed remarkable speech techniques for choral writing by working with a small, permanent ensemble which devoted extensive amounts of rehearsal time to the preparation of such pieces as Gaburo's own *Maladetto* (recorded on CRI S-316).

Ingram Marshall has been one of the first to teach the subject of text-sound composition in the U.S. His classes at California Institute of the Arts were offered in 1972-74, and it was there that he produced his four-track piece *Cortés* (1973), an electronic-sounding work composed with only *musique concrète* techniques of filtering and speed changes.

Steve Reich's loop phase voice pieces are well known through his Columbia and Odyssey recordings. Pauline Oliveros' music has taken the direction of sonic meditation, often concerned with the relationship of the voice to the human organism. The same is true of the recent pieces of Bill Maraldo, who creates electronic drone chants of great beauty in collaboration with members of the Tantra Research Institute of Oakland.

Poet Jim Rosenberg concentrates on speech inflection in his *Pure and Applied Mathematics.* The piece consists of phrases from the Senate Watergate hearings. Only the dates are heard, spoken by witnesses and senators. These are spliced out of the continuous hearings and strung one after the other, isolated by silences of varying lengths. Often the dates are heard in repetition, as if on continuous tape loops. Thus the manner of speaking the dates becomes so accentuated that the speech rhythms take on a musical character.

Toby Lurie has involved audiences in his performances, encouraging rhythmic chanting of phrases which retain their denotative functions and which reflect his studies of counterpoint and polyrhythms with Darius Milhaud. Sculptor Carl André has produced pieces for three simultaneous readers scored by typing one line above another in the desired juxtaposition.

Alvin Curran, who has lived in Rome since the mid-1960s, has utilized tape delay procedures to create settings of two of Clark Coolidge's more minimal works. His settings of "will term" and "of about," poems published in Coolidge's book *Space* (Harper and Row), are extremely rich and beautiful. Curran has been associated with the live-electronic improvisation group Music Elettronica Viva and continues to produce pieces which incorporate ambient sound recordings such as *The Rubber Bee* and *A Day in the Country*.

Other U.S. artists involved in text-sound composition are W. Bliem Kern, John Payne, Daniel W. Schmidt, Ira Steingroot, Sheila Booth, members of the Poetry Out Loud group (Klyd Watkins, Linda Watkins, and Peter Harleman), Charles Levendosky, and Stephen Ruppenthal.

Like Robert Ashley, Alvin Lucier has made remarkable voice pieces with theatrical elements. Lucier often incorporates his own natural stuttering habit in his pieces which regularly evokes an incredulous reaction from his audience. Most don't know if he is imitating a speech defect or if he actually *has* one, and the ambiguity creates an uneasiness which stimulates closer listening and an appreciation of Lucier's performances. In his *I Am Sitting in a Room,* published on an LP included in *Source Magazine* No. 7-8, Lucier reads and records a statement, then plays it back into a room for re-recording by an air microphone, so that the quality is intentionally degenerated. This process is repeated until, after twenty minutes, the sounds are unrecognizable as words.

Among American composers who have attempted to break language down to its smallest components and then formalize relationships of various musical parameters such as pitch and timbre in accordance with textual cues, Milton Babbitt has figured prominently. Also working in this area have been Charles Wuorinen, Godfrey Winham, James K. Fandall, and Edward Levy.

Copyright © 1981 by Charles Amirkhanian.

A Voice in the Wilderness: Seance vs. Vision Music

Charlie Morrow

THE SINGLE MOST striking aspect of music in our culture is its relationship to death. The "highest" music is performed in a special insulated and vibrant indoor location where listeners sit motionless and soundless while darkly dressed, carefully schooled and carefully moving musicians play the music of a dead person.

This seance is magic made possible by the written note. With the written note, the musician becomes the medium through which ideas and energies of the long gone spirit live again. Image and sound recording expand this process.

In most of the world, written music and written words are just recently entering verbal and musical traditions. And learning orally means learning the personal style of the teacher, not just a melody, words and a general style.

In this age when death is more abundant and violence more colossal than in the past, the reality of death is farther and farther from consciousness. Food is never seen as dead animals and plants. Killing and death are divorced in many minds. Our old people and old traditions are packed away, named and coded, and disappear from daily life.

As a performer, one allows the audience to enter his place, his mind, his spirit. You open up the possibility of behavior not acceptable in other areas of life. Social dancing is one area where music and musicians let the people act crazy.

As people enter my space, I consider what makes that process possible, not just in music, but in all performing arts, religious ritual, sports, the performances of everyday life. And how does this relate to death transcendence?

Death transcendence is the highest magic, and is the extremest form of the physical, mental and emotional changes that "being in someone else's place" affords. It is the entering of a person's place, commonly associated with sexual activity, that is the highly charged process. And trickiness is necessary to bring it off: heroic skills, wondrous memory, charismatic personality, inventive and revelatory ideas, an evocative body, androgynous appearance, etc. These tricks turn up in mythology as the play of the gods: Zeus as swan, bull; God as the word, the whirlwind; Coyote as creature upstream from washing women who sends his penis downstream and gets them all; schools as seminaries.

In [Carlos Castenada's tales of] Don Juan, Don Gennaro, the old sorcerer, leaps from stone to stone down a perilous cataract. And the high artist is the high sorcerer who can do a trick a culture wants to believe.

But it is magic within all of us that is being tapped in these tricks. And in finding myself being entered, I want to know what is the magic in everyone and where do my tricks begin. This common ground is what must be established to prevent exploitation of people hungry for transformation but ready to buy the politics of franchised religion. The stranglehold that organized religion has on magic and spiritual processes, most of which reside in the individual, is a most unnecessary monopoly.

The common ground is our bodies and minds . . . BREATH, VOICE, GESTURE. Over and above this common matrix are the "codes" of language and customs of our species, countries, regions, neighborhoods, social & professional clans.

Breath is unique as the universal carrier of information. Its range of colors and rates is enormous. We know emotional and physical states from each other's breath. And breathing, to some degree, is the basis of cross-species understanding. Each species has its own range of clock rates, with corresponding physical (respiration, heartbeat) states.

This "tracking" procedure seems able to transmit anybody's state. If so, we probably can and do know a lot about each other in all the transactions of life. The power of this breath transaction also suggests that the reaction we get from much of performance comes from the breath level, and not all from the verbal and musical languages, which are further illuminations.

The voice is the fundamental illumination of the breath, filling breath of many colors with sound of many colors. The rhythm of voice in relationship to the rhythm of breath seems to affect time perception.

275

(Gesture seems to be in an equal place wth voice.)

Voice enters breath as resonances in the body. The bell, with low vibration at the rim and higher partials up to its dome, is an idealized respiratory column: low vowels and grumbles in the belly, higher and higher through the chest, throat, to mouth and nasal space. All can ring in different ways at once. In many chant systems the vibrating parts of the body serve particular ends. The use of bell & gong sound can serve to focus on the body ringing.

Voice, coming from various resonating combinations, tells of states of self, regions of the world, and stereotypes invoked. The voices of musical instruments function similarly.

Voice is also what we hear from our sound environment, animate and inanimate. It is easy to understand the world as filled with various spirits & voices. Imparting cognition and volition to the wind, etc., is naturally another issue. Imitation of voices reflects the way images have entered our personal space.

Imitating voices comes in several ways: I hear something and respond spontaneously, or I imitate something consciously, or I dream something and do it, or I study something and present it. The response to the original voice in each case is delayed differently and colored differently. But all relate to the reflex response.

Little children play with the sound world, answering reflexively; field frogs and other signalling creatures play with the reflex, taking turns leading and following. There is both a compulsion to answer and the desire to evoke and answer. This game is a fundamental music, linguistic music. In music where there is only melody, most of the world's music, the role shifting in answering and counterpointing expands this game. Basic forms are echoing, dialogue, and follow the leader.

Chanting, as a way of traveling between or dwelling on various body resonances and voice locations, is found in all cultures. By chanting, I mean vocal music where voice is primary and if there are instruments, they propel and punctuate. From breathing we know our moods and gross physical states. From chanting we know ourselves better as "bells," and collections of voices (places in and out of ourselves). From playing with our unisons and reflex responses, we join with each other and our environment as active spirits.

And we know our artists as magicians who trick us in ways we want to be tricked. The common matrix of breath, voice and gesture can be tapped by anyone. But an artist, athlete, priest, or any transcendor is expected to go beyond what everyone can do within that matrix. In social dancing, for example, anyone keeping the beat can begin something, but a good band gets you farther.

So as a living performer confronted with such high things, I know people will not enter my body without a seductive process.

In stating this overview publicly, there is my hope that when the ritual context is established for any activity, that activity can then be that much higher.

PLACING

Charlie Morrow

The Breath

one does not place the breath
the breath is a place

in breathing one emits a constant steam of life information
    how you feel
    how healthy your body is
    how you are in the moment/situation
    how you are in the location—the space around you
                    the larger spaces

other people can read this
other breathing things can read this

the colors of the breath &
the rhythms of the breath &
the articulations of the breath
1. can be followed & duplicated by others
2. are a basis for world view

Breath Chant

form a circle of people (a circle can be two people)
one person breathe audibly in any patterns & everyone track & imitate
then another person take over until the circle has been
then another & another until the circle is done at least once

multiple times around the circle deepen the process

some people like to talk between segments

eye contact: some lead eyes closed & some eyes open
              some follow eyes closed & some eyes open

Breath Chant as a Healing Piece

The patient is touched by the other members of a group.
The patient breathes audibly & inaudibly.
The group tracks audibly & inaudibly.
The end comes by itself.

Placing the Word (Sound) on a Breath

A word can be placed anywhere on a breath, exhale & inhale.

Gently breathing, say a word.

Now repeat it, perhaps moving its location on the breath.

Continue this process of breathing & speaking.

Charles Olson's concept of breath in poetry is
the inspiration for a language that notates the
breath, in which the reader breathes with the
breath patterns and reads the words in their
locations. This has particular application for
nonrealtime language, where time can be controlled
like tempo in music.

For live readings or group silent reading, one
person can control the breathing of the others.

Placing the Word (Sound) on the Voice

THE WORD CAN BE LOCATED ANYWHERE IN THE VOICE.
That is the word can be said in any voice.
Voices are located in many places in the body.

Choose a word.
Speak it.
Repeat it in the same or different voice.
Continue the process.

This may include codes & sign languages.

Placing the Voice

THE VOICE IS IN MANY PLACES AT ONCE.

1. The Voice is in the breath

the voice occupies as much or as little time as it needs

2. The Voice is in the body

the voice can ring from any place in the respiratory column
        can vibrate any place on the body

3. The Voice is in the space around it

the voice can ring the space around it

the voice can expand & contract that space by calling, whispering & &

4. The Voice is in the world
people from certain places like to use the voice alike
all things have their sound

5. The Voice is in the Mind/Universe

connections as sensed & felt

I & the voices that speak thru me: my father, the wind
All sound & no sound

Voice & Time in the Beating (OMitted beating) is TRAVELLING
                                                    DWELLING

Voice & Stage of Life: young, old, etc.

Voice & Gender: male, female, androgyny

SOME NOTES RE SOUND, ENERGY, AND PERFORMANCE

Steve McCaffery

W hen considering sound it is energy not meaning that is the essential form of communicated data.

And on the supposition that form is frozen energy (Reich) and that form is conventionally goal, target, destination, that which is arrived at through com-position (Aristotle)

then what the sonic poet practices is the frontal de-formation of language treating form as that state of language which constitutes a point of departure.

This not to be achieved alone. In isolation with the single voice anchored to a unilinear vector. But through group soundings. The poem as community. A living syntax in the bioenergetic interweavings of multiple voice and multiple bodies.

Theater?
Polis?

Perhaps. But like the Inuit throat poetry audience becomes dispensable by absorption.

I had worked five years in sound performances before I realized that the focused factor throughout every performance was the dialectic of the occasion: the actual syntax and configuration of energies and feelings that the interface of audience and performer created together. This was no ordinary informational circuit but a structure best likened to the parallelism of two dynamos or rhyming energy fields constantly charging and recharging. And this was possible—natural in fact—because the communicative goal was non-informational and non-cortical. Cortex, being that interface of matter colliding with language, the acoustic poem was directed away from that interface transmitting energy as fragmented linguistic particles through sound and vibration to the spinal column. Energy up the spine. Through the CNS. Which makes of conventional intellection and critical response to sound poetry irrelevant. What is needed is a critical vocabulary, a rhetorical set that is relevant to the neural direction and spinal implications of the sound-sign-calorie.

The abstract sound as the signification of an energy referent. A circular sign. A dynamo charge with sign and referent poles. Terminals. Abstract sound then diagrams energy flow and in performative context has a geomantic relevance. It realigns the flow created from audience and performer's energy.

Fracture on the plane of lexeme and syntagm both result in energy release in the eventist field of phoneme and subphoneme. Sound abstracted and reconfigurationalized becomes an extension of verbal sign into its immediate presence as event. Entity. Ball's "plasticization of the word."

The sound poem as a way of returning language to its own matter. Concretization of the referent by cutting the referent line. Compaction and release and the replacement of the linear thrust of sign (through signifier to signified to referent) with the dilation of the energy flow, a constant process of extending outwards, a rounding and marginalization of a kinetic frame.

Sound: the somatic property in language. Non-functionally experienced. Listen to that

Paint
   a surface on a surface.
Sound
   an event on an event.

Language. Physis. The somatic nexus. *La poeme c'est moi*. And yet the absolute annihilation of the subject. Body in sound in dilation. What is it? What it is.

Sound when autodemonstrative, when at the service of no verbal meaning, becomes its own referent.

And the rhyme of the language and the soma. Give an audience that. What is called a self-discovery. The rhymes being possible: lips. lungs. generative organs. testes (tes tes O'Huigan). eyes. Plus the rhythms and vibrations in pulse. beat of heart. intercourse. breath. the compulsory rhythms of the body finally articulate.

Then after the knock comes the silence. The audience listen. They answer. The door opens. It is formed.

To return the body to those energy zones previously repressed and chanelled into rubric and frigidity.

Freedom to.

Not freedom from however. To suggest by this not an apoetics of anarchy but the return to a state that gives the freedom to construct pragmatically and spontaneously one's own rule structures. Good for one performance. And hence the audience as witnesses and co-participants alike. Structures modified in accord with the unique relationship of audience to performer no. But audience and performer. Two audiences perhaps. As Stein says defining genius as the simultaneous expression and reception of a sound. Who speaks. Who listens. Who speaks as listening. THAT.

Finally the text. Text as a dialectic term. The antithetical surface from which a performer reacts, responds projecting out into the unique synthetics of performance. Unique. Unrepeatable. The life of a piece is its total sum of performances. The sound text leading to a constructed multiple through time action and memory patterns. A non-ideational text, a predenotative, absolutely improvisatory product. It must have this freedom for energy knows no duplicated shapes. Energy is reactive to the form that freezes it. What the body frees. The text freezes. Hence a text permitting multiple access with wide graphic possibilities. Opto-phonetic scoring based upon the procedural rhyme of typographic size and audible volume. Pitch values assigned to the traditional geography of the page; the transformation of north to high, south to low and the east west axis: normal pitch. Graph paper for immediate, ready-made time units.

Syntax: as much a biologic as linguistic space.

Sound the event not the servant of semantic becomes a possible antidote to the paradox of sign. That a thing need not be a this standing for a that but immediately a that and so free of the implications of the metaphysics of linguistic absence.

Steve McCaffery with The Four Horsemen   Photograph by Stephen Ruppenthal

SCORE FRAGMENT: THE SAME LANGUAGE

Stephen Ruppenthal

The Same Language is the opening work of a seven-part composition exploring sonically the middle ground between verbal/nonverbal communication. The representational modes of text and nontext are realized in such a manner to achieve a balance within a closely related background-foreground environment. It is the composer's intent to revitalize and invoke the "spirits" and energies of the words/text through vocal fragmentation and integration with the psychological powers inherent in a dronelike sonic meditation.

Totemic Illusions, BMI, 1977. Based on an Eskimo text, "Magic Words," with English working by Edward Field, from Knud Rasmussen. Used by permission.

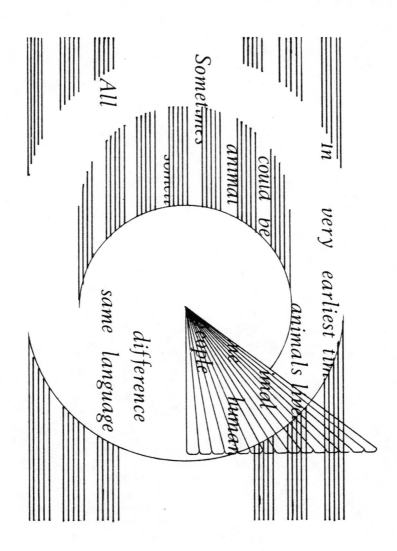

All

Sometimes

In very earliest th...

animal

coud be

animals b...

someti...

difference

same language

human

SOUND SCORES

Larry Wendt

the technological and natural worlds.
By the confrontations of humanity
with their environment, words have been
fragmented and split open by the blos-
soming technologies: their vital substan-
ces are spilled upon the new occurances
and the archaic phenomena which gave
birth to them to form subtle onomatopo-
etic analogies. Through the rules genera-
ted by these analogies, a sound will sug-
gest another and the connection between
primitive formations and their most abs-
tract derivations are erased by technology
to lead one on an endless quest for ety-
mologies. The text is no longer a crypto-
graphic signature of the world which
demands an interpretation from us but
rather its presence is a force which di-
rectly impresses itself upon our minds and
bodies to color all of our pains and pas-
sions.
We are therefore speaking here of a
language of electrical fluctuations,
mechanical noises, animal sounds, bio-
rhythms, Fibonancci constants, mythic

This is a documentation of life and
work in the *Silicon Valley* of California:
an area south of San Francisco which
contains the major semiconductor indus-
tries of the United States. The large-scale
manufacturing of high-density integrated
circuits provides the worker with some of
the most sophisticated and tedious labor
on the planet. This text-sound composi-
tion could be the story of any person's
job, from welders to chemists, and about
the eroding processes of modern labor
which reduces us to the automatic levels
of the machines which we work upon.

the microcosm between humanity and its
environment.
    Over the past few years, it has been
noticed that many natural and man-made
phenomena share certain statistical char-
acteristics in regards to their periodicity.
For example, such cited events as sun-
spot activity, the changes in river levels,
the membrane currents of the nervous
system, the noise produced by certain
semiconducting devices, the fluctuations
of traffic flow, the programming upon
radio, and most music all exhibit a subtle
property of spectral density which ap-
proximates the inverse proportion of
their frequency of occurrence. All of
these events display some order of re-
gularity but they also simultaneously ex-
hibit an element of uncertainty; they lie
in between the random collisions of par-
ticles known as *white noise* and the de-
terminable bounces of a particle locked
within a box known as Brownian Move-
ment. Such *in between* events have been

The 1978 Toronto Sound Poetry Festival

Larry Wendt

O
n October 1978, in Toronto, the Eleventh International Festival of Sound Poetry brought together more than forty performers from seven different countries for an intense week of activities. For the first time, a sound poetry event of this proportion took place on the North American continent.

The international festivals began in 1968 when the Literary Unit of the Swedish Broadcasting Corporation and a Swedish avant-garde performing society known as Fylkingen hosted three consecutive performances of sound poems by practitioners from France, England, Germany, and Sweden. The intent was to present material which would not have been allowed at a conventional poetry reading or a contemporary music concert. The performances dealt almost exclusively with works utilizing the then-current technological developments in the manipulations of vocal material—pieces which the people at Fylkingen had given the title "Text-Sound Composition"; hence the festival title: International Festival of Text-Sound Composition. Its emphasis on technologically assisted productions of linguistic art separated this festival from previous sound poetry festivals. Later festivals lost their emphasis on this technological mode of sound poetry. In 1974, when the festival moved to London, "Text-Sound Composition" was dropped from the title to be replaced by "Sound Poetry."

Sound poetry can be traced back to the literary experiments of Futurism and Dada. Many of the avant-garde art movements in the first half of the twentieth century were involved with producing literary works which were paradoxically "nonliterary" and which belonged somewhere in between poetry, music, and performance. These works placed an emphasis upon the physical sonorities of language rather than on semantics. A more deliberate and self-conscious attempt to produce sound poetry became evident in the 1950s, largely as a result of the invention of the tape recorder, which both aided in a wider distribution of the material and provided more potentials for its production.

The Toronto festival continued to place heavy emphasis on acoustical sound poetry. Though sound poetry ideas have been distributed throughout the world by recordings on disk and tape (and by the rare radio station), recordings alone can lead the listener into limited or erroneous conceptions about the work of a particular artist. Sound poetry is a performing art; as such, it has to be seen to be fully comprehended. Although many "regulars" from the earlier European festivals were at Toronto, several new faces appeared from Canada and the United States. Participants' experience in the field ranged from a few years to more than twenty-five, so the variety in performance styles was immense.

Sound poetry remains an experimental artform. Many of its ideals are far from being fulfilled or exhausted, and it lacks clear theoretical definition. Several tendencies were apparent at Toronto. Both acoustic and technically augmented works were presented. Both group presentations, of sound poems and solo performances were given. Some performers used elaborate movements and theatrical gestures; others used material which displayed a strong influence from ethnographic sources.

Greta Monach, a Dutch sound poet, gave a "classic" performance. Her work represents a highly evolved phonetic poetry whose roots can be traced back to *Die Sonata in Urlauten* by Kurt Schwitters. This work is made up of phonetic fragments—"nonsense" syllables which lack any kind of semantic reference. Monach arranged the fragments entirely for their musical effect, although they were spoken rather than sung. Monach's "Automaterga" series is composed of possible, though not actual, Dutch single syllables placed in complex auditive and visual arrays with the aid of a computer. In her performance at Toronto, Monach "read" a printed score of one of these pieces held in a music stand. Her vocalizations were rhythmically articulate and her "performing presence" was very much like that of the singer of a contemporary music score. Another work she performed had a more semantic basis. Its text was derived from a children's story, in English, called "Otto the Rhino." The actual English words and syllables read in this work were given a musical character by vocal distortions and by being placed in rhythmical and repeating juxtapositions. Once again the text was read precisely and skillfully. This style of reading became funny and delightful when combined with the childlike, humorous semantics of the piece.

A conception of sound poetry more like Hugo Ball's could be observed in the performance style of the New York poet, Bliem Kern. A performer with remarkable stage presence, Kern first appeared clanging two long aluminum vacuum cleaner tubes together, wearing knit ski gloves, a green corduroy suit, and red plastic boots, and chanting in "ooloo" (his own synthetic language) amid the stick incense he had placed about the performing area. Kern's work is on the boundary between serious ritual and satire. He often appears to be using influences from other cultures, and in many of his pieces he speaks "in tongues" and takes poses which resemble Egyptian icons. Kern's works are largely phonetic in nature. He often begins with recognizable words and phrases which he alters into unknown words by naturalistic and seemingly casual methods. He also makes frequent use of pantomime; in one instance, he did a perfect imitation of a barnyard chicken. Kern's shorter works appeared elaborately choreographed in terms of movements related to the sounds he was vocalizing.

A more serious use of ethnopoetic materials used as sound poetry appeared in the work of the well-known American poet and anthologist, Jerome Rothenberg. He performed pieces from his translations of the Navaho "Horse Songs." The "Horse Songs" are "total" translations of Indian chant-poems: an attempt to translate the nonsense syllables and performance context as well as the words. The poems were chanted by Rothenberg who accompanied himself with a horn rattle. He also read some of the songs with a multi-track tape. Rothenberg's voice recorded several times reading the same text has the effect of a chorus of singers; he has translated the Indian group singing situation into a technological multi-voiced context. Rothenberg ended with a tribute to the Dadaist and Surrealist Tristan Tzara that included a sound poem by Tzara, a Kabbalistic sound poem made up of the letters of the name of God, and a more conventional poem about Tzara. Rothenberg's poetry is a true synthesis of many cultural aspects. The balance between these factors is difficult to achieve and form into an honest expression of our culture, but Rothenberg, with skill and naturalness, makes his work very much a part of the American experience.

Another American, Charlie Morrow, also makes use of this kind of ethnic material as a source of inspiration. Morrow also uses folk instruments; he entered the performance space in Toronto with a chorus of ocarina players. Unlike Rothenberg, who uses recognizable words in all of his pieces, Morrow deals with skillful multiphonic chants and songlike structures. In Toronto, he did a "trance" piece in which he chanted in a high-pitched voice while striking a gong. He then spoke to the audience about the visions he had seen while chanting. He ended the performance by taking the whole audience out of the performance hall and instructing them to produce dronelike sounds in harmony with the Toronto traffic and night sounds.

The performers at Toronto often made gestures and body movements an integral and important part of their presentations. Many times, as in the work of Bill Bissett, the body movements were of an accentual character, produced as a result of a particular vocalism. In other cases, as with Kern, the movements were semantic. A fine example of this semantic movement could be seen in the work of the master Italian sound poet, Arrigo Lora-Totino. Part mime and part Commedia del'Arte, Lora-Totino had the Toronto audience gasping with laughter with very short phonetic pieces which consisted of Italian puns acted out in pantomime. These "athletic poems" included actions such as the feeling out of the spatial dimensions between "finite/infinity," the hand-shaking of a politician working himself up to a heart attack, and the vomiting of phonetic fragments from eating too many food-words. Lora-Totina also used a hornlike device filled with water to modulate his voice for a series of "liquid poems." At one point he threw the entire contents of the horn on the audience.

A tendency toward group recitation of acoustic sound poetry, especially among English and Canadian sound poets, was also prevalent at the Toronto festival, moreso perhaps than at any previous festival. Most of the Canadian groups did acoustic sound poems. Even a simple public address system was often excluded, and they depended upon the strength of their voices. Perhaps most exemplary of the Canadian sound poetry groups was the Horsemen: Rafael Barreto-Rivera, Paul Dutton, Steve McCaffery, and bp Nichol. A real crowd pleaser, their performance filled St. Lawrence Hall with applause and laughter as the high-energy group gesticulated with slaverings of phonetic atomizations, ejaculatory glossolalia, and paroxysmal wheezes (often well-lubricated, as in the case of McCaffery, with copious amounts of saliva). Their work explored the oral manifestations of speech in a variety of ways ranging from the semantic to onomatopoeia and abstract phonetics. One of their more semantic works consisted of a fixed sentence pattern repeated by McCaffery and Dutton in which an exchange of insults was generated by changing the object with each repetition. Dutton usually received the raw end of the transfer. Their more phonetic works were usually accompanied by wild and humorous theatrics: During the performance of the phonetic masterpiece "OP Relations," McCaffery gargled with a soap solution, with bubbles emerging in a sickening fountain from his mouth. During another piece, each member of the group had a towel wrapped around his mouth to prevent meaningful articulations. Though much of their material is improvisational, their performances are highly structured, polished, and tight, with few vocalisms or gestures wasted. The intensity of their expression and the skill with which they project their energies toward the audience clearly illustrates their eight years of working together.

Another Canadian group of four was Owen Sound: Michael Dean, David Penhale, Steven Smith, and Richard Truhlar. Obviously influenced by the Horsemen, their material was a bit different and was presented in a less intense and more improvisational fashion. In one piece, *"Kinderspielgesang,"* children's "noise-making" toys piled upon a card table were picked up and played: the performance was more reminiscent of Mauricio Kagel or an early Dada "noise" orchestra rather than a piece of sound poetry. Another interesting piece was performed by Richard Truhlar, who wore a black cloak and a dark grotesque mask and used highly amplified breath sounds.

The English group Koncrete Canticle has performed together off and on since 1971. Each of its members—Bob Cobbing, Paula Claire, and Bill Griffiths—is also well-known as a solo sound poet. Bob Cobbing was the first explorer of sound poetry in England and is a long-time experimenter in visual and performance poetry. During their performance, the members of Konkrete Canticle would often wander through the audience while reading from pages of paper. A "text" was used for all of the readings. For one piece, a few rocks were ritually read by the members of the group; in another, a piece about plutonium, the burn markings of a soldering iron on paper was the text; still others used fragments of letters and words that resembled the works of the Abstract Expressionists. Many of these poems or "scores" were on large sheets of paper which were thrown about the stage as the reading was completed. The markings or "signatures" were given vocallic expression as well as some sort of gestural articulation. In one piece, a woman wearing a large white bag with a letter-fragment similar to the score the group was reading slowly crept and erotically gyrated across the stage while the group vocalized the piece to the audience. This way of "reading" a text, developed by Cobbing and his associates, has since been "picked up" and used by other sound poets in the world and was prevalent at Toronto.

Jackson Mac Low is a solo performer who also writes a number of pieces to be performed by groups. He has been a seminal American poet for over thirty years because of his pioneering use of indeterminacy in poetry. His performance at Toronto contained perhaps the largest variety of sound poetry forms that was made use of by any acoustic sound poet. He did works for single voices, small groups, and large groups (made up of other participants at the festival who performed the works expertly). These works were composed of fragmented, simultaneous, and permutated texts (such as a "found" text from *Scientific American*). Mac Low also performed a long series of pieces with a piano, and with an "8-voiced canon" for tape, "The Black Tarantula Crossword Gathas."

Some of the performers already mentioned used prerecorded tapes to emphasize certain qualities of the human voice beyond its physiological limitations. Technically-aided sound poetry can "accent" or "amplify" acoustical parameters of speech which are below routine awareness levels. As with purely orally manipulated sound poetries, this increase of the perceptible dimensions of language increases the amount of information which it can contain. The use of technology also introduces the added advantage of being able to explore areas which the "mere human" cannot.

One of the founding pioneers in the use of the tape recorder for the production of sound poetry is Henri Chopin, who presently resides in England. His performance at Toronto gave a sampling of his use of "micro-vocallic particles" (his term for fragmented phonemes) and intensely amplified "body" sounds (swallowing, rubbing the microphone against the unshaven cheek, farting, and so on). He also made occasional use of conventional words to yield, by means of extensive superimpositions, multi-layered aural works that are sonic representations of physiological processes. At Toronto, Chopin not only augmented his tapes with on-stage vocalizations but also conducted, in a very idiosyncratic manner, the person playing the tape to indicate the amplitude levels. Chopin's tapes also cued his responses in that particular performance situation. What would probably appear crude and superficial in the hands of another was done by Chopin with style, wit, and charm. It would be extremely difficult to imagine anyone doing sound poetry as uniquely expressive as that of Chopin.

Another pioneering French artist of *poesie sonore* at Toronto was Bernard Heidsieck. Heidsieck's pieces, more semantic and grounded in words and syntax than Chopin's, are a "mixage" of words and phrases with sociological ramifications. Often the sounds of the environment of the words and phrases are included. In performance Heidsieck usually supplements the gut-rending intensity of his tapes with a live reading. His presence reminded me of an over-wound alarm clock about to explode. His most recent work, *"Démocratie,"* involves several superimpositions on tape of his voice reading the names of the French prime ministers since the Revolution: Starting from the back of the performance area, Heidsieck moved slowly forward after each name was heard on tape and simultaneously read from a tightly clutched slip of paper which was discarded after being read. In the piece "Vaduz," the names of all the different races in the world were read from a long scroll of paper. This reading was also simultaneously heard on a multi-voiced tape. In these pieces the text functions more as a prop than as a score; the tape actually provides the performance cues. Several of Heidsieck's sound poems performed at St. Lawrence Hall and A Space were concerned with making such day-to-day things as shaving in the morning, eating snacks, and hearing and seeing cliches in the streets into a tightly contained, powerful experience. The most trivial of events was transformed into an intense poetry.

Unlike the "hot," emotionally-charged performances of Chopin and Heidsieck, Sten Hanson's work is cool and involving. Presently the director of Fylkingen, Hanson's techniques for manipulation of the human voice are skillful beyond comparison. He purposely restricts his processing of vocal material to "subtractive" and filtering techniques. His text-sound compositions are often humorous and political in content. In most cases at Toronto, the tapes which he played cued his gestural responses, such as bowing continually during "How Are You?" or performing an elaborate choreography with his back with another tape. He also presented a projected sequence of slides augmented by tape, and he played his tape masterpiece of verbal kineticism, "OIPS," in the dark. He ended his performance with "AU 197,0" in which he acted out the part of the "God of Materialism" with vocalisms and tape.

A performance of live or "real-time" electronics was presented by Stephen Ruppenthal, an American. In "Cloud Forests," two performers simultaneously read a text which progressed by oral manipulations into phonetic fragmentations while, at the same time, Ruppenthal electronically processed his own voice and gradually returned it to normal. This piece was also augmented by musical sounds from a voltage-controlled processor.

The Baltimore group, CoAccident, gave a performance which made use of nearly every means of doing sound poetry presented at Toronto. Along with the core members of CoAccident—Alec Bernstein, Kirby Malone, Chris Mason, and Marshall Reese—an indeterminate number of people were involved in their performance at A Space. A large technical system was used which consisted of eighteen video monitors (in a wide array of playback modes), visual poetry on slides, real-time electronics and synthesizers, and "found" and conventional musical instruments. Absurd and surreal costumes and theatrics were employed by the performers. During one part of their presentation, large letters on sheets of paper were "read" by several individuals rolling upon them while screaming. Most of the action was generated by three or four (or five?) performers moving about wildly and generally acting lobotomized.

The works presented at Toronto could not be ascribed to a single art movement but rather to a mode of working that is as multi-faceted as a medium such as painting. Certainly one could detect similar ways of working and particular continuities of influence among groups of performers, often along nationalistic lines. More often than not though, the performers presented unique and individualistic interpretations of what they believed sound poetry

Larry Wendt   Photograph by Stephen Ruppenthal

to be. "What is sound poetry?" was the question most often asked by visitors and journalists to the Toronto festival. As Steve McCaffery answered, "You would think that after twenty years of work in this field, we wouldn't be asked this question anymore." But the question appears to be a fundamental aspect of sound poetry. After each evening's performance, small bands of likeminded practitioners would roam the Toronto streets and congregate in the isolated confines of hotel rooms, late-night restaurants, or bars and say, "That was interesting, but is it sound poetry?" What was revealed was that tastes are individual, that there is no single clear conception of what sound poetry is, and that sound poets are an especially diverse group with little contact between factions.

With the disappearance of several internationally distributed sound poetry publications in the early seventies (*Stereoheadphones, OU, Kontexts,*), sound poetry festivals have remained the major vehicle and point of contact for the transfer of ideas about sound poetry. Because of financial problems, Toronto may have been the last festival of its kind. In the future, we will likely see more specific or regional festivals put on in several places around the world. A "running dialogue" in the form of publications of theoretical documents and recorded anthologies will have to be maintained and increased in order for a cohesive artform to continue to exist. Otherwise sound poetry will become just an aspect of several other artforms.

For some, sound poetry is a "tool": a momentary resting place between what people are doing and where they are going. To others, it is a way of life, a way of focusing their reality, and a search for what is unique and whole in the human communicative processes. The Toronto festival, despite its limitations, allowed interactions between artists who have widely different experiences and conceptions about sound poetry. The scope and variety of performances at Toronto has undoubtedly generated relationships in the world of sound poetry that will resonate for years to come.

Oroonoko

Charles Amirkhanian

critical Poe
tin tinder tin
banjo makeup
cakewalk
gumption
blunder reel

fat
'n tarry Sambo
'n dog
dilemma dancing
dancing

steak
'n bagel barter
steak steak
'n bagel barter bait bunt

critical Poe
tin tinder tin
tin tinder
banjo makeup
Poe Poe

    for four voices
    leader reads all lines
    leader joined on underlined phrases by
        Stanza One: reader two
        Stanza Two: reader three
        Stanza Three: reader four
        Stanza Four: all in unison, whispering

    for Peter Garland
    30 November 1973. Amsterdam

Copyright © 1973 by Charles Amirkhanian

The argument for the page:

Space Printing : Social Mode.

Automatic memory.

THE PRINTERS

Work by *Frances Butler, Alistair Johnston, Holbrook Teter &*
Michael Myers, Graham Mackintosh, Betsy Davids &
Jim Petrillo, and Cheryl Miller

. . . And of course the question came up of reading poems aloud. The world is mad, MAD on this subject. Would somebody start Meditation places of silence, so silent you couldn't help but hear the sound of your page without opening your mouth and reading books would come back. . . . "

—Lorine Niedecker in a letter to Cid Corman (July 12, 1967), *Truck* magazine.

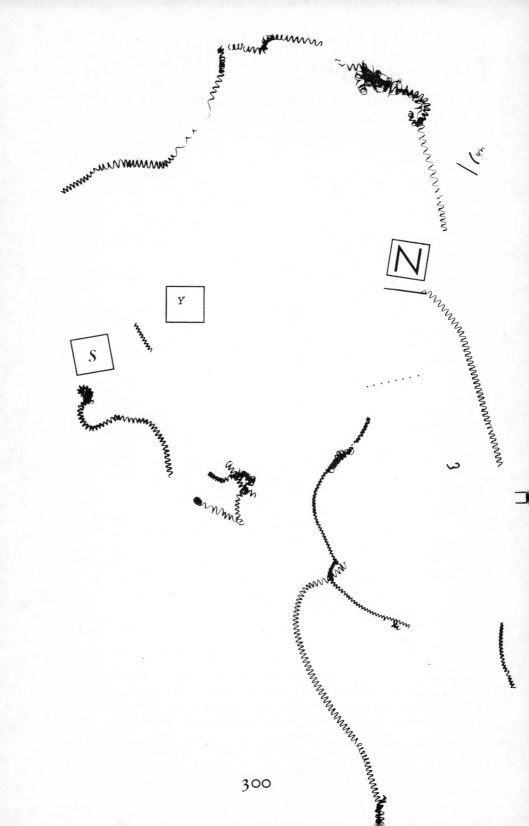

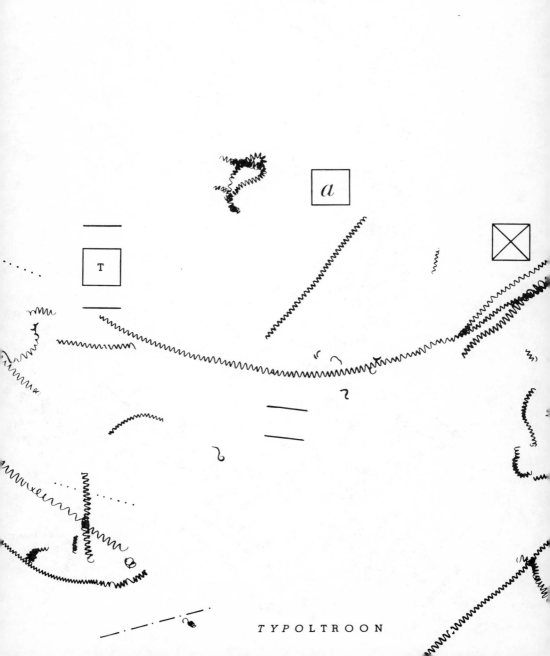

TYPOLTROON

a better
about
usually
s prefig...het to cove
...eenth ce...
ntury.
...to...
...nym...
...specimen...ano...
– for want
...y the al...indus

...d deb...
all the w...wh...kers in
...dents fo...s, the
...langud tr...inde
...ge-ori...

neers
...nders'
artists

M W...
O...nte...rk-In-Pro...
...wd do, n...sh...
...t the ...CIS...
...rete o...work of th...
typo-...
books o...
Futurists...isual poet...
...i the nine...

to a large...
the printin
urge...

of...
...naire and
...ti-faceted
...his form...
Apol...
...ginnings of th...
...raced back...
Shocks.
...of nine...
Marinetti...
which...
C. L...

...wledg...grou...
The...
artists wh...
Tod...
...to hist...

H...
...pe...
Latter
n Jabber...
ist & art
as is
al...

...ured...
...with occ...
...attemp...
Dod...Lew...disser...
...lity...the b...
...een...
Th...

302

Its raining ladies shoes

like I dont remember what

can you keep up this patter indef

carbon clouds have a certain resonance

listen if disdain & reglet flood the garden w
                                              t
                                              h
                                              e
                                              i
                                              r

ANTECEDENTS OF CONCRETE POETRY
‖Alastair Johnston‖

W HILE not attempting to establish precedents for all the wayward trends in dadaist & post-modern language art, the author's work-in-progress, *The Literature of Nineteenth Century Typefounders' Specimens* will demonstrate that the work of the Futurists and others credited as pioneers of concrete or typo -visual poetry was prefigured in typefounders' specimen books of the nineteenth century.

The Fellowship of Bohemian Scribes.

AN HOUR

for

SIMULTANEOUS WRITING

Throughout the World.

MINE
FREDSELE
TRAMONFORE
HENDS persona
SHURENOD hermione
REDINBURGH present form
REAN BIRMINEH unsdem emodan
THORNEAR TUSMIN retarded changers
MANCHESTER EXCURSIONS cremantile for measures
CRYSTAL REFRESHMENT ROOMS mention these arrangements

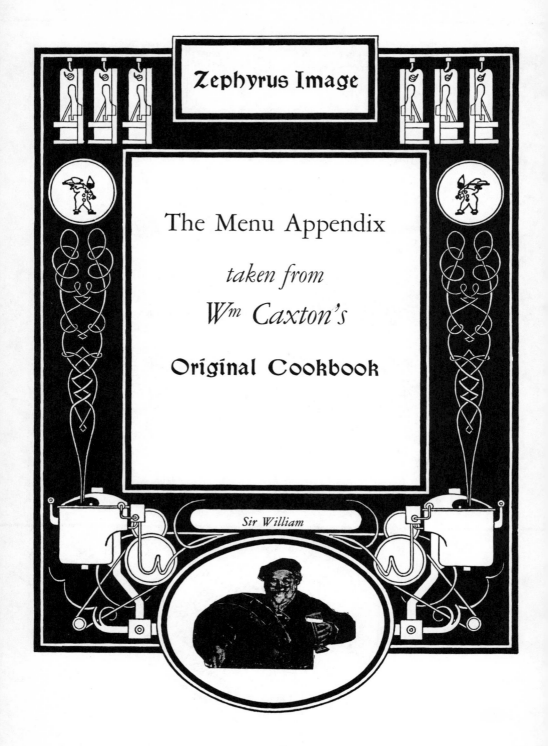

Zephyrus Image

The Menu Appendix

taken from

Wᵐ Caxton's

Original Cookbook

Sir William

Breakfast

Kerns & Whey
Bowl O' Kels   Buffalo Chapbook
Pickled Hairlines   Off-their-pigs-Feet

Eggs Palatino   Ham & Aldus
Hammond Eggs   Relievo-on-a-Shingle
Kerned Beef Nash   Fish Heads Sans Gill

Hot buttered Friskets
Jelly Rollers   French Paste-ups   Muts Melba

Folio Margarine

Spanish Flywheels
Frozen Uncials   Fruits Van Dyke

x-height x-presso
Caps Pacino   Thunderbird
Type Punch

Sir Real

Lunch

Stuffed Octavos
Smorrisbord   Colt-type Cuts   Ultra Bologna
Cloister Oysters   Helvetica on a Half Shell

Deep Dish Dene
Swash Kebab   Colophon Casserole   Mat Loaf
Stempel Shtew   Bodoni & Cheese

Candied Cams
Zincs Allemands   Basted Title Bâtarde
Bold Face Potatoes   Compuker Grotesque

Water Cresci
Soilant Green Futura, Belt Dressing
Romaine du Roi   Word Salad

Mould-made Jello
Stauffacher Jack Cheese   Goudy Cheese
Cheltenham Chip Cookies   Toasted Marsh Border

Sir Loin

Dinner

Boul' Miche Bouillabaisse
Aldus Minestrone   Bembo Gumbo
Hairline Soup

Printer's Thumb Paté
42-Line Lasagna   Pied Pica   Shrimp Shrdlu
Arrighi and Meatballs

Quoin Keys & Cabbage
Koch au Vin   Doves Ashendene
Ourhen Press Duck   Ground Roxburgher

Platen au Gratin
Corn-on-the-cob-Sanderson   Business Chard
Chandler & Rice

Butterscotch Roman
Stephenson Cake   Franklin Mints
Jock Full o' Nuts   Draw Sheet Cake

Zapfindel   Old Crow   Quoin Chianti

Sir Upp

Good FOOD

Mis-en-page (singular)

Mis[mises?]*-en-page*

These examples of placing *mis* on the page are, hopefully, self explanitory, and the astute student will realize the importance of placement goes beyond the French subject matter. Indeed, it ultimately leads us away, out from the gutter.

Mis-en-page

No doubt one of the most annoying aspects of modern trade books
the "pinching" that goes on in the gutter. It is annoying because
hile some bad or compromising things are unavoidable in book
oduction usually for reasons of economics or bad taste, there are
 reasons for crowding the text into the gutter. No particular
onomy is effected and the final appearance ultimately transcends
d taste and enters into the realm of dumb.
Type, or image, can be put easily anywhere on the page. Presses
d binding equipment are completely indifferent to this aspect of
e business, so why, then, does this practice persist?
My guess is that type or image on a single unbound page does look
st in the classical stance—that is: the top margin is no more than
's (.72%) of the bottom margin and the binding edge margin no
ore than ¾ of the thumb-edge. Books on typographic design give
untless examples of this, and visually it is quite true. A page so
yed out would make a very nice wall print or broadside but when a
hole bunch of them are gathered together and glued along the edge
 make a book the result is awful. One must either thrust one's
umbs deep into the crevice and torturously twist and bend back
til the spine breaks or simply ignore the first few words of the left
nd margin on the right hand page and the last few words of the
ht hand margin on the left hand side. Clearly both options are
or.
What I am getting at here is that the classical models must be
vised in light of today's actual manufaturing techniques if they are
 retain some semblance of pleasing proportion. This is called *mis-*
-page. A French term I presume, though my mastery of this lan-
age is incomplete. *Page* means, of course, page; and *en* means on. I
 not sure if *mis* is singular or plural though plural would seem
ore likely. In any case, here are several examples of *mis-en-page* by
ay of illustration:

't h e   b o w l   s p e e c h' by J u d y   G r a h n

art is like a bowl, meant to be both beautiful in itself, and to hold
other things within it . . .

art is not a way out, there is no way out. there is only what we've
got and how to turn it around to reinforce our fighting genius; to
clarify and point out what has been stolen from us and that we
must take it back or continue with nothing.

moving art is never only personal, it is never only self-expressive
and is never produced solely for the purpose of publication, for
museums or for record companies. nor do artists ever know when
they have produced it; only other people can judge a bowl by its
usefulness to them.

at its best, art comes from our bitterest anger, our most expansive love, our most courageous hopes, our most vital visions, our most honest insights, our fiercest determination. and this is a collective feeling; if the collective is fragmented, then the art will speak of loneliness and alienation, of longing and isolation. if the collective is together, the art even at its best, catches only the thinnest glimmer of what we all feel, when we allow ourselves to show how we feel, and of how we all act, when we push ourselves and each other to act. now it is time to forget about the word *bowl* since that is simply an analogy of something which is socially useful and at this particular time a bowl is not socially useful although it should be. perhaps the work instead shapes itself into a long shiny surface which someone holds up and we all peer into it saying yes, that is a face i recognize, that is an event i formed, that is what determination looks like, that is how resistance sounds. many people have pretended to see the bowlmaker in the shiny surface but she is not there, she is over here holding up a piece of clay; sometimes people see the shine and say, every witch must have a knife and then someone else will say hey i just cut myself on that image while someone else will take it and bury it in her enemy's heart, that is what i mean by socially useful, that is what i mean by moving art.

Copyright 1975 by Judy Grahn. Reprinted by permission.

*First in a series of broadsides printed for friends
& neighbors of Interval Press.*

THREE HATTED LADIES,","

YOUR BASIC MIDWESTERN LADIES,,

TAKING A WALK.

I tell
the lady
next to me
that this is EXACTLY
what my life is like
isn't just a walk; we
from one place to another
◆ We're climbing steeply;
these days. This
women are traveling
place for a REASON.
this is a building we're
climbing over; it's a CHURCH ROOF: we somehow missed
the street & got onto this church instead, & now we have
to climb over it to get down to the street again. ◆ The
lady next to me loses her hat and complains that she's the
fourth generation in her family to make this climb, and the
footing is very precarious; as a matter of fact, there are nails
on this roof. ◆ Oh, I say, it's nothing UNUSUAL.

fresh worth

I'm listening to someone talking about a new toothpaste called WORTH. Health-food people like it. The someone wants to mix up a fresh batch of WORTH for a bazaar. Usually you can only buy year-old WORTH with a preservative in it; if he were selling FRESH WORTH, he could make a real killing.

Now I'm looking at a tube of WORTH and watching a TV commercial. The tube says WORTH is "silver-free." The tube says: people call it THE SILENT ONE. The media voice says: "Do YOU talk with pink gums flapping? You can learn to talk more silently with WORTH."

& next to me is Jim Petrillo showing this slide show and mocking the TV demonstrator. He smiles with pink gums showing, then pretends to speak with only the edges of his teeth visible. He says "SHAKESPEARE."

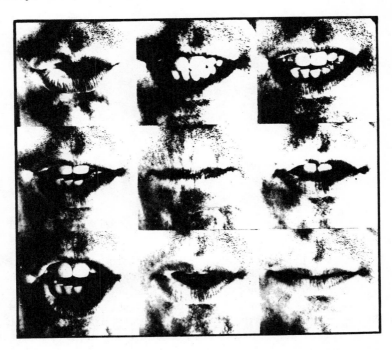

I say: not a chance! with a soft voice like mine I'd never be audible the silent way. I'll always be stuck with showing my gums.

_et_Uo_e _=OP_e
_h_e _e_=S_ol_ed_e
_eic'_t _e _O_t_t_e
_sh_t

The pieces included here evolved from text & typography by Davids and images by Petrillo. *Three Hatted Ladies* is an excerpt from *Books & Changes*, a narrative performance piece for slides & voice, and was originally published in 1976 as a Rebis performance ticket & keepsake. The lady on the left is B. Davids. *Fresh Worth* is the 1976 broadside version of a performance piece based on a dream account & usually performed in its heyday with American Sign Language translation. *Ceviche de Turista* is a Mexico tourist joke & the first in an ongoing series of typographic takes on Kufic calligraphy & was originally published in Fe Mail Art/Vile No. 6, 1978.

AGAINST READINGS

Ron Sukenick

WHILE I AM NOT ONE to pass up a reading, it seems to me that the reading circuit has had some negative as well as some positive effects on poetry. A few things to think about:

A reading puts emphasis on the performance, not the poem.

Some good poets are bad readers.

Some bad poets are good readers.

If the essence of poetry is its performance in public, why not hire trained actors for readings?

If it is essential for the poet to read his or her own poems, what right have we to say that John Ashbery is better than Rod McKuen? Or is he?

Some poems perform well, some don't. Which are better? How do you decide?

Reviews of readings are not reviews of poems. Reviews of readings divert attention from the quality of poems.

Oral traditions come out of traditional folk cultures. Most of us don't have such a culture and can't impose one on ourselves.

Oral poems are not written down and then read aloud later. They are composed and transmitted orally. Nor are they the property of an individual poet. The closest thing we have to an oral tradition is the blues.

What is the need for books? Why not just bypass them? Burn them?

In the unlikely event I feel the need for some poetry between readings, what do I do? Buy the record?

Instead of books, what about movies of poems?

From now on instead of getting up in the morning and confronting my manuscript and my typewriter, I will get up and mutter to myself. I just hope I remember what I say.

Did you ever attend a Gary Snyder reading, with three quarters of the audience applauding at the wrong places?

If living performance is the thing, what happens after the poet has died?

If recordings replace books, Bob Dylan beats Allen Ginsberg every time.

Is there a difference between oratory and poetry? If so, what is it?

In a live audience situation, the tendency is to try to please the audience. You find yourself reading things that are most effective for live audiences. Oh well, that's show biz.

What about the individual, reading alone, and thinking about what he or she reads?

The pen is mightier than the word.

THE POEM AS OBJECT

Ted Pearson

THE ORAL PRESENTATION of poems written to be read on the page may be said to constitute a provisional form of publication, making available, however momentarily, to an audience of prospective readers, poems otherwise not yet "in print," as well as published poems unknown to all or part of a given audience.

When the writer of poems written to be read on the page is involved in such a presentation, it is "understood" that he or she is in fact reading *from* a text *to* an audience and is not giving a performance *of* a text *for* an audience. It is further "understood" that the text as such is complete in itself and is neither dependent on such presentation for its existence nor intended to serve as an element in a matrix of elements coherent in the term and act of performance.

These conventions, whose purpose may be aided by a manner of presentation which both acknowledges and attempts to minimize the mediating role of writer as performer, are necessary adjuncts to a premise which insists on the primacy of the text as the appropriate object of attention.

The text of a poem written to be read on the page is neither script nor score, nor, strictly speaking, and regardless of its intrinsically evidential character, is it transcript or documentation. Simply: Any and all relevant procedural data is present in the completed text, singularly, and by definition.

It is useful to reflect on the grounds on which a poem written to be read on the page is only provisionally available to an audience (as distinct from a readership) to which it is orally presented. In these reflections it is well to remember that such a poem is not written *for* the page, but *on* it. Writing requires a surface, by definition. The text exists for the reader.

Serious readers of poems are aware of the intimate and diverse pleasures to be had from the reader/text relation. The possibility of determining for oneself what, how much, at what pace, and in what manner one will, in the event, read, as well as the option of *re*-reading, as one goes, or over whatever period of time; that is, the varying degrees of attention one is moved to bring to a text—all this, and more, as we say, is solely within the province of the reader.

The writer (as reader of the text which he or she is writing) shares in the awareness of these possibilities and is (as writer of the text to be read) complexly subject to this awareness. That the poem *is* written—of necessity—comprises an event of a separate order from that in which what is written *may* be read. The context in which the poem as such exists is that of "all poems."

Any attempt to further limit (qualify) this context inevitably results not only in the diminution of the poem's access to its own possibility but also in the unwarranted restriction of possible reader/text relations. This result obtains regardless of any *a priori* specification (on the part of the writer) of who the reader, actually or virtually, is, or might be.

Given that a poem is *written,* its content is, without exception, language. By definition. Speech has nothing to do with this. Neither do words, as such. Poems have been written without words, poems which cannot be spoken. But no poem is, or can be, written without language. Language as such. Not "yours," not "mine," though once such proprietariness is dismissed, it is necessarily one's own language, thus restored to its use-value, and as it becomes available from within oneself, to oneself, through the quality of one's attention to it, that leads one, from the inside out, to "secrets objects share."

To insist on the literal object-status of the text is to insist on the obvious. To insist that its content is language is, or should be, no less obvious. When the reader of the text is moved to recall the primacy of these terms, then he or she has regained a vista above and beyond the welter of contentions that result from forgetting to include the obvious in any sighting of "what is." And in thus regaining such prime ground, the reader is enabled to perceive and enjoy the ongoing transformations of the give (old:new) that the text is empowered to disclose.

"The best way to find out about poetry is to *read* the poems." Louis Zukofsky (italics mine). And Williams, commencing *Spring and All:* "If anything of moment results—so much the better. And so much the more likely will it be that no one will want to see it."

From "Big Talk and Small Business"

Francis O. Sinclair

THE FOLLOWING WAS OVERHEARD at the Small Business Expo, a business opportunity show held recently in the [San Francisco] Hyatt Regency's Embarcadero Exhibit Hall.

ASHLEY BENSON, Chicago: "I used to be a dancer in a small club and then I became a hypnotist's assistant in a bigger club and right before I moved I was dressing up like a rabbit and helping out a magician work out a new act. So you can say I've had some odd jobs. I'm looking to start a little business for myself. I don't even care if I flop.

"The guy over there just took me for a tour of his printing business. I was thinking of opening up a speedy print-out franchise, because everyone needs stuff in a hurry. Right? I used to have a boyfriend who was a poet—Ah, the old days, right? Everyone was a poet!—and he'd run into those speedy print-out places and get a thousand of his poems and hand them out at bus stops.

"Even poets rush around, right? I was working for the hypnotist at the time. The poet would be in the audience every night. He'd get hypnotized, then go in the back room and write until closing time.

"I know what you're thinking. You think I want to open one of those places in hopes my poet will walk in one day and we'd fall in love all over again over one thousand copies.

"Well, you're wrong. The guy became a Buddhist monk, and moved to Canada. Gave up poems, women and meat at the same time."

From "Big Talk and Small Business," by Francis O. Sinclair, *California Living, The Sunday Chronicle-Examiner,* June 22, 1979.

THE SILICON NATIVITY

Hilton Obenzinger

CHRISTMAS 1979 was the Silicon Nativity. The marketplace was flooded with computer toys that sold out weeks before Christmas Day. The silicon chip had fully come of age as the new mass commodity. Now what?

Computers and calculators are already being used in schools, and plans exist for even more extensive use. One prototype computer, using the famed silicon-chip circuitry, is the size of a slightly overlarge clipboard. Equipped with a video screen and a memory many times larger than the original UNIVAC, this clipboard computer is being tested as the student's textbook of the future. Math games, logic problems, individualized programs on any topic can be easily stored. Plugged into the central memory—the "main library"—it's possible that many students could read the same "book" at the same time as the words array themselves across each student's video screen.

Computers are being developed and marketed for home use as well. The bills could be filed, the oven turned on automatically, the alarm set, all according to program. Computers are being developed that can respond to a person's voice—or that can speak themselves.

The possibilities are enormous and are fast appearing before our eyes. Given the nature of capitalism, when a low-cost technological invention such as the silicon chip arrives, a market suddenly lunges into view. Next to the TV, the "memory" shall soon sit.

What does it all mean? Well, the speculations vary, but obviously the impact—on education, business, at home—is both inevitable and great. I'm sure the profits will be as well. But, speaking as a writer, as a poet, certain speculations tickle my fancy.

If books can be read from video screens, our notions of the page need to be revised. The movement of words arrayed across a screen? A continuity no longer cut off by the bottom of the sheet? Since words can be "typed" on the screen, it's possible for a poet to control the breath (or line or meter) visually. Would you like a dramatic pause or perhaps an enjambment? Just program your book for a slight hesitation. Perhaps a jerky, breathy, excited passage? Program it.

Perhaps this could be matched with a simultaneous reading. The audience could read the book (as the words move across the screen) and hear it read at the same time. The poetry "reading" can become a mass form.

Concrete poems, word-pictures, and other types of artful graphicisms could quite naturally be a part of the computer-poet's repertoire. But what about computer games, games of logic? What of those poets who see themselves as passionate scientists of language? What possibilities could they unfold by the marriage of mathematics and language? Could the poet create a language game, skillful and poetic, that engages both the poet and the reader? "Honey, I think I won't watch TV tonight. I feel like playing 'Paradise Lost' on the Compupoem. Wanna play?"

Many ideas are already being put into practice. I just received a copy of a Coach House Press Manuscript Edition. It's a manuscript, nicely typed and bound, of a poem labeled "First Draft, June 1979." They describe themselves this way:

Coach House Press Manuscript Editions are computer line-printer copies of works in progress—long poems, poetry collections, etc. They are run off and bound up as orders are received at the Press. The compositional date and number of the particular draft are clearly marked and as the manuscript is revised by the author these revisions are typed into the computer and the compositional date and draft number altered accordingly.

It is our hope with these editions to allow readers and writers more access to each other during the compositional process.

Hopefully, after requests come in for readings of drafts of a work, the readership will offer on-going criticisms to the author. A very helpful idea. It could, I suppose, develop into the basis for an entire style itself. Perhaps audience participation. Or serializations upon request like a soap opera or Dickens.

The computer format definitely helps a press in dealing with its sometimes risky marketing problems. How many editions have ended up stored away in some basement until the book finally sells out? With a computer that publishes upon request, it's possible that more works could reach the public, and at very little cost. I guess this might be similar to the advent of the mimeograph machine upon the world of the little magazines.

These are just speculations, small starts. But they are growing possibilities nonetheless. An area for language is being presented to us. Implications arise as to the relation between form and content—the development of new forms, and the like—that await exploration. It's exciting—as well as fearful.

Why apprehension? Without waxing too philosophical, modern technology is not an easy thing, nor is it neutral and always benign. Often it's used against us, against people. This misuse arises from social causes, not mechanical ones, as a rule—and the solutions are social. But technology makes a qualitative impact. It's not only *who's* using it (which class, society and the like) but the thing itself. Nuclear energy is a case in point. Or genetic modifications. Won't the advent of cloning do more than become good plot material for horror movies? The big question is: Will we become appendages of our own creations, or will human consciousness achieve new heights of knowledge and wisdom? So I think it's good to be wary. They probably asked the same thing when someone came up with a wheel and someone else fell under it.

To poets, as many of us seek warmth, the video screen seems a cold hearth indeed. Perhaps. The transition from handwritten manuscripts to moveable type was also disorienting, but it expanded language and literature enormously.

It seems so ephemeral, the word flashed on a screen. It's not substantial, heavy, like a book. And what about the smell of ink on a page as you press it against your nose? The feel of the page? A wonderful letterpress imprint? We should remember that sabotage lurks deep within our own best-loved devices. The way paper and inks are currently produced, most books are expected to self-destruct in about thirty or forty years. How's that for immortality? My goddamn words are gonna get eaten right off the page by some lousy acid! Perhaps a silicon chip holds at least as much chance for survival.

The writing, the artistry, or anything is still the telling part. Because art can be programmed—well, it still needs to be art. Poets are among the forefront of consciousness *or* appendage. We explore the choice. And we are well-known troublemakers. Soon, I am sure, we'll be deep inside a circuit, thrashing, giving solace and joy, making rebellion. The poet's program is inescapable.

EPILOGUE

The Editors

poetry, performance, and silence
   art as spiritual activity, as a functioning social entity that seeks to destroy self
   language pieces, exploration of language in context, the problem of work out of context that any printing of it, judging of it, talking about it on any level but an involved level, implies
   the audience involved in the piece, the paradox of our printing the traces of these social, transitory acts, the silence at the end of any book, last page turned, alone with how it entered you

Stephen Vincent
Ellen Zweig
Spring, 1981

Appendices

SELECTED BIBLIOGRAPHY OF NEW POETRIES

Larry Wendt

Selection of listed material is necessarily limited to personal interests and is by no means comprehensive. This list was compiled both to show the variety of twentieth-century poetic forms and to aid those who wish to seek more extensive and specialized sources. Categorical headings are used only as a rough means of generalizing this material and are not intended as absolute labels.

Performance

Books

ARTAUD, Antonin. *The Theatre and Its Double*. New York: Grove Press, 1958.

BAUMAN, Richard. *Verbal Art As Performance*. Rowley: Newbury House, 1977.

BENAMOU, Michel, and Charles Caramello, eds. *Performance in Postmodern Culture*. Center for Twentieth-Century Studies, University of Wisconsin at Milwaukee. Madison: Coda Press, 1977.

FRIEDMAN, Ken, ed. *Fluxshoe*. Catalogue. Cullompton: Beau Geste Press, 1972.

KAPROW, Allan. *Assemblage, Environments and Happenings*. New York: Harry Abrams, Inc., 1964.

KIRBY, E. T. *Total Theatre*. New York: E. P. Dutton and Company, Inc., 1969.

KIRBY, Michael. *Futurist Performance*. New York: E. P. Dutton and Company, Inc., 1971.

KULTERMANN, Udo. *Art and Life*. Translated by John Gabriel. New York: Praeger, 1971.

SCHECHNER, Richard, and Mady Schuman. *Ritual, Play and Performance*. New York: Seabury Press, 1976.

SOHM, H., ed. *Happening & Fluxus*. Catalogue. Cologne: Im Kölnischen Kunstverein, 1970.

Articles

CLAIRE, Paula. "Statement on My Performance Poems." *Rawz* (Summer 1977).

"Fluxus." Special issue. *Flash Art*, No. 84–85 (Oct.–Nov. 1978).

FRANK, Peter, Glenn Loney, Lenora Champagne, and Ron Blanchette. "Special Report: European Festivals and Performances." *Performing Arts Journal*, vol. II, no. 2 (Fall 1977).

"How We Met or a Microdemystification." Special Fluxus issue. *AG* 16 (1977).

KIRBY, Michael, ed. "Black Theatre." Special issue. *The Drama Review, vol.* 16, no. 4 (Dec. 1972).

MONK, Meredith. "Our Lady of Late." *The Painted Bride Quarterly,* vol. 3, no. 2 (Spring 1976).

MOTTRAM, Eric. "'Declaring a Behavior': The Poetry Performance." *Rawz* (Summer 1977).

MUMMA, Gordon. "The Once Festival and How It Happened." *Arts in Society,* vol. IV, no. 2 (1967).

ROTHENBERG, Jerome. "Some Notes Toward a Poetics of Performance." *Performance in Postmodern Culture* (Dec. 1977).

Records

AMIRKHANIAN, Charles, producer. *New Music for Electronic and Recorded Media.* Berkeley: 1750 Arch Street Records (S-1765), 1977. Johanna Beyer, Annea Lockwood, Pauline Oliveros, Laurie Spiegel, Megan Roberts, Ruth Anderson, and Laurie Anderson.

ASHLEY, Robert. *Private Parts.* New York: Lovely Music (LML 1001), 1977.

GEORGE, B., producer. *Airwaves.* New York: One Ten Records, 1977. Vito Acconci, Jane Haimsohn, Terry Fox, Julia Heyward, Dennis Oppenheim, Meredith Monk, Diego Cortez, Jim Burton, Leandro Katz, Connie Beckley, Laurie Anderson, Jacki Apple, and Richard Nonas.

KAPROW, Allan. *How To Make a Happening.* New York: Something Else/Mass Art Inc., n.d.

MONK, Meredith. *Our Lady of Late.* Minona Records, 1973.

———. *Key.* New York: Lovely Music (LML 1051), 1977.

MUMMA, Gordon. *The Dresden Interleaf* 13 *February* 1945/*Music From the Venezia Space Theatre/Megaton for Wm. Burroughs.* New York: Lovely Music (VR 1091), 1979.

WEINER, Lawrence. *Having Been Done At/Having Been Done To—Essendo Stato Fatto A.* Rome: Sperone Gian Enzo and Fischer Konrad, 1973.

Cassette Publications

ROBERTSON, Clive, ed. *Voicespondance.* Toronto: Arton's Publishing Inc. Includes:
  VSP 1 (1975): Fluxshore, Albert Mayr, Suzy Lake, Davi Det Hompson, Graham Challifour, Paul Woodrow, Dick Higgins, David Zack, Clive Robertson.
  VSP 2 (1976): Robert Filliou, Image Bank, Ray Johnson, COUM, General Idea, Vic d'Or.
  VSP 3 (1976): Dick Higgins and Emmett Williams. SP 4 (1978): Robert Filliou
  VSP 4 (1978): Robert Filliou and John Oswald.

Text-Sound Composition and Phonetic Poetry

Books and Text-Scores

BALL, Hugo. *Gesammelte Gedichte.* Zurich: Peter Schifferli, 1963.

———. *Flight Out of Time.* Translated by John Elderfied. New York: Viking Press, 1974.

LURIE, Toby. *New Forms, New Spaces.* San Francisco: Journeys into Language, 1971.

———. *A Handbook on Vocal Poetry.* San Francisco: Journeys into Language, 1974.

———. *Mirror Images.* Millbrae: Celestial Arts, 1974.

———. *Conversations With the Past.* Woodinville: Laughing Bear Press, 1977.

MAC LOW, Jackson. *Stanzas for Iris Lezak.* Barton, Vt.: Something Else Press, 1972.

————. *phone*. New York and Amsterdam: Printed Editions & Kontexts Publications, 1978.

————. 21 *Matched Asymmetries*. London: Aloes Books, 1978.

————. *First Book of Gathas*, 1961–79. Milwaukee: Membrane Press, 1979.

MARINETTI, F. T. *Zang Tumb Tuuum*. Milane: Edizioni Futuriste di "Poesia," 1914.

————. *Dune*. Firenze: *Lacerba* review, no. 4, 1914.

————. 8 *Anime in una bomba*. Milane: Edizioni Futuriste di "Poesia," 1919.

McCAFFERY, Steve, and bp Nichol. *Sound Poetry: A Catalogue*. Catalogue for the 11th International Festival of Sound Poetry. Toronto: Underwhich Editions, 1978.

MON, Franz. *Artikulationen*. Pfulligen: Günter Neske, 1959.

————. *Texte über Texte*. Berlin: Neuwied, 1970.

MONACH, Greta. *Compoëzie*. Utrecht: Samson Automatisering Servic Centrum bv., 1973.

ROBSON, Ernest M. *The Orchestra of the Language*. New York: Thomas Yoseloff, 1959.

————. *Transwhichics*. Chester Springs: Dufour Editions, 1975.

————. *Vowel and Diphthong Tones: New Procedures for Sound Poets*. Chapbook. Parkerford: Primary Press, 1977.

————. *Transcualisticas*. Bilingual Spanish Edition. Parkerford: Primary Press, 1978.

RÜHM, Gerhard. *Ophelia und die Wörter*. Darmstadt: Herman Luchterhand, 1972.

RUPPENTHAL, Stephen. *History of the Development and Techniques of Sound Poetry in the Twentieth Century in Western Culture*. San Jose: Master's Thesis, Music Department, San Jose State College, 1975.

SCHOLZ, Christian. *Zur geschichte der Lautdichtung: Vorstufen und entwicklung bis zum ende des Dadaismus*. Erlangen: Staatsexamesarbeit Unv. Erlangen, 1975.

SCHONING, Klaus, ed. *Neues Hörspiel: Essays, Analysen, Gespräche*. Frankfurt: Suhrkamp, 1970.

STIKKER, U. G. *Auchemie*. Groningen, 1968.

ZDANEVICH, Ilya (Iliazde). *LidantJU f Aram*. Paris: 41°, 1923.

————. *Poesie de mots inconnus*. Paris, 1949.

Articles

CHOPIN, Henri. "Naissance de L'Art Nouveau." *Cinquième Saison*, no. 14/15 (1962).

————. "Les mutations poetiques." *Les Lettres*, ser. 8, no. 30 (1963). Paris.

————. "Why I am the author of sound poetry and free poetry." *Artes Hispanicas*, vol. 1, no. 3/4 (1968).

————. *"Poesie sonore . . . apres vient la musique."* *Opus International*, no. 40–41 (Jan. 1973).

————. "La venue de la poésie phonetique." *De Tafelronde*, vol. 1, no. 10, Antwerp.

"Henri Chopin." *Ceolfrith* 18 (May 1972).

COBBING, Bob. "Between Poetry and Music." *isis*, no. 1507, Oxford (1966).

DOHL, Reinhard. "Fussnote und chronologischer Exkurs zur akustischen Poesie 1." *Die Sonde*, vol. 4, no. 33, Frankfurt am Main (1964).

DUFRÊNE, François. "Le Lyrisme, c'est ce qui nous chante." *Bizarre*, no. 32–33 (1964).

————. "Le crirythme et le reste." *De Tafelronde*, vol. 2, no. 13 (April 1967).

————. "Le Lettrisme et toujours pendant." *Opus International*, no. 40–41 (Jan. 1973).

EDBERG, Ulla-Britt. "'Sound Poetry' the Swedish Way." *Current Sweden*. Swedish Institute, no. 90 (Sept. 1975).

GARNIER, Pierre. "Manifest fur eine neue seh-und Lautposie." *Texturen*, no. 7, Munich (1963).

———. "Manifeste pour une poésie nouvelle, visuelle et phonique." *Les Lettres,* ser. 8, no. 29 (Jan. 1963).

———. "La poème phonétique." *Neue Texte,* 8/9 (March 1972).

GASSIOT-TALABOT, Gerald. "Bernard Heidsieck—notes et contresens." *Opus International,* no. 40–41 (Jan. 1973).

GIBBS, Michael. "Langwe Art." Review of the 10th International Festival of Sound Poetry. *Art Contemporary,* no. 9 (1977).

GLASMEIER, Michael C. "Auswahl-Bibliographie zur Theorie der Phonetischen Poesie." *Sprache in technischen Zeitalter,* no. 55, Stuttgart (July-Sept. 1975).

HAUSMANN, Raoul. "Introduction a l'Histoire du Poeme Phonétique." *German Life and Letters,* vol. xix, no. 1 (1965).

———. "Manifesto on the Lawfulness of Sound." *Form,* no. 4, Cambridge (1967).

———. "Meaning and Technic in Phonetic Poetry." *Form,* no. 5 (1967).

HEIDSIECK, Bernard. "Poésie action, poésie sonore 1955–1975. *Factotumbook,* 2, "Poesia Sonora 1." Brescia, n.d.

JANDL, Ernst. "Phonic Poetry." *Form,* no. 3 (1967).

JOHNSON, Bengt Emil. "Fylkingen." *Source,* vol. 4, no. 2 (1970).

JOLLAS, Eugen. "From Jabberwocky to 'Lettrism.'" *Transition,* second series, no. 1 (Jan. 1948).

KOSTELANETZ, Richard. "Text-Sound Art: Survey, Parts One and Two." *Performing Arts Journal* (Fall–Winter 1977).

KRIWET, Ferdinand. "Elektronische Musik und Hortexte." *diskus,* 15 (1965).

KUCHARZ, Lawrence. "Time-Form and Serial Procedures." *Ear Magazine,* vol. 3, no. 1, New York (Feb. 1977).

LORA-TOTINO, Arrigo. "Poesia da ascoltare." Venice: catalogue "poesia concreta," exhibition biennale venezia, 1969.

———. "Poesia orale: la componente fonica nella poesia d'avanguardia." *Arte e Poesie,* no. 11/14. Rome (1971).

MAYER, Peter, ed. "Bob Cobbing and Writers Forum." *Ceolfrith,* 26 (Oct. 1974).

MON, Franz. "Artikulieren und Lesen." *Nota,* no. 3 (1959).

OHUIGIN, Sean. "Eighth International Sound Poetry Festival." *Open Letter,* vol. III, no. 3 (Fall 1975).

PETRONIO, Arthur. "Verbophonie." *Les Lettres,* ser. 8, no. 31 (1963).

RIHA, Karl. "Übers Lautgedicht." *Sprache im technischen Zeitalter,* no. 55, Stuttgart (July-Sept. 1975).

ROBINSON, Ann. "Three Phonetic Poets (Cobbing, Jandl, Chopin)." *If's, Wimbledon School of Arts Magazine,* no. 3, London (1966).

RUPPENTHAL, Stephen, and Larry Wendt. "Vocable Gestures: A Historical Survey of Sound Poetry." *Art Contemporary,* no. 9 (1977).

TZARA, Tristan. "Poemes Negres." Translated by Piette Joris. *Alcheringa,* New Series, vol. 2, no. 1 (1976).

Sound Poetry Journals and Publishers

COBBING, Bob. *Writers Forum.* London. Visual and sound poems. Issue no. 1 (June 1963); Issue no. 100 (Oct. 1973).

———. *And,* no. 1 (July 1954), no. 2 (Feb. 1961), no. 3 (Feb. 1963), no. 4 (March 1966), no. 5 (Sept. 1969), no. 6 (Oct. 1973).

———. *Krocklock* with dom silverster houedard and Peter Mayer as editors. A historical and contemporary anthology of sound poetry texts. Issue no. 1 (1971), no. 2 (Sept. 1971), no. 3 (Dec. 1972), no. 4 (n.d.).

CHOPIN, Henri. *Cinquième Saison.* Paris and then after 1968 England. "First review in France (1958) for audiopoems." Concrete poetry and objective poetry. Nineteen numbers, 1958 to 1963.

————. *Review OU.* First anthology in the world for sound poetry. Poems, texts, manifestos, "livres-objets," and sound poetry recordings. First series: 13 numbers from 1964 to 1972. Second series: a cassette-text publication, beginning in April 1979.

Records:

20/21: Heidsieck, Gysin, Chopin.

23/24: Rotella, Heidsieck, Gysin, Chopin, Dufrêne.

26/27: Hausmann, Heidsieck, Chopin.

28/29: De Vree, Dufrêne, Chopin.

30/31: Chopin.

33: Wolman, Dufrêne, Chopin, Heidsieck.

34/35: Cobbing/Dufrêne, Cobbing/Lockwood, Dufrêne, Chopin.

36/37: Novak, Hanson, Chopin, Davies, Heidsieck.

38/39: Bekadrt, Hansen, Chopin.

40/41: da Silva, Burroughs, Heidsieck, Gysin, Chopin.

42/43/44: Burroughs, Hodell, Amirkhanian, Novak, Rimbaud, Chopin.

DAMAN, Herman. *AH.* Utrecht. Ten issues, 1966 to 1972. Poems and manifestos. Two issues with records:

AH no. 8: Gils, Nannucci, de Vree/Doesburg, van der Kooy, Daman.

AH no. 0: Daman.

FYLKINGEN SOCIETY FOR EXPERIMENTAL ART, pub. *Fylkingen International Bulletin.* Stockholm. First issue, Winter 1967. Critical and theoretical documents. A special issue in 1969 contained a comprehensive list edited by Sten Hanson of text-sound compositions and phonetic poems produced up to 1969. Fylkingen also produced the following record anthologies:

No. 1 Stockholm Festival 1968, RELP 1049: Hodell, Dufrêne, Cobbing.

No. 2 Stockholm 1968. RELP 1054: J. and S. Hammarberg-Akesson, Laaban, Klintberg, Hanson, Heidsieck, Johnson.

No. 3 Stockholm 1969, RELP 1072: Hodell, Rot/Williams, Hanson, S. Bodin.

No. 4 Stockholm 1969, RELP 1073: L. G. Bodin, Heidsieck, Chopin, Novak, Thygesen.

No. 5 Stockholm 1969, RELP 1074: Johnson, Gils, Cobbing, Laaban, Novak, Lille.

No. 6 Stockholm 1970, RELP 1102: Key-Aberg, Chopin, Novak, S. Bodin.

No. 7 Stockholm 1970, RELP 1103: Mon, Cobbing, Mellnäs, Laaban, Heidsieck.

Text-Sound Festivals—10 Years, RELP 1010: L. G. Bodin, Hanson, Hodell, Johnson, Laaban, Amirkhanian, Chopin, Cobbing, Heidsieck, Lora-Totino.

GIBBS, Michael. *Kontexts.* England and Amsterdam. Ten issues, 1969–1977. Generally a "Language Art" anthology with "News and Reviews" of recent international work. Issue no. 8 is a tabloid sound poetry "newspaper" which contains the following titles: "William Burroughs and Brion Gysin in Geneva," "Vocabulary" by Jackson Mac Low, "Poesie Sonore" by Henri Chopin, "Verbotecture" by Arrigo Lora-Totino, and "Computer Poetry" by Greta Monach.

REESE, Marshall, and Carl Eugene. *E.* Baltimore. Visual and sound poems. Two issues so far; a record is planned for the third.

SARENCO AND PAUL DE VREE. *Factotum-Art.* Brescia. Texts, visual and sound poetry.

1977 I-1: Bellora, Shohachiro, Pignotti, Perfetti, Hausmann (contains his extensive correspondence to de Vree), Bory, Mucci, Mussa, Heidsieck, Guarneri,

Boezem, de Vree, Aubertin, Sarenco.

1978 no. 2: Sarenco, Chopin, de Vree.

1978 no. 3: Higgins, Wendt, Hampl, Trinkewitz, Sarenco, Gerz, Aubertin.

Factotumbook: Issue no. 2: "Poesia Sonora 1," de Vree, Heidsieck, Miccini, Sarenco, Verdi; "Poetsia Sonora 2," Wendt, Chopin, Amirkhanian, de Rook, Lora-Totino. Issue no. 3: "Esenin and Majakowskji S. P. A.," Sarenco.

SCHRAENEN, Guy. *AXE.* Antwerp. Poems, texts, objects-art, and records.

Issue 1, April 1975: Record: Chopin, Gysin.

Issue 2, November 1975: Record: Dufrêne, Gysin.

Issue 3, November 1976: Record: Hanson.

Also publishes cassette editions and record books:

Dufrêne, François. *Oeuvre Desintegrale.* Three cassettes, 1976.

Heidsieck, Bernard. *Encoconnage.* Recordbook.

———. *Portrait-Petals.* Recordbook.

Radovanovic, Vladan. *Becoming Distinct/Indistinct.* Cassette.

Carrion, Ulises. *The Poet's Tongue.* Cassette.

ZURBRUGG, Nicholas. *Stereo Headphones.* Suffolk. "An occasional magazine of the new poetries." Important critical documents, sound-texts, visual poems, and "news and reviews." Last issue: no. 7, Spring 1976. To resume again sometime in the near future in Australia.

Records

AMIRKHANIAN, Charles. *Lexical Music.* Berkeley: 1750 Arch Records (1779), 1979.

BISSETT, Bill. *Awake in the Red Desert.* Vancouver: See/Hear Productions, 1971.

———. *Medicine My Mouth's on Fire.* Recordbook. Canada: Oberon Press, 1974.

BODIN, Lars-Gunnar. "Dedicated to you II" plus Bengt Emil Johnson's "Through the Mirror of Thirst" and Sten Hanson's "L'inferno de Strindberg." *Music for Tape/Band—Musik.* Stockholm: Caprice (RIKS LP 35), 1973.

BODIN, Lars-Gunnar. "*Den Heter Ingenting, den Heter Nog 'Seans II'*" plus Bodin and Bengt Emil Johnson's "*Vietnam*" and Johnson's "*Släpkoppel.*" Stockholm: Sveriges Radio Förlag (RELP 5016).

BRAU, Jean Louis. *Instrumentation Verbale.* Paris: Achèle, 1965.

CHOPIN, Henri. *Audiopoems.* London: Tangent (TGS 106), 1971.

COBBING, Bob. *ABC in Sound,* plus Ernst Jandl's *Sprechgedichte.* London: Writers Forum, 1969.

———. *e colony—a version.* With Peter Finch. A record included in *Typewriter,* 4, New York, 1973.

DODGE, Charles. *Synthesized Voices.* New York: CRI (SD 348), 1976.

DUFRÊNE, François. "*U 47.*" With J. Baronnet. Included on *Images Fantastiques.* Chicago: Mercury/Limelight, n.d.

———. *Crirythme Dédié à Jean Louis Brau.* Paris. Ache: Achèle, 1965.

DUFRÊNE, François, and Pierre Henry. *Fragments pour Artaud.* Phillips, 1967.

DUGUAY, Raôul. *Vivant Avec Tôullmônd.* Quebec: Capitol–EMI Records, 1978.

FAHLSTRÖM, Öyvind. *Fylkingen and Sveriges.* Stockholm 1961.

FOUR HORSEMEN (Steve McCaffery, bp Nichol, Rafael Barreto-Rivera, Paul Dutton). *Canadada.* Toronto: Griffin House, 1974.

———. *Live in the West.* Toronto: Starborne Productions, 1977.

GARNIER, Pierre, and Ilse Garnier, and Seiichi Niikuni. *Poems Phonetiques sur Spatialisme.* Tokyo: Columbia Records, 1971.

GIORNO, John. *Raspberry, Pornographic Poem.* New York: Intravenus Mind, 1967.

HEIDSIECK, Bernard. *Exorcisme (1962)*. Paris: Vaga group. Included in *l'Humidite*, no.
8, Moderna (Jan. 1972) and *KWY*, no. 11 *(1963)*.
———. *Trois Biopsies, un Passe-partout*. Paris: Multitechniques, 1972.
———. *Partition V*. Six records and book. Paris: Le Soleil Noir, 1973.
———. *Poèmes Partition D2 and D3 Z*. Two records and book. Ingatestone: Collection
OU, 1973.
HELMS, Hans G. *FA: M' AHNIESGWOW*. Cologne: Dumont, 1959.
HODELL, Åke. *General Bussig*. Stockholm: Igevär, Kerberos förlag, 1965.
———. *Verbal Hjärntvätt*. Stockholm: Kerberos Verlag, 1965.
———. *Lagsniff*. Recordbook. Stockholm: Raben & Sjögren, 1966.
———. *Stokely Carmichael: BLACK POWER* and *U.S.S. Pacific Ocean—a story
about the World Police*. Stockholm: Raben & Sjögren, 1968.
———. *Law & Order Inc.* and *Mr. Nixon's Dreams*. Recordbook. Stockholm: Raben
& Sjögren, 1970.
HUELSENBECK, Richard. *Four Poems from Phatastische Gebete*, 1916. In *Aspen* maga-
zine, 5, 1967.
ISOU, Isidore, and Maurice Lemaître. *Le Lettrisme*. Paris: Columbia, 1965.
JANDL, Ernst. *Laut und Luise*. Berlin: Klaus Wagenback, 1968.
———. *Das Röchelm der Mona Lisa* and Helmut Heissenbüttel's *Max Unmittelbar
Vorm Einschlafen*. Neuwied: Luchterhand, 1970.
———. *Die Kunstliche Baum*. Neuwied: Luchterhand, 1970.
———. *Hosi und Anna*. Berlin: Klaus Wagenback, 1971.
KRIWET (Ferdinand). *Modell Fortuna, Hörtext VIII*. Düsseldorf: Art Press Verlag, n.d.
LADIK, Katalin. *Phonopoetics*. Beograd: Galerija Studentskog Kulturnog Centra, 1976.
LEMAÎTRE, Maurice. *La Lettre et Le Silence. Au Dela des Mots*. Paris: editions Saravah,
n.d.
LORA-TOTINO, Arrigo. *english phonemes* 1970. In *Source*, vol. 4, no. 2, 1970.
———, and P. V. Fogliari. *Musica e poesia liquida: Il liquimofono e l'idromegafono*.
Turan-Milane: studio informazione estetica and V. Scheiwiller, 1968. Recordbook.
MAC LOW, Jackson. *From Stanzas for Iris Lezak*. In *Alcheringa*, 4, 1972.
———. *Young Turtle Asymmetry*. In *Aspen* magazine, 8.
MARINETTI, F. T. *La Battaglia di Adrianopli (1926)*. Milan: La Voce del Padrone, n.d.
———. *Il Futurismo*. *(1935–1938)*. Milan: La Voce del Padrone (3c 065–179), n.d.
NICHOL, bp (with Sean OHuigin and Ann Southam). *Appendix*. Windsor: Black Moss,
1978.
———. *Motherlove*. Toronto: Allied Records, 1978.
NOVAK, Helga. *Fibelfabel aus Bibelbabel*. Neuwied: Luchterhand (DGG 2574 033),
1973.
OHUIGIN, Sean, and Ann Southam. *Sky Sails*. Toronto: Berandol, 1974.
OWEN SOUND (Michael Dean, David Penhale, Steven Smith, Richard Truhlar). *Meaford
Tank Range*. Recordbook. Toronto: Wildpress, 1977.
ROTELLA, M. *Poemi Fonetici* 1949–1975. Milan: Plura Edizioni, 1975.
ROTH, Dieter, Gerhard Rühm, and Oswald Wiener. *Selten Gehörte Musik von den 3.
Berliner Dichterworkshop*. Stuttgart: Edition Hansjorg Mayer, 1973.
———. *Novembersymphonie, 2. Berliner Musikworkshop*. Stuttgart: Editions Hans-
jorg Mayer, 1974. Two LP records.
RÜHM, Gerhard. *Ophelia und die Wörter* and Wolf Wondratschek's *Paul oder die
Zerstorung eines Hörbeispiels*. Neuwied: Luchterhand (DGG 2574 006), 1973.
———. *Wahnsinn Litaneien*. Recordbook. Munich: Carl Hanser Verlag, 1973.
Schwitters, Kurt, and Ernst Schwitters. *An Anna Blume/Die Sonate in Urlauten*.
London: Lords Gallery, 1958.

334

WILLIAMS, Reese. *Sonance Project.* Berkeley: Line, 1977.
WOLMAN, Gil J. *Improvisations—Megapneumes.* Paris: Barclay, 1965.

Record Anthologies

AMIRKHANIAN, Charles, ed. 10 + 2:12 *American Text Sound Pieces.* Berkeley: 1750
Arch Records (1752), 1975. Ashley, Coolidge, O'Gallagher, Gysin, B. Sanderson,
Gnazzo, Amirkhanian, Dodge, Saroyan, Giorno, Cage.
ARTS COUNCIL OF GREAT BRITAIN. *Experiments in Disintegrating Language/Konkete
Canticle.* London, 1971. Mills, Verey, Clark, Cobbing, Claire, Chant.
BITZOS, Anastasia, ed. *Konkrete Poesie—Sound Poetry—Artikulation.* Bern, 1966.
Bremer, Gomringer, Jandl, de Vree, Mon, L. Greenham, Bense, Döhl, H. de
Campos, Geissbühler.
———. *Text und Aktionsabend* 2. Two 17-cm. records and booklet. Bern, 1967.
Bremer, Blaine, Geissbühler, Bory, Döhl, Ulrichs.
BROWN, Jim, ed. *See/Hear* 1. Vancouver: Talonbooks, 1969. Bissett, Brown, Kearns,
Nichol, and others.
DUFRÀENE, François, ed. *L'Autonomatopek* 1. Opus Disque International. Paris, 1973.
Dufrêne, Cobbing, Spacagna, Brau, Chopin, Isou, Wolman.
GREENHAM, Lily. *Internationale Sprachexperimente der 50/60 Jahre.* Frankfurt: Edi-
tion Hoffmann, 1971. Greenham reads her own work as well as the work of Peter
Greenham, Heissenbüttel, Jandl, Mills, Arias Misson, Molero, Morgan, Pignatari,
Rühm, Sanmark, Steen, Asins, Azeredo, Bense, Braga, Augusto de Campos,
Haroldo de Campos, de Melo e Castro, Cobbing, Draper, Garnier.
LORA-TOTINO, Arrigo. *Futura, Sound Poetry.* Milane: Cramps Records, 1978. Seven-
record anthology with bilingual booklet.
    1. Marinetti, Balla, Cangiullo, Depero, Farfa.
    2. Majakovskij, Khlebnikov, Kamenskij, Kručenych, Zdanevič, Albert-Birot,
       Pétronio.
    3. Morgenstern, Scheebart, Ball, Tzara/Janco/Huelsenbeck, Hausmann,
       Schwitters.
    4. Artaud, Dufrêne, Chopin.
    5. Heidsieck, Mon, Rühm, Einhorn, Novak, Claus.
    6. Gysin, de Vree, Cobbing, Isou, Lemaître, Altagor, Vicinelli, Spatola.
    7. Nannucci, Stratos, Lora-Totino, Concento Prosodico Group.
MON, Franz. *Phonetische Poesie.* Neuwied: Luchterhand, 1971. Khlebnikov,
Kruchenik, Malevich, Hausmann, Schwitters, Lemaître, Dufrêne, Chopin,
Cobbing, Greenham, de Vree, Lora-Totino, Novak, Rühm, Jandl.
NANNUCCI, Maurizio, ed. *Poesia Sonora.* Italy: CBS/Sugar CBS 69145, 1975.
Nannucci, Cobbing, Chopin, de Vree, Dufrêne, Gysin, Hanson, Heidsieck, Jandl,
Lora-Totino, Mon, Petronio.
STEDELIJK MUSEUM. *Sound Texts, Concrete Poetry & Visual Texts.* Amsterdam (RSC
246), 1970. Chopin, Dufrêne, Heidsieck, de Vree, Johnson, Hanson, Cobbing,
Novak, Jandl.

Cassette Editions and Tapes

ALLELUIA, Dominic. *Sounds for Dance.* San Jose: Frog Hollow, 1979.
AMIRKHANIAN, Charles. *Ode to Gravity.* KPFA radio program (since 1970) on avant
garde music and literature. Los Angeles: Pacifica Tape Library.
BUCK, Paul, and Ulli McCarthy. *xxxx 7, Rooms (& Trophies).* Pressed Curtains, Tape
2/3, 1977.

EINHORN, Nicolaus, and Michael Kohler. S-Press Tonband Verlag. Dusseldorf. Cassettes and open reel. Include the following:
Amirkhanian. *Five Text-Sound Pieces* (1975).
Cage. *Mureau* (no. 14).
Chopin. *Le Voyage Labiovelaire & Le Cri* (no. 9).
Coolidge. *Polaroid* (n.d.).
Dufrêne. *Crirhythmes* (1977).
Giorno. *Johnny Guitar* (23/24, 1976).
———. *Balling Buddha* (38/39, 1976).
Gomringer. *Konkrete Texte* (no. 13).
Gysin. *The Brion Gysin Show "Where Is That Word"* (no. 32).
Harig. *Sprechstunden für die Schone Bunte Kuh* (no. 12).
Hausmann. *Phonemes* (no. 3).
———. *R.L.Q.S. Varie en 3 Cascades* (no. 4).
———. *Soundreel* and *Interview Avec les Lettristes* (no. 5).
Heissenbüttel. *Texte* (no. 6).
Khelebnikow. *Uebertrgungen* (1977).
Mac Low. *The 8-voice Stereo-Canon Realisation (11/25/73) (for Kathy Acker)—August 1973—of the 'Black Tarantula Crossword Gathas'* (no. 33).
Heidsieck. *Poeme Partition J (1961)* and extract of *Carrefour de la Chausse d'Antin (1972)* (no. 18).
Nebel. *Zuginsfeld (Ausschnitte)* (no. 1).
———. *Unfeig (Ausschnitte)* (no. 2).
Rothenberg. *Horse-songs and other Soundings* (no. 25/26).
Rühm. *Abhandlung über das Weltall* (no. 8).
———. *Litaneien 1* (no. 34/35).
———. *Dialektgedichte* (no. 46/47).
Schuldt. *Deutschland Aufsagen/Deutschland Nachsagen* (no. 10).
GREENHAM, Lily. *Tune in to Reality*. Tape. London: Edition OT, n.d.
KERN, William Bliem. *meditationsmeditationsmeditations*. Cassettebook. New York: New Rivers Press, 1973.
KOSTELANETZ, Richard. *Experimental Prose*. New York, 1975.
———. *Opening & Closing*. New York, 1975.
KRIWET (Ferdinand). *Ball Hörtext X*. Tape. Zwei-Spur, 1973/74.
LA MAMELLE, INC. *AUDIOZINE*. San Francisco. Includes:
No. 3: Dominic Alleluia. *New Work*.
No. 4: Stephen Ruppenthal and Larry Wendt, ed. *Variety Theatre: An Anthology*. Amirkhanian, Wendt, Ruppenthal, Heidsieck, Chopin, Weisser, McCaffery, Oswald, Strange, Alleluia, Lurie, Rasof, Abbatecola. 1977.
No. 8: Peter Plonsky. *Mind Emission*.
No. 9: Anna Banana and Bill Gaglione. *Futurist Sound Poems*.
MALONE, Kirby, and Marshall Reese. *Duo O Accident*. Baltimore: Widemouth no. 8601.
MCCAFFERY, Steve, and Ted Mosses. *Black Aleph 1 to 4*. Toronto: Underwhich Editions, 1978.
———. *Three Sound Compositions*. Toronto: Underwhich Editions, 1978.
———. *Research on the Mouth*. Toronto: Underwhich Audiographic Series no. 1, n.d.
———, Sean OHuigin, and Ann Southam. *Names for Cricket*. Toronto: Underwhich Editions, 1978.
MONACH, Greta. *Automaterga—72–73*. Utrecht, 1974–1976.
NICHOL, bp. *bp Nichol*. Toronto: High Barnet, 1972.

OTHER BOOKS, pub. *Sound Proof No.* o. Amsterdam, 1978. de Rook, Monach, Gibbs, Carion.

ROBSON, Ernest. *Names in the Cosmic Ocean.* San Jose: Frog Hollow, 1979.

SARENCO, ed. *Edizioni Amodulo. Poesia Sonora.* Bresca, 1970. Includes:
No. 1: *Poemi audio-visuali.* Paul de Vree.
No. 2: *Political Poems.* Sarenco.
No. 3: *Poemi technologici.* Gruppo 70.
No. 4: *Verbosonies.* Herman Damen.

SPATOLA, Adriano, ed. *Baobab* 1. Phonetic informations of poetry. Italy, 1977. Bisinger, Blaine, Abbate/Gambaro, Higgins, Hoogstraten, Niccolai, Spatola, Tiziano, d'Aurelio, Lora-Totino.

WENDT, Larry. *Mythologiques.* Los Gatos: Ocean Records/Composers Cassettes, 1976.

———. *New & Slightly Used Text-Sound Compositions.* San Jose: 451 Books, 1977.

———. *Metropolitan Fractalizations.* San Jose: Frog Hollow, 1978.

Visual Poetry

Books

ARAGON, and Raoul-Jean Moulin. *Jiři Kolář.* Paris: Editions George Fall, 1973.

CARUSO, Luciano, and Stelio M. Martini. *Scrittura visuale e poesia sonora futurista.* Firenze: Palazzo Medici Riccardi, 1977.

COBBING, Bob. *a peal in air.* Collected poems, vol. 3, 1968–1970. Toronto: Phenomenon Press, 1978.

———, and Peter Mayer. *Concerning Concrete Poetry.* London: Writers Forum, 1978.

DE ROOK, g.j. *anthologie visuele poëzie.* Utrecht: Uitgeverij bert bakker den haag, 1975.

FINCH, Peter, ed. *Blats.* Cardiff: Second Aeon Publications, 1972.

———. *Typewriter Poems.* New York: Something Else Press/Second Aeon Publications, 1972.

FINLEY, Ian Hamilton. *Honey by the Water.* Los Angeles: Black Sparrow Press, 1973.

GOMRINGER, Eugen. *The Book of Hours and Constellations.* Translated by Jerome Rothenberg. New York: Something Else Press, Inc., 1968.

———. *Konstellationen ideogramme stundenbuch.* Stuttgart: Philipp Reclam. 1977.

———, ed. *Konkrete Poesie.* Stuttgart: Philipp Reclam, 1972.

HIGGINS, Dick. *George Herbert's Pattern Poems: In Their Tradition.* New York: Unpublished Editions, 1977.

JESSOP, John. *International Anthology of Concrete Poetry,* vol. 1. Toronto: Missing Link Press, 1978.

KOSTELANETZ, Richard. I *Articulations/Short Fictions.* New York: Kulchur Foundation, 1974.

———, ed. *Language & Structure in North America.* Catalogue. Toronto: Kensingen Arts Association, 1975.

MCCAFFERY, Steve. *Carnival,* the first panel: 1967–70 and the second panel: 1970–75. Toronto: The Coach House Press, 1973 & 1975.

MON, Franz, ed. *Movens: Dokumente und Analysen zur Dichtung, bildenden Kunst, Musik, Architektur.* Wiesbaden: Limes Verlag, 1960.

ROBSON, Ernest. *Prosodynic Print.* Chapbook. Parkerford: Primary Press, 1976.

ROT, Dieter. *Books and Graphics* (part 1). Collected Works vol. 20. Stuttgart: Edition Hansjorg Mayer, 1972.

RÜHM, Gerhard, ed. *Die Wiener Gruppe: Achleitner, Artmann, Bayer, Rühm, Wiener: Texte, Gemeinschaftsarbeiten, Aktionen.* Reinbeck bei Hamburg: Rowohlt, 1967.

SARENCO, and Paul de Vree, eds. *Il Libro 1968–71*. Brescia: Edizioni amodulo, 1971.
SOLT, Mary Ellen. *Concrete Poetry: A World View*. Bloomington: Indiana University Press, 1968.
SPATOLA, Adriano. *Zeroglyphics*. Los Angeles: Red Hill Press, 1977.
WILLIAMS, Emmett. *Sweethearts*. New York: Something Else Press, 1967.
———. *A Valentine for Noel*. New York: Something Else Press, 1973.
———, ed. *Anthology of Concrete Poetry*. New York: Something Else Press, 1967.

Articles

DE CAMPOS, Augusto and Haroldo, and Decio Pignatari. "Plano-Pilõto Para Poesia Concreta." *Noigrandes* no. 4, 1958. Reprinted in *Teoria da Poesia Concreta*, Sao Paulo: Edições Invenção, 1965.
FÄHLSTROM, Öyvind. "Manifesto for concrete poetry (1953)." Translated by Karen Loevgren and M. E. S. *Bord-Dikter* 1952–55. Stockholm, 1966.
WEAVER, Mike. "Concrete Poetry." *The Journal of Typographical Research*, vol. 1, no. 3, July 1967.

Ethnopoetics

Books

DORIA, Charles, and Harris Lenowitz. *Origins: Creation Texts from the Ancient Mediterranean*. New York: Anchor Books, 1976.
ROTHENBERG, Jerome, ed. *Technicians of the Sacred*. New York: Doubleday Anchor, 1972.
———. *Shaking the Pumpkin*. New York: Doubleday Anchor, 1972.
———. *A Big Jewish Book*. New York: Doubleday Anchor, 1978.

Articles

BENAMOU, Michel, and Jerome Rothenberg, eds. "Ethnopoetics: A First International Symposium." Special Issue. *Alcheringa*, New Series, vol. 2, no. 2 (1976).
"Oral Cultures and Oral Performance." Special Issue. *New Literary History*, vol. 8, no. 3 (Spring 1977).

Journals

ROTHENBERG, Jerome, ed. *New Wilderness Letter*. New York: New Wilderness Foundation.
TEDLOCK, Dennis, ed. *Alcheringa: Ethnopoetics*. Boston: Boston University. Biannually, with record.

Records

ROTHENBERG, Jerome (with David Antin, Jackson Mac Low, and Rochelle Owens). *Origins and Meanings: Primitive and Archaic Poetry*. New York: Broadside Records (BR651), 1968.
———. *From a Shaman's Notebook: Primitive and Archaic Poetry*. New York: Broadside Records (BR652), 1968.

Cassette Editions

MORROW, Charlie, ed. *Audiographics*. New York: New Wilderness Foundation. Includes:
    7701A: Philip Corner. *Uhhm (after a deep and Tibetan image)* and OM 'pot' breathconstant.

7702A & 7702B: Leonard and Mary Crow Dog. *Peyote Songs.*
7703A: Spencer Holst. *Spencer Holst Stories.*
7703B: ———. *The Institute for the Foul Ball.*
7703C: ———, and Tui St. George Tucker. *There Are Different Kinds of Writing.*
7705A: Jackson Mac Low. *Word Event.*
7705B: ———. *Homage to Leona Bleiweiss.*
7705C: ———. Continuation of *Homage to Leona Bleiweiss.*
7706A: ———. Charlie Morrow. *Personal Chants.*
7706B: ———. Continuation of *Personal Chants.*
7706C: ———. *Hour of Changes.*
7707A: Jerome Rothenberg. *Six Horse Songs for Four Voices.*
7708A: Armand Schwerner. *Recent Poetry.*
7708B: ———. Spohocles' *Philoctetes.*
7710: Hanna Weiner. From the *Clairvoyant Journals.*
7712A: Alison Knowles. *Sound Performance Pieces.*

Oral Tradition and Oral-Formulaic Theory

Books

ABRAHAMS, Roger D. *Deep Down in the Jungle . . . : Negro Narrative from the Streets of Philadelphia.* Chicago: Aldine, 1970.
FINNEGAN, Ruth. *Oral Poetry.* Cambridge: Cambridge University Press, 1977.
———. *Penguin Anthology of Oral Poetry.* Harmondsworth: Penguin, 1977.
JACKSON, Bruce, ed. *"Get Your Ass in the Water and Swim Like Me": Narrative Poetry from Black Oral Tradition.* Cambridge: Harvard University Press, 1974.
LORD, Albert B. *The Singer of Tales.* Cambridge: Atheneum, 1960.
WEPMAN, Dennis, and Ronald B. Newman, and Murray B. Binderman, eds. *The Life, the Lore and Folk Poetry of the Black Hustler.* Philadelphia: University of Pennsylvania Press, 1976.

Articles

CASSIDY, Frederic G. "How Free Was the Anglo-Saxon Scop?" *Franciplegius.* New York, 1965.
FREDMAN, Stephen. "Out Loud." *Panjandrum IV* (Fall 1975).
MAGOUN, Francis P. "The Oral-Formulaic Character of Anglo-Saxon Narrative Poetry." *Speculum* 28 (1953), pp. 446–67.
NAGLER, Michael. "Towards a Generative View of the Oral Formula." *Transactions and Proceedings of the American Philological Association* 98 (1967), pp. 269–311.
"The Oral Impulse in Contemporary American Poetry." Special issue. *Boundary, 2,* vol. IV, no. 3 (Spring 1975).

Records

GINSBERG, Allen. *William Blake.* MGM (FTS 3083), n.d.
HARLEMAN, Peter, and Klyd Watkins, eds. *Poetry Out Loud.* Ten records. St. Louis: Out Loud Productions. Issue no. 1, 1969.
NOWLIN, Bill, Bill Phillips, and Mark Wilson. *Hollerin'.* Rounder Records (0071), 1976.

Jazz, Blues, and Rock Poetry

Books

DYLAN, Bob. *Tarantula*. New York: Macmillan, 1971.
————. *Writings and Drawings*. New York: Knopf, 1977.
GINSBERG, Allen. *First Blues*. New York: Full Court Press, 1975.
JONES, LeRoi. *Blues People*. New York: William Morrow & Co., Inc., 1963.
KOFSKY, Frank. *Black Nationalism and the Revolution in Music*. New York: Pathfinder
    Press, 1970.
MELTZER, R. *The Aesthetics of Rock*. New York: Something Else Press, 1970.
MINGUS, Charles. *Beneath the Underdog*. New York: Knopf, 1971.
SACKHEIM, Eric, ed. *The Blues Line*. New York: Schirmer Books, 1969.
SMITH, Patti. *Babel*. New York: G. P. Putnam's Sons, 1978.

Articles

HENDERSON, Stephen. "The Forms of Things Unknown: Black Speech and Black Music
    as Poetic References." *Understanding the New Black Poetry*. New York: William
    Morrow, 1973.

Records

HUGHES, Langston. *The Black Verse: 12 Moods for Jazz*. Buddah Records (BDS
    2005/Sunday Series), n.d.
LAST POETS, THE. *This Is Madness*. Douglas Records, 1971.
————. *Jazzoetry*. Douglas Records (ADLP 6001), 1976.
————. *Delights of the Garden*. Douglas Records (NBLP 7051), 1977.
————. *At Last*. Blue Thumb Records (BTS 52), n.d.
SCOTT-HERON, Gil. *The Revolution Will Not Be Televised*. Flying Dutchman (BDL
    1–0613), 1974.

Casette Editions

ST. MAWR, Erin, ed. *St. Mawr*. A jazz poetry tape cassette periodical. Middlebury, Vt.

The Poetry Reading

Books

BROWN, Zoe, ed. *Charles Olson Reading at Berkeley*. Coyote, 1966.
LYKIARD, Alexis, ed. *Wholly Communion: International Poetry Reading at the Royal
    Albert Hall*. New York: Grove Press, 1965.
NELSON, Sonja, ed. *The American Poetry Archive Audio Tape Collection 1954–1971*.
    San Francisco: The Poetry Center at San Francisco State University, 1978.
ROBSON, Ernest. *Poetry as a Performance Art On and Off the Page*. Chapbook.
    Parkerford: Primary Press, 1976.
ZIEGLER, Alan, Larry Zirlin, and Harry Greenberg, eds. *Poets on Stage: The Some
    Symposium on Poetry Readings (Some no. 9)*. New York: Release Press, 1978.

Articles

ALBERT, Barry. "David Antin—Jerome Rothenberg." *Vort*, no. 7 (1975).
————. "Jackson Mac Low—Armand Schwerner." *Vort*, no. 2 (1975).
OLSON, Charles. "Projective Verse." *Human Universe and Other Essays*. New York:
    Grove Press, 1967.

Records

FERLINGHETTI, Lawrence, and Kenneth Rexroth. *Poetry Readings in the Cellar*. Fantasy
   Records (7002), n.d.
GINSBERG, Allen. *Howl and Other Poems*. Fantasy Records (7013), n.d.
JOYCE, James. *Meeting of James Joyce Society*. Folkways (FL 9594 B), 1951.
LINDSAY, Vachel. *Reading the Congo and Other Poems*. Caedmon (TC 1041), n.d.
POUND, Ezra. *Ezra Pound Reading His Poetry*. Caedmon (TC 1122), 1960.
SITWELL, Edith. *Facade. Canticle of the Rose*. Caedmon (TC 1016), n.d.
STEIN, Gertrude. *Gertrude Stein Reads from Her Works*. Caedmon (TC 1050), n.d.
WILLIAMS, William Carlos. *William Carlos Williams Reading His Poems*. Caedmon
   (TC 1047) n.d.

Record Anthologies

GIORNO, John, ed. Giorno Poetry Systems. New York. Includes:
   The Dial-A-Poem Poets, GPS 001–002. T. Berrigan, Brainard, Brownstein,
      Burroughs, Cage, Carroll, K. Cleaver, Coolidge, Creeley, di Prima, Ginsberg,
      Giorno, Gysin, Henderson, Kandel, B. Mayer, Mead, O'Hara, Sanders, A.
      Saroyan, Schiff, Seale, Sinclair, Waldman, Whalen, E. Williams, H. Williams.
   Disconnected, GPS 003–004. Amirkhanian, Ashbery, Baraka, Berson, Blackburn,
      Brainard, Brownstein, Burroughs, Cage, Carrol, Clark, Coolidge, Corso,
      Creeley, di Prima, Dorn, Fagin, Ginsberg, Giorno, Lima, McClure, Malanga,
      Mayer, O'Hara, Olson, Orlovsky, Owen, Padgett, Perreault, Plymell, Sanders,
      Spicer, Thomas, Trungpa, Wakoski, Waldman, Whalen, J. Wieners.
   William S. Burroughs and John Giorno, GPS 006–007.
   Totally Corrupt, GPS 008–009. Amirkhanian, Baraka, Berrigan, Brownstein,
      Bukowski, Burroughs, Cage, Curtis, Dorn, Ginsberg, Giorno, Heidsieck, Howe,
      Huggins, Kesey, Knott, Kyger, McClure, Mac Low, Mead, Merwin, O'Hara,
      Olson, Orlovsky, M. Owen, R. Owens, Plath, Rothenberg, Sanders, Spicer, Towle,
      Waldman, Weatherly, W. C. Williams.
   Biting Off the Tongue of a Corpse, GPS 005. Adams, Ashbery, Berrigan,
      Burroughs, Cage, Denby, di Prima, Duncan, Giorno, Koch, Levertov, O'Hara,
      Olson, Sanders, C. Stein, Snyder, J. Wieners.
   John Giorno and Anne Waldman, GPS 010–011.
   Big Ego, GPS 012–013. Adam, L. Anderson, Ashley, Brodey, Brown, Burroughs,
      Curtis, DaVinci, Elmslie, the Fugs, Giorno, Glass, Gnazzo, Greenwald,
      Hamilton, Heidsieck, Johnson, Lally, Levertov, Lowell, Monk, Myles,
      O'Hara, Oldenburg, Oppenheimer, Padgett, Reed, Sanders, Schiff, P. Smith,
      Thomas, Tropp, Waldman, Wendt, Wilson/Knowles.
GIORNO SOUND-SYSTEM ALBUMS. 222 Bowery, New York, New York 10012.
   The Nova Convention. Burroughs et al. November 30, 1978–December 2, 1978).
   Disconnected. The Dial-A-Poem Poets (1974).
   Biting Off the Tongue of a Corpse. The Dial-A-Poem Poets (1975).
   The Big Ego. The Dial-A-Poem Poets (1978).
   Totally Corrupt. The Dial-A-Poem Poets (1976).

Cassette and Tape Editions

AUSTIN, Alan, ed. "Breathing Space. An Anthology of Sound Text and Other Exten-
   sions." *Black Box No. 15*. Washington D.C.: Black Box, annually, n.d. Cage, Kern,
   Rasof, Wellman, Prins, Mac Low, B. Anderson, Kostelanetz, Corner, B. Andrews,
   Quasha, C. Stein, Morrow, T. Johnson, Lockwood.

BLY, Robert. *For the Stomach: Selected Poems,* 1974. Washington D.C: Black Box, n.d.
GINSBERG, Allen, and Anne Waldman. *Reading at Naropa Institute.* Boulder:
    Vajradhatu Tapes, 1975.
OLSON, Charles. *The Maximus Poems I.* Washington D.C.: Black Box, 1975.
ROBSON, Ernest and Marion. *Selected Poems of Ernest Robson.* Parkerford: Primary
    Press, 1978.
SCHWERNER, Armand. *The Tablets I–XVIII.* Dusseldorf: S-Press, 1975.
SHEPPARD, Robert G., John C. Purdy, and Tony W. Parsons. 1983. A tape poetry
    magazine. Brighton: Supranormal Cassette, 1975. Includes:
    Issue No. 1: Harwood, Sheppard, Peret, Finch, Honston, MacSweeney, Pickard.
    Issue No. 2: Brown, Sheppard, Woods, Chopin, Row, Griffiths, Harwood.
SNYDER, Gary. *There Is No Other Lite: Poems 1954–1974.* Dusseldorf: S-Press, 1975.
Audio Arts Magazine. London. Includes:
    Vol. 1, no. 1: Art Language Proceedings.
    Vol. 2, no. 1: Joseph Beuys.
    Vol. 3, no. 4: Marcel Duchamp.
    Vol. 3, no. 2: Art and Experimental Music.
    Vol. 3, no. 4: Documenta 6. From a Coded World.

Miscellaneous

Books and Articles

BEILES, Sinclair, William Burroughs, Gregory Corso, and Brion Gysin. *Minutes to Go.*
    San Francisco: Beach Books, 1968.
BAYARD, Par Caroline, and Jack David. *Avant-Postes/Outpost.* Interviews. Ontario:
    Press Porcépic Ltd., 1978.
BERNER, Jeff, ed. *Astronauts of Inner-Space: An International Collection of Avant-
    Garde Activity.* San Francisco: Stolen Paper Review editions, 1966.
BURROUGHS, William S. *The Job.* New York: Grove Press, Inc., 1974.
———, and Brion Gysin. *The Third Mind.* New York: Viking, 1978.
CAGE, John. *Notations.* New York: Something Else Press, 1968.
———. *M.* Middletown: Wesleyan University Press, 1974.
———. *Empty Words.* Middletown: Wesleyan University Press, 1978.
———. *Writing Through Finnegan's Wake and Writing for the Second Time Through
    Finnegan's Wake.* New York: Printed Editions, 1978.
CAVELLINI, Guglielmo Achille. *Nemo Propheta in Patria.* Brescia: Nuovi Strumen-
    ti/Piero Cavellini, 1978.
CELANT, Germano. *The Record As Artwork from Futurism to Conceptual Art.* Cata-
    logue. Fort Worth: The Fort Worth Art Museum, 1977.
COOLIDGE, Clark. *The Maintains.* San Francisco: THIS, 1974.
CORK, Richard. *Vorticism: An Abstract Art in the First Machine Age.* Two volumes.
    Berkeley: University of California Press, 1976.
CORMAN, Cid. *Word for Word.* Santa Barbara: Black Sparrow Press, 1977.
CROSBY, Harry. *Shadows of the Sun.* Edited by Edward Germain. Santa Barbara: Black
    Sparrow Press, 1977.
DAVIDS, Betsy. *Bathtub.* Oakland: Rebis, 1975.
DAVIES, Hugh, ed. *International Electronic Music Catalog.* New York: M.I.T. Press,
    1968.
DE LOACH, Allen, ed. *The East Side Scene.* New York: Anchor Books, 1972.
———, ed. *Intrepid Anthology: A Decade and Then Some.* Buffalo: Intrepid Press,
    1976.
FLANAGAN, James Cotton. *Speech Analysis, Synthesis and Perception.* Berlin, New

York: Springer, 1972.

GAGLIONE, William John, and Anna Banana. "Special International Double Issue." *VILE*, no. 2/3. San Francisco: Banana Productions, 1976.

GIBBS, Michael, ed. *Deciphering America*. Amsterdam: Kontexts Publications, 1978.

GRENIER, Robert. *Cambridge M'ass*. Berkeley: Tuumba Press, 1978.

GROSS, Ronald. *Pop Poems*. New York: Simon & Schuster, 1967.

————, and George Quasha. *Open Poetry*. New York: Simon & Schuster, 1973.

HEISSENBÜTTEL, Helmut. *Das Textbuch*. Darmstadt: Hermann Luchterhand, 1966.

HIGGINS, Dick. *A Dialectic of Centuries*. New York: Printed Editions, 1978.

HOROVITZ, Michael, ed. "Big Huge." *New Departures*, no. 7/8 and 10/11 (last issue). London: New Departures, 1975.

JAROSIŃSKI, Zbigniew, ed. *Antologia Polskiego Futuryzmu I Nowej Sztuki*. Wroctaw: Zaktad Narodowy Imienia Ossolińskick-Wydawnictwo, 1978.

KENNER, Hugh. *The Pound Era*. Berkeley: University of California Press, 1971.

KOSTELANETZ, Richard, ed. *Breakthrough Fictioneers*. Barton: Something Else Press, 1973.

————, ed. *Essaying Essays*. New York: Out of London Press, 1975.

MAFFINA, G. F. *Luigi Russole e l'Arte dei Rumori*. Torino: Martano Editore, 1978.

MARKOV, Vladimir. *Russian Futurism: A History*. Los Angeles: University of California Press, 1968.

MCCAFFERY, Steve, ed. "The Politics of the Referent." *Open Letter* (Spring 1978).

————, and bp Nichol. *The Story So Four*. Toronto: The Coach House Press, 1976.

MCCLURE, Michael. *Ghost Tantras*. San Francisco: Four Seasons, 1969.

MILLER, Joni K., and Lowry Thompson. *The Rubber Stamp Album*. New York: Workman Publishing, 1978.

MOHOLY-NAGY, L. *Vision in Motion*. Chicago: Paul Theobald, 1946.

MOTHERWELL, Robert. *The Dada Painters and Poets*. New York: Wittenborn and Schultz, 1951.

NATIONS, Opal L. *The Private Affairs of Heliomann and How the Various Parts of His Body Lived Apart from the Whole*. San Francisco: Empty Elevator Shaft Poetry Press, 1974.

NICHOL, bp. *The Martyrology*, Books 1 and 2 and Books 3 and 4. Toronto: The Coach House Press, 1977 and 1978.

PORTER, Bern. *Found Poems*. New York: Something Else Press, 1972.

RICHTER, Hans. *Dada: Art and Anti-Art*. New York: McGraw-Hill, n.d.

ROBISON, Mark, ed. *Improvised Poetics*. An interview with Allen Ginsberg. Anonym, 1971.

ROBSON, Ernest. *Thomas Onetwo*. New York: Something Else Press, 1971.

————. *I Only Work Here*. Chester Springs: Dufour Editions, 1975.

————, and Jet Wimp, eds. *Against Infinity*. An anthology of mathematical poetry. Parkerford: Primary Press, 1979.

ROTHENBERG, Jerome, ed. *Revolution of the Word*. New York: Seabury Press, 1974.

SHATTUCK, Roger. *The Banquet Years*. New York: Vintage Books, 1968.

SILLIMAN, Ron. *Ketjak*. San Francisco: THIS, 1978.

————, ed. "A Symposium on Clark Coolidge." *Stations*, no. 5 (Winter 1978).

SPOERRI, Daniel. *An Anecdoted Topography of Chance*. New York: Something Else Press, 1966.

STRANGE, Allan. *Electronic Music: Systems, Techniques, and Controls*. Iowa: Wm. C. Brown Company, Publishers, 1972.

TISDALL, Caroline, and Angelo Bozzola. *Futurism*. New York: Oxford University Press, 1978.

343

TOMKINS, Calvin. *The Bride and the Bachelors*. New York: Viking, 1971.

TOOP, David, ed. *New/Rediscovered Musical Instruments*. Vol. 1. London: Quartz/ Mirliton, 1974.

WALDMAN, Anne. *Fast Speaking Woman*. San Francisco: City Lights, 1975.

——, and Marilyn Webb, eds. *Talking Poetics from Naropa Institute*. Vol. I. Boulder: Shambhala, 1978.

YOUNG, La Monte, and Jackson Mac Low, eds. *An Anthology*. New York: Heiner Friedrich, 1970.

YOUNGBLOOD, Gene. *Expanded Cinema*. New York: Dutton, 1970.

Records

ASHLEY, Robert. "Purposeful Lady Slow Afternoon." *Sonic Art Union*. Mainstream (MS/5010).

——. *In Sara, Mencken, Christ and Beethoven There Were Men and Women*. Milane: Cramps Records, nova musicha, no. 3 (CRSLP 6103), 1973.

BERIO, Luciano. *Thema: Omaggio a Joyce*. Turnabout Vox no. TV 34177.

EIMERT, Herbert. *Epitaph für Aikichi Kuboyama*. Wergo no. 60014.

FERRARI, Luc. *Music Promenade*. Wergo no. 60046.

HENRY, Pierre. *Le Voyage, d'après le Livre des Morts Tibétain*. Philips 836 899.

——. *Messe de Liverpool. Phonemes et collaboration vocale: Jacques Spacagna*. Philips 6510 001.

——. *La Noire à Soixante; Granulométrie (1962–1968) en collaboration avec François Dufrêne*. Philips 836 892.

——, and Pierre Schaeffer. *Symphonie pour un homme seul (1949–1950)*. Philips 6510 012.

LA BARBARA, Joan. *Voice Is the Original Instrument*. Wizard Records, RVW 2266.

——. *Tapesongs*. New York: Chiaroscuro Records, CR 196, 1977.

LUCIER, Alvin, director. *Extended Voices*. Brandeis University Chamber Chorus performing the work of Pauline Oliveros, Alvin Lucier, John Cage, Robert Ashley, Toshi Ichyanagi, Morton Feldman. Odyssey 32 16 0156.

REICH, Steve. *It's Gonna Rain*. Columbia MS-7265.

——. "Come Out" on *New Sounds in Electronic Music*. Odyssey 32 16 0160.

SCHNEBEL, Dieter. "Deuteronomium 31, 6 für 15 Solostimmen," on *Neue Chormusik 1*, Wergo no. 60026.

STOCKHAUSEN, Karlheinz. *Gesange der Junglinge*. DGG no. 138811.

WISHART, Trevor. *Red Bird*. York, England, 1977.

Contributor's Notes

ALTA's most recent volume is *The Shameless Hussy: Selected Stories, Essays & Poetry* (The Crossing Press).

CHARLES AMIRKHANIAN is a poet, composer, percussionist, and one of America's leading practitioners of text–sound composition. He has served as music director of radio station KPFA (Berkeley, California) since 1969. His album, *Lexical Music,* recently released by 1750 Arch Records, contains six of his text–sound pieces.

DAVID ANTIN is currently a member of the Visual Arts Department at the University of California at San Diego, where he lives on a sagebrush ranch behind Del Mar. He is the author of *Dialogue* (Santa Barbara Museum) and a book of "talk" pieces, *Talking at the Boundaries* (New Directions, 1976). *Who's Listening Out There* is due shortly from Sun & Moon Press, College Park, Maryland. His current project is a book that explores "a model of coming to a 'common knowing' called 'Tuning,' to replace our disastrous term 'understanding.'"

FRANCES BUTLER of Poltroon Press is a printer and illustrator who teaches typography and book design at the University of California at Davis. Her latest works include *Career Options* and *New Dryads (Are Ready For Your Call).*

CID CORMAN edits *Origin* and Origin Press books (4th series). He is currently working on a dozen or more books, as well as setting up a dessert shop in Boston.

VICTOR HERNÁNDEZ CRUZ was born in Aguas Buenas, Puerto Rico, twenty miles from the Equator. He came to the United States as a young child. His three volumes of poems include *Snaps, Mainland,* and *Tropicalization.* In 1982 Momo's Press will publish *By Lingual Wholes.* He currently lives in New York City.

BETSY DAVIDS and JIM PETRILLO of Rebis Press & Performing Arts Company (P. O. Box 2233, Berkeley, CA 94702) are variously involved in word&image art, bookmaking, and performance. The latest in their series of unUsuaL Rebis books is a 13-part invention called *Big Mac,* an accordian-fold book version of their all-time favorite performance piece.

THULANI NKABINDE DAVIS, author of *All the Renegade Ghosts Rise,* lives and works in New York City. Currently she is working on several projects for theater, performing with a number of musicians, and looking for a publisher for a new manuscript of poems, *Sweet Talk and Stray Desires.*

345

BARRY EISENBERG lives with his wife and daughter in Mendocino County. His life is divided between his family, farming, and working on a lifetime project—a quintet of fantasy novels.

DON GRABAU is a poet and video gypsy. His most recent correspondence is from Colorado where he is active in educational projects focused on the perils of uranium mining.

From 1976 to 1978, DAVID GUSS lived in Venezuela, with the Makiritare (So'to) Indians of the Upper Orinoco area, particularly in the village of Adujaña on the Paragua River. He translated the creation epic of the Makiritare, known as the *Watunna*, which has been publisehd by North Point Books. The piece in this book is taken from a book now in progress about his experiences with the Makiritare: their myths, their land, and their culture.

JESSICA TARAHATA HAGEDORN currently lives in New York City. She is the author of *Dangerous Music* (Momo's Press, 1975). Her forthcoming book, *Tropical Apparitions*, a mix of stories and poems, will be published by Momo's in the Fall of 1981.

JAMES HUMPHREY lives with his wife and son in a renovated railroad station in Attleboro, Massachusetts. His one-act plays have appeared in Cambridge and off-Broadway. His fourth book of poems, *The Re-Learning* (Providence: Hellcoal Press, 1976) was a Pulitzer Prize and National Book Award finalist. He is currently working on his autobiography, *Abuse,* to be published by Harper & Row.

FRANCES JAFFER, a resident of San Francisco and Marshall, California, wrote *Any Time Now* (Effie's Press) and *She Talks to Herself in the Language of an Educated Woman* (Kelsey Street Press). She has taught "Feminist Journal Writing" in the Women's Studies Program at San Francisco University and is working on her third book, *Milk Song.*

ALASTAIR JOHNSTON of Poltroon Press in Berkeley is a printer, poet, pianist, lecturer in typography at the University of California at Berkeley, and bibliographer of Auerhahn Press. He is presently engrossed in typo-historical works, such as the literature of nineteenth-century typefounders' specimens.

FAYE KICKNOSWAY is well known as both a poet and an artist. Her latest books are *The Cat Approaches* and *Nothing Wakes Her.* Her drawings, which have won awards in museum shows, can be found in a number of her books. Currently she is at work on new collections of short stories and poems.

HARRY LEWIS, a native of Brooklyn, is one of the founding editors and publishers of *Mulch* magazine and press, and is now co-editor of # magazine and Press. He gives many readings in New York and other areas, often collaborating with jazz musicians. He has published four books of poetry, including *Home Cooking.* His most recent collection of poetry, *The Wellsprings,* will be published by Momo's Press. His current project is a new translation of the poems of Vladimir Mayakovsky.

STEVE McCAFFERY of Toronto, Canada, is a writer and performance artist. He co-founded the Toronto Research Group and is a member of Four Horsemen, a performance poetry ensemble. He is an artist-in-residence at York University, where he is researching the application of computer hyperspace to current literary theory. Other current projects include poetry *(The Abstract Ruin, Mind of Pauline Brain),* 4 *Intimate Distortions: A Displacement of Sappho,* 1978, and *Dr. Sadhu's Muffins* (Vol. 1 in a trilogy of homolinguistic translations).

LINDA MONTANO is a conceptual performance artist and lives in California. In 1977 she received an NEA award in visual arts. She has taught courses in performance at San Francisco State and the San Francisco Art Institute, as well as workshops throughout the country. She is currently interested in collaboration.

GRAHAM MACKINTOSH is not a variety of apple. He can be found at Mackintosh & Young at 631 State Street in Santa

346

Barbara. A book designer and printer, he is most well known for his work with White Rabbit Press and Black Sparrow Press.

JACKSON MAC LOW, an American poet, composer, playwright, and performance artist, has read and performed in a variety of locations, including Sound Poetry Festivals in London (1975, 1978), Glasgow (1978), and Toronto (1978). His most recent books include *phone* (New York and Amsterdam: Printed Editions and Kontexts, 1979) and *Assymetries (1960) 1–260* (New York: Printed Editions, 1980). He is currently preparing for publication *Representative Works* (Santa Barbara: Ross-Erikson) and *First Book of Gathas* (1961–79) (Milwaukee: Membrane). The work reprinted in this book is from *The Pronouns, A Collection of 40 Dances—for the Dancers, 3 February–22 March* 1964 (with photographs by Peter Moore) (Barrytown, New York: Station Hill, 1979).

CHERYL MILLER has been a letterpress printer and publisher for ten years. Currently she divides her time between teaching and operating her Interval Press. If you would like to be on her mailing list for broadsides and announcements of new publications, write to her at 128 Downey Street, San Francisco, CA 94117.

CHARLIE MORROW is a ceremonial musician and event maker. "Voice in the Wilderness" was first published in *Big Deal* magazine, no. 4, Fall 1976. *Placing* is in a manuscript collection of his essays edited by Michael Byron for which he is seeking a publisher. *Chanting*, a xeroxed book publication, is available from New Wilderness.

HOWARD NORMAN's translation of the stories of Paulé Bartón (Haitian), *The Woe Shirt,* was published this fall by Penmaen Press. In 1979 he received the National Book Award in translation for *The Wishing Bone Cycle (Tales of the Swampy Cree).* His radio play, *The Ice Donkey,* was recently performed on National Public Radio.

HILTON OBENZINGER's *This Passover or the Next I Will Never Be in Jerusalem,* a sequence of poems, stories and interviews, explores the roots and issues of Jewish identity in America. It was published this past winter by Momo's Press.

PETER OGBANG AND LINUS EDE IGBAGIRI. True to the prophesy in Linus's poem, Dr. Peter Ogbang has twice served the Nigerian government in administrative positions. In 1975, under the military government, he was appointed civil commissioner for education in the Cross River State. Subsequently he was appointed federal commissioner of health. Currently, he and his family live in Lagos where he is now national director of organization and research for the Nigerian People's Party (NPP). Linus Ede Igbagiri, true to the wish of his song, eloped with Eliza. They now have five children and a house in the village. He works for the Health Ministry in Calabar and is active in the state's Cultural Centre Board.

TED PEARSON is the author of *The Grit* (1976) and *The Blue Table* (1979), published by Trike Books, San Francisco, California.

ROBERT PETERS is co-director of the writing program at the University of California at Irvine and the author of numerous books of poems and criticism. Among his books are *The Gift To Be Simple, Gauguin's Chair: Selected Poems,* a massive edition of John Addington Symonds's letters, and a forthcoming book of poems, *The Picnic in the Snow: Ludwig II of Bavaria.* He is also on the staff of *The American Book Review.* A collection of his essay, *The Great American Poetry Bake-Off,* has just appeared and is in a second printing.

CHARLES POTTS's book *Valga Krusa* (Litmus Press: 1977) contains perhaps the most intense and personal account of the Bay Area poetry reading scene between 1966 and 1968. It's available direct from the author for $7.77 at 525 Bryant, Walla Walla, Washington 99362.

JEROME ROTHENBERG is the author of over forty books of poetry and poetics, including *Poland/1931, Poems for the Game of Silence, A Seneca Journal, Vienna Blood* (all from New Directions), and the anthology—assemblages *Technicians of the Sacred, Shaking the Pumpkin, America A Prophecy,* and *A Big Jewish Book.* He founded *Alcheringa* in 1970, and he now edits *New Wilderness Letter,* a magazine of poetics throughout the spectrum of the arts.

STEPHEN RUPPENTHAL lectures at San Francisco State University in the Center for Experimental and Interdisciplinary Art and teaches electronic music in the music department. His MA dissertation at San Jose State was *History and Techniques of Sound Poetry in the Twentieth Century.* He currently performs with the Electric Weasel Ensemble and is involved in the production of *Totemic Illusions,* a continuing series of works in the text–sound and electronic-music media.

JAMES SCHEVILL is a professor of English and theater at Brown University. Recent books, published by Copper Beech Press, include *The Arena of Ants* (1977), *The Mayan Poems* (1978), and *Fire of Eyes* (1979). His *Collected Short Plays* (Chicago: The Swallow Press) is forthcoming in 1981. In their 1980–81 season, The Trinity Square Repertory Co. of Providence presented his new play, *Mother O, or The Last American Mother.*

TOM SCHMIDT performs with the Emery, Schmidt, & McCann band, teaches songwriting in elementary schools, and manages The Harmony Grits Dance Company. As a CETA artist, he recently wrote an *Arts Resource Guide to Sacramento,* with Connie Miottel.

EILEEN SHUKOFSKY created the text, music, and movement for *Grace,* a musical which she produced and directed in Mobile, Alabama. She has also sung and composed music for various dance productions, including David Lusby's *The Medicine Wheel* at The Kitchen in the Soho and Bill Setters' ballet, *Gathering Together,* performed at Oberlin College. She is currently rewriting *Grace* and working on a long piece of fiction, *The LuAnne's.*

RON SILLIMAN's books include *Ketjak* (This Press, 1978), *Tjanting* (The Figures, 1980), and *The Age of Huts* (Pod Books, 1980).

NORMA SMITH lives and works in Oakland, California. She is currently working on productions for KPFA radio, a Berkeley Pacifica station, including prose and poetry readings, interviews, and documentaries. She has taught classes and workshops in poetry and prose writing and has coordinated readings, including a series at the Grand Piano, a San Francisco coffeehouse.

RON SUKENICK's latest novel is *Long Talking Bad Conditions Blues* from The Fiction Collective (Braziller). His previous work includes the novels *Up, Out,* and *98.6.*

HOLBROOK TETER and MICHAEL MEYERS are responsible for Zephyrus Image books and broadsides. They invite inquiries and can be reached at 4460 Pine Flat Road, Healdsburg, California 95448.

CAROL SUE THOMAS has presented her one-woman mime shows at many locations, including Richmond Shepard's Theater in Los Angeles and the Intersection Theater in San Francisco. She has also performed in television and film. Until recently she performed regularly as Suggs the Mime outdoors at The Cannery, a warehouse shopping complex in San Francisco.

STEPHEN VINCENT's poetry can be found in *Five on the Western Edge* (Momo's Press, 1977) and in *Now Everyone Knows Childcare* (Momo's Press, 1979). He is the former poetry review editor for the *San Francisco Review of Books,* and the editor and publisher for Momo's Press. His new book of poems, stories, and interviews is called *Father* (Momo's Press, 1981).

LARRY WENDT is an electronic technician for the music department at San Jose State University. His computer-aided, generated text, "Earthworm," for performance and live computer electronics, has recently been published in *Cenizas,* no. 6 (San Francisco). He is currently co-editing a two-record anthology of American and Canadian sound poetry for an Italian label.

ELLEN ZWEIG's book *Performance Poetry* is forthcoming from Ross-Erik-son. She has performed her own poems in New York, San Francisco, Paris, Amsterdam, and elsewhere. Her present project is *Soundcards,* five hundred ways a postcard can make sounds, for Alternative Press.

ACKNOWLEDGMENTS

The "Sour Grapes" selection by WILLIAM CARLOS WILLIAMS is from *The Autobiography* of William Carlos Williams. Copyright© 1951 by William Carlos Williams. Reprinted by permission of New Directions.

The excerpt from "Projective Verse" by CHARLES OLSON is from *Selected Writings* by Charles Olson. Copyright© 1959 and © 1966 by Charles Olson. Reprinted by permission of New Directions.

"The Poetics of Performance" by JEROME ROTHENBERG was previously published in two sections. The opening section appeared in *Alcheringa,* New Series Volume II, no. 2, edited by Michel Benamou and Jerome Rothenberg. "A Post-Script" was published in *Performance in Post Modern Culture,* edited by Michel Benamou, Milwaukee, Wisconsin: Coda Books, 1978.

The selection from "The Duende: Theory and Divertissement," by FEDERICO GARCIA LORCA, is from *Poet in New York* by Federico Garcia Lorca, a new translation by Ben Belitt. Copyright © 1954 by Ben Belitt.

"Three Dances and Notes" by JACKSON MAC LOW are from *The Pronouns, A Collection of 40 Dances—for the Dancers,* 3 February–22 March 1964 (with photographs by Peter Moore). (Barrytown, New York: Station Hill, 1979). Reprinted by permission of the author.

"The First All-Women's Poetry Reading/Berkeley" by ALTA is an excerpt from *Momma, a start on all the untold stories* by alta. (Times Change Press). Copyright © 1974 by Alta Gerrey. Reprinted with the permission of the author.

"Speech: As It Falls: Is Poetry (more notes on oral poetry)" and "Continuing Oral Poetry" by CID CORMAN are reprinted in *Word for Word/Essays on the Arts of Language,* vol. I (Santa Barbara: Black Sparrow Press, 1977). Copyright © 1977 by Cid Corman. The selections from these pieces appear by permission of the author and Black Sparrow Press.

The selection from "Big Talk and Small Business" by FRANCIS O. SINCLAIR is from *California Living,* the Sunday magazine of the *San Francisco Examiner & Chronicle,* June 22, 1979. Copyright© 1979 by the San Francisco *Examiner.* Reprinted with permission.

The selection "Art with No Name" by RON SILLIMAN was originally published in *State of the Arts* published by Cultural News & Services. (Vol. 1, no. 10, November 1977). Reprinted by permission of the author.

MOMO'S PRESS

Magazine

Shocks No. 1   Poetry & Criticism—The Bay Area and
   Northern California   O/P
Shocks No. 2   Poetry & Criticism—The Bay Area and
   Northern California $5
Shocks No. 3/4   Poetry & Criticism—The Bay Area and
   Northern California   O/P
Shocks No. 5   The Day Book—a Collective Journal with
   work by Andrei Codrescu, Beverly Dahlen, Susan
   Griffin, Jessica Hagedorn, Roberto Vargas and
   Stephen Vincent $5
Shocks No. 6   The Androgyny Issue—men looking at the
   women in themselves, women looking at the men in
   themselves—poetry, essays, fiction, a play & graphics   O/P

Books

Dangerous Music (poems & a story) Jessica Hagedorn   paper $4.95
Pet Food & Tropical Apparitions (poems, stories & a
   novella) Jessica Hagedorn   paper $5.95
                                                            cloth $15
The Wellsprings (poems) Harry Lewis   paper $5.95
                                                            cloth $12.50
Lorca/Blackburn Poems of Federico Garcia Lorca chosen
   and translated by Paul Blackburn; *Bilingual Edition*   paper $4.95
                                                            cloth $10.00
This Passover or the Next I Will Never Be in Jerusalem
   (poetry & prose) Hilton Obenzinger   paper $4.95
                                                            cloth $12.50
The Ballad of Artie Bremer (a long poem) Stephen Vincent   paper $5

Anthologies

Omens from the Flight of Birds: The First 101 Days of Jimmy Carter (A Collective Journal by Writers & Artists including Alta, K. Abbott, B. Barich, B. Dahlen, J. Hagedorn, L. Hejinian, D. Henderson, F. Jaffer, H. Obenzinger, R. Silliman & others)   paper $4.95

Five on the Western Edge (An Anthology of Men in Transition) Beau Beausoleil, Steve Brooks, Larry Felson, Hilton Obenzinger and Stephen Vincent   paper $4.95

Forthcoming Titles (Spring/Summer 1981)

By Lingual Wholes (poetry & prose)
Victor Hernandez Cruz   paper $5.95
     cloth $15

Fathers & Lovers (poetry & prose) Stephen Vincent   paper $5.95
     cloth $15

A Reading (mixed forms) Beverly Dahlen   paper $5.95
     cloth $15

Please address all inquiries to **Momo's Press,** 45 Sheridan Street, San Francisco, California 94103